THERE WAS A MAN

The Saga of Gordon Kahl

A True Story

by

Capstan Turner with A. Jay Lowery

Library of Congress No. 85-90500
IBSN 0-9614465-0-1

SOZO PUBLISHING COMPANY
Nashville, Tennessee 37202-3541
Phone: (615) 885-0198

Gordon Wendell Kahl

Dedicated to
Those Such As Penny Wilson
Who Share the Following Beliefs:

"How many men *are there to a square thousand miles in this country? Hardly one.*

"It is not a man's duty, as a matter of course, to devote himself to the eradication of any, even the most enormous wrong; he may still properly have other concerns to engage him; but it is his duty, at least, to wash his hands of it, and if he gives it no thought longer, not to give it practically his support ... if (injustice) is of such a nature that it requires you to be the agent of injustice to another, then I say break the law. Let your life be a counter friction to stop the machine. What I have to do is to see, at any rate, that I do not lend myself to the wrong which I condemn ... under a government which imprisons any unjustly, the true place for a just man is also a prison.

"In literature it is only the wild that attracts us. Dullness is but another name for tameness ... as the wild duck is more swift and beautiful than the tame, so is the wild - the mallard - thought ... a truly good book is something as natural, and as unexpectedly and unaccountably fair and perfect, as a wild flower discovered on the prairies of the West ... in short, all good things are wild and free."

- Henry David Thoreau, *Essays*

"Government is not reason, it is not eloquence, it is force! Like fire, it is a dangerous servant and a fearful master."

-George Washington

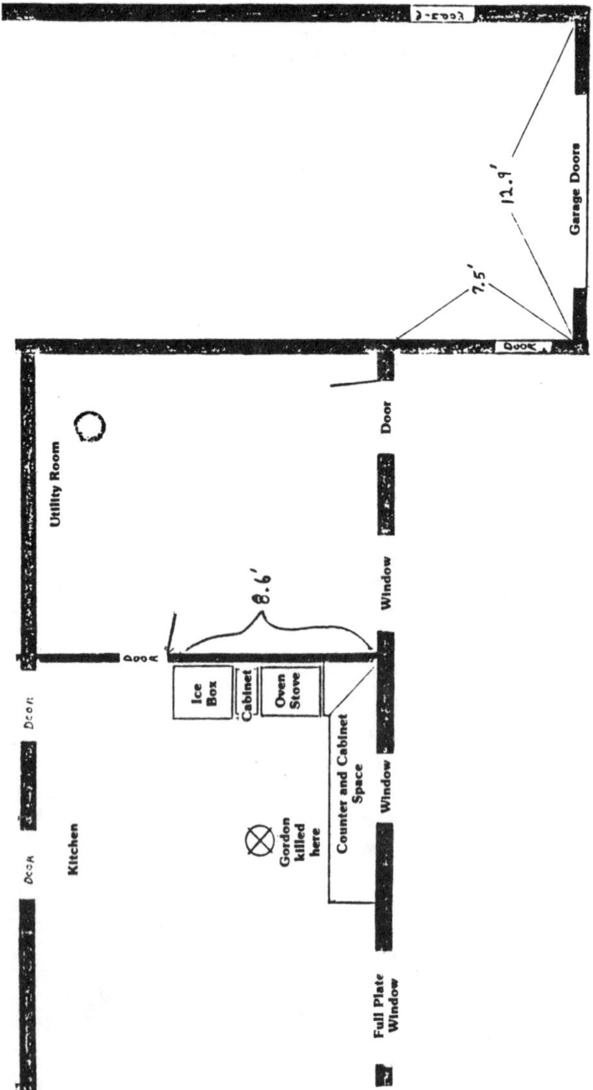

Ginter house outline

Contents

Foreword

My comments are those I think my late husband, Gordon, would have me make.

Some things there are you must not tolerate. Yes, some things you just never stop considering to be unbearable: injustice and oppression and dishonor and shame. Doesn't matter how young you are or how old you've gotten. Not for accolades nor for money; for publicity with your picture on TV nor for cash in the bank, either. That's the long and short of it!

One of the unbearables is the infanticide of a million and a half unborn babies each year under the pretext of "freedom of choice". Ever since *Roe v. Wade,* this had been Gordon's primary reason for refusing to directly support a government which endorses and subsidizes such atrocities. This book talks much about "murder", but it won't hold a candle as murder and butchery.

William Penn said, "Man will ultimately be governed by God or ruled by tyrants." Just as Peter said, when admonished not to preach Jesus Christ, "Am I to obey man's laws or God's laws?" The choice is one each person must make for himself, but if one is to stand for God and freedom, he must count the cost. Injustice anywhere is a threat to justice everywhere. If you are never scared or maligned or embarrassed or mistreated or hurt, it means you never take any chances, never do anything brash. Gordon dared to tell the government, "You are wrong!" Gordon's primary technique for *action* was to follow the advice of a sage who wrote in the 1500's: "If you participate in an evil structure which you oppose, just cease to support it, and it will fall of its own weight." It only takes guts and God to do this.

Gordon was a small, ordinary man who figuratively stood ten feet tall. He followed Thomas Jefferson's advice, "In matter of principle, stand like a rock..." He learned patience and gained strength from his long tenure with the prairie trees. He was the type of person in front of whom a friend could think and speak aloud without reservation.

He always tried to give away kindness, but was not too successful at it, as kindnesses are often returned. "A man's greatness is measured by his willingness to be kind," someone once said. Gordon understood that success was a journey and not a destination. He was a farmer, whom Washington Irving described well:

"In rural occupation there is nothing mean and debasing. It leads a man forth among scenes of natural grandeur and beauty; it leaves him to the workings of his own mind, operated upon by the purest and most elevating of external influences. Such a man may be simple and rough, but he cannot be vulgar."

Goethe said, "It is not doing the thing we like to do, but liking the thing we have to do, that makes life blessed." Gordon believed that.

Gordon was a good husband and father, even though his family was deprived and sacrificed somewhat in pursuit of his altruistic goals. He realized that having a child to teach was the way adults learned. His pursuit of happiness was inextricably interwoven in walking with God and being with his family. He worked hard, realizing that better luck often follows from greater effort. When times got tough, Gordon had the tenacity to hold on, when necessary, and the wisdom to "let go, and let God" when appropriate, requiring and acquiring greater strength.

Gordon lived in a country where two thirds of the crimes, including half the violent crimes, go unreported. Yet, we incarcerate a larger proportion of citizens than all but two countries. Even with 40 percent of our resources spent or transferred by government, many believe fallaciously that the king (the government) can do no wrong; that government officials and agents do not perpetrate any crimes. Gordon knew better.

Some do not agree with Gordon's aims and beliefs, and that's all right. One nice thing about being imperfect is the joy it brings to others. As a Kristofferson song says, "Everyone needs someone to look down on." On the other hand, Gordon had many superb attributes. In learning of these, some may join Voltaire, who said, "By appreciation, we make excellence in others our own property."

Among the few times the government mentioned God, other than in profanity, was by a marshal in an Arkansas court, who said, "...God save the United States and this court." In this vein, I would like to add my own prayer, "God bless this country *again*, as was done when it was founded, and return freedom to the people." After all, as Capstan Turner wrote in another book, *"The Years the Locusts Stole"*, "The history of mankind is little more than a continual struggle for liberty."

Enjoy the book. When you finish, the central question will remain: Are you and I alive to serve the government, or is it to serve us? Are we to be the slaves or masters of government?

In Macaulay's "An Essay on Milton," the following quotation about the Puritan could equally apply to Gordon Kahl, patriot:

"Thus the Puritan was made up of two different men, the one all self-abasement, penitence, gratitude, passion; the other proud, calm, inflexible, sagacious. He prostrated himself in the dust before his Maker; but he set his foot on the neck of his king. In his devotional retirement, he prayed with convulsions, and groans, and tears. He was half-maddened by glorious or terrible illusions. He heard the lyres of angels or the tempting whispers of fiends. He caught a gleam of the Beatific Vision, or woke screaming from dreams of everlasting fire. Like Vane, he thought himself intrusted with the sceptre of the millennial year. Like Fleetwood, he cried in the bitterness of his soul that God had hid his face from him. But when he took his seat in the council, or girt on his sword for war, these tempestuous workings of the soul had left no perceptible trace behind them. People who saw nothing of the godly but their uncouth visages, and heard nothing from them but their own groans and their whining hymns, might laugh at them. But those had little reason to laugh who encountered them in the hall of debate or in the field of battle. These fanatics brought to civil and military affairs a coolness of judgement and an immutability of purpose which some writers have thought inconsistent with their religious zeal, but which were in fact the necessary effects of it. The intensity of their feelings on one subject made them tranquil on every other. One overpowering sentiment had subjected to itself pity and hatred, ambition and fear. Death had lost its terrors and pleasure its charms. They had their smiles and their tears, their raptures and their sorrows, but not for things of this world. Enthusiasm had made them Stoics, had cleared their minds from every vulgar passion and prejudice, and raised them above the influence of danger and of corruption. It sometimes might lead them to pursue unwise ends, but never to choose unwise means. They went through the world, like Sir Artegal's iron man Talus with his flail, crushing and trampling down oppressors, mingling with human beings, but having neither part nor lot in human infirmities; insensible to fatigue, to pleasure, and to pain; not to be pierced by any weapon, not to be withstood by any barrier."

As Albert Schweitzer said, "Example is not the main thing in influencing others. It is the only thing." Gordon Kahl provided the example which Goethe had in mind when he wrote, "Let everyone sweep in front of his own door, and the whole world will be clean." He was like Stevenson's saint, defined as a sinner who keeps trying. As John Gardner said, "Some people strengthen society by being the kind of people they are." That was Gordon. He lacked the money and power and influence of others, but he had a greater asset - enthusiasm.

I close with the following quotation from Daniel Webster:

"Let our object be: our country, our whole country, and nothing but our country. And, by the blessing of God, may that country itself become a vast and splendid monument, not of oppression and terror, but of Wisdom, of Peace, and of Liberty, upon which the world may gaze with admiration forever!"

Joan Kahl

Preface

This is a story about a man, Gordon Wendell Kahl, who many think was persecuted by federal authorities because of his religious and political beliefs. Some of these beliefs were at variance with existing statutory or administrative civil law. Gordon Kahl's predictable response would probably be, "God's law is the supreme law; government actions are to be in harmony with the higher law. Our rights come from God, not from government, and are therefore inalienable, cannot be taken away by public officials. Agents of Satan have taken over many of the power positions in government. Whenever these evil would-be rulers in this great land attempt to oppress the people under the color of a law which is contrary to the Constitution, they are acting lawlessly. The laws which they seek to enforce are null and void. The Constitution strictly limited the powers and sovereignty of the federal government. The people are sovereign. Those attempting to change the Constitution by judicial "interpretation", executive edict, or legislative mischief are guilty of nothing less than usurpation and treason. For example, a Federal judge, D.W. Suttle, directed me not to mention the name of Jesus Christ or the Constitution in his court room. They were my defense.

"Everyone should study the Bible, the Declaration of Independence and the Constitution," Gordon Kahl might have said. "Article 1, Section 10 of the Constitution is quite explicit about money. We don't have any dollars anymore, just illegal debt instruments issued by a private central bank controlled by an international elite group, in which the Rothschilds and alien powerholders predominate. These bills, until just lately, had printed on them 'redeemable in lawful money,' but this statement has now been removed. How can you pay a debt with a debt? The way this scam works is that the government prints these federal reserve notes and sells them for about 2 cents each to the bank, who then lends them to the government at interest. Or, the government borrows checkbook money from a commercial bank. It is the same thing; just printed debt. A result is that one of these unit bills won't buy what a dime would in 1930. The government and bankers can then do such nonsense as re-lend this borrowed 'money' to farmers, enticing them to become overburdened and pay exorbitant interest. Fact is, any interest at all is usurous on fiat money that is just printed up! I think that the big plot is to foreclose-out the small family farmers, letting a relatively few agri-businesses do the farming and own the land.

"We need to return to Christian common law under which this nation was founded. For example, the federal government really has no right meddling in education; it has no power to do so. Thomas Jefferson endorsed public (government) schools primarily because religious instruction would be a benefit to both the individual and society. The schools have been transformed into tools of atheistic secular humanists and socialist welfare state forums for propaganda and indoctrination. Little Johnny is still not taught to read and compute properly, much less to think for himself," Gordon would continue.

"The biggest piece of nonsense that ever came out of Washington was when Charles Evans Hughes said the Constitution meant whatever the Supreme Court said it did, 'legal realism'. Actually, the Constitution is a simple document which states quite plainly what it means. Putting an apple on the table and saying that it is an orange does not make it so. Any doubts are quickly dispelled by reading the *Federalist Papers* and the *Documents Illustrative* published by the 69th Congress to determine meaning. The bottom line is that power rests with the people, not with the officials and bureaucrats. It is not a perfect document. The fact that I had relatives fighting on both sides during the War for Southern Independence speaks to that. Some issues require interpretation, it is admitted. But rewriting the Constitution under the guise of interpretation is a different kettle of fish, especially when the net result is to centralize power and strip citizens of their rights," Kahl would assert.

"The proper role of government is to protect the citizens from one another, from foreigners, and from their own regulations. God endowed us with resources, to be combined with our labor to produce the products we need to sustain life. Thus life, liberty and property are basic to our pursuit of happiness. Government should protect the individual and family — the historic basic social unit — in this regard. Instead of this, our government has sought to enslave us in the name of assuming responsibility for any and all personal or group problems. Government cannot give anyone anything; it can only take from one and give to another, stifling the incentives of both in the bargain, and peeling off a good chunk for the bureaucrats in the process.

"Why should government think it is responsible for every social ill? Once it commences to fight one problem, is it not logically responsible for all problems, then? The truth is, government has no responsibility for any of it, and the record is clear: that which government attempts to change and those whom it might try to help end up being victims in the long run, where the solutions are inevitably worse than the ills. More harm is usually caused than good is done, regardless of intentions.

"The self-serving tyrants who contrive our wars and demolish our Constitution use devious and ingenious devices to gain their ends. One method is to get vast hordes to work for them in controlling the people, by promising the military and bureaucracy huge pensions to be paid, not by the current populace, but by the posterity who are taxed for this 'social contract' commitment without representation. Similarly, working sheep are sheared of their wool in the name of social security programs. Little squawking was heard because those in the early decades of the program stood to receive vastly more in transfers than they would pay into the treasury. Thus, the monstrous fraud of taxing people who work in order to give to those who do not work was institutionalized. The success of this giant pyramid game — a chain letter pure and simple — depended on each generation of workers having larger real incomes, and those receiving the transfers remaining at a low ratio numerically. This has not happened, and the game is about up in this rip-off. The house of cards is tumbling.

"Another great ill of our country," Kahl would say, "is the adoption of the second plank of the Communist Manifesto - the progressive personal income tax. (It has not been ratified into law.) As anyone who has studied the subject knows, this is patently unconstitutional and is legalized plunder by government to obtain funds which it uses for improper government functions. Since the government knows this, and the Supreme Court will not review an IRS case because of this, the income tax is called 'voluntary'. It exists without legal basis. Can you realize the word 'income' is not even defined in the internal revenue code? This is no accident; if it were defined, the code would be invalid on its face. Even though millions do not bother to file income tax 'returns' — return what? — the sons of Satan still selectively murder or prosecute a handful, such as me, in order to terrorize the remaining people who might protest the illegal confiscation, the plunder. Most people, then, yearly send their tithes to the synagogue of Satan out of both ignorance and fear — terror! The IRS operates largely outside the law; it views itself as being above the law or its own code book. Only the KGB can be compared to it as a government tool of oppression.

"A great number of individuals or organizations unwittingly assist the power elite in subduing the free people of America. However, top leaders in some organizations are certainly accessories to the plot. The elitists use many fronts, like the Freemasons, the human cattle (goyum), to further their aims. The Masons are in an organization as anti-Christian and pro-Satan as one can possibly get, but most don't know it. You will never hear the word 'Jesus' in any Lodge. Only the very highest Masonic degree-holders fully understand its Satanic objectives. Often, with their burn hospitals and such, Masonic orders appear as angels of light (Lucifer) or as wolves in sheep's clothing. We must pray that each member becomes aware of this and resigns from this anti-Christ group, which is doing so much to undermine our American heritage.

"The erosion of our freedoms has been gradual or

Fabian Socialism, named after the Roman general Fabius, who wore his enemies down, inch by inch. The trend may well accelerate in the future," Kahl would add. He had read Gulliver's Travels, with its threads of tyranny ... one strand at a time ... until freedoms are gone and we are bound with the chains of tyranny.

"Grouping the various 'isms', they appear as a picture of CONSPIRACY. At this late hour in their timing, different names are used to achieve power. Those who aspire to rule the world refer to it as their New World Order. The Humanists may talk of 'Global 2000', from reports submitted to the Carter administration, proposing that the Humanist Millenium should begin in that year. Cultists may talk in terms of the 'New Age' or 'The Rainbow' or the 'Aquarian Conspiracy'. Groups such as the Illuminati, Trilaterals, Council on Foreign Relations or International Bankers all promote one world government, through such evil devices as the Holocaust Convention (treaty). Whatever the name, all of the foregoing promote, in the final analysis, a War Against Christianity, which connotes an attack on Biblical morality, private property, free enterprise and individual liberty. Whatever the 'ism' or the stated aims, the final objective entails the establishment of a World Government, a total destruction of family life as we know it, and a new world religion where 'The State' is the only god that can be worshipped or discussed."

The above is a sampling of the beliefs firmly held by Gordon Kahl. This book is not particularly concerned with Kahl's beliefs; it is neutral. However, the story is quite concerned with a person's right to embrace unconventional convictions and with his right to propose them to others. Among other things, the story tells of how the government treated Gordon Kahl, his family and his friends. One should note the Gordon Kahl affair is no anomaly, not an isolated instance in recent years.

Take a person who despises and shuns white-shelled eggs and condemns those who eschew the "much superior" brown eggs at every opportunity. How should he be treated by a society in which 97 percent of the people use white eggs exclusively? Is he ostracized? Should he be investigated, prosecuted and penalized by one sanction or another? The trouble with such an oversimplified analogy is that the stakes are much higher in the real-life Kahl case. Should he be wrong, the errors of his opinions will be evident in due course with little damage done. However, were his conclusions to be correct, our Constitutional Republic, as we know it, is on its last legs. Instead of the government and its agents being servants of the people, the roles will switch with the bureaucrats ruling the populace; with the accompanying demise of individual liberty. What makes one pause is that Gordon Kahl, a quite intelligent man, reached his conclusions after years of intense investigation and study. The rest of us generally have values and opinions predicated on casual exposure to the controlled mass media, uninformed associates, apathetic relatives, government schools, and a desire to conform to the prevailing norms and to be socially acceptable. Kahl believed this to be the road to slavery!

As Gordon's granddaughter narrates the Kahl story in late 1985, the reader is invited to determine which actors are the serious lawbreakers. Those familiar with the Constitution can do this best, but which public schools teach it in depth? It suffices to rely on one's innate sense of justice. The central objective of the U.S. Constitution was, in Jefferson's words, "To bind government officials with the chains of the Constitution to keep them from their mischief."

This story will illustrate its dismal failure to put shackles on the government. Bureaucrats are primarily concerned with their internal regulations, not the Constitution. Legislators have their eye on the short-term political expedient of the moment, as they ever seek higher taxes and more controls on the people, for the people's own good, of course. Courts are much more concerned with precedent than with the Constitution. Thus, the noble and supreme document is rendered relatively ineffectual in hamstringing the immediate goals of those in seats of power. Gordon Kahl sought nothing less than a complete turnaround of this trend and for the government to cease "destroying the people".

One may say that conditions are different now from when the Constitution was written. The answer to that is simple: the Constitution provides the machinery for amending or revising its provisions. Usurpation by officials of the intent of the framers of the document, whether separately or in concert, is not the proper way.

Upon receiving his Nobel prize in literature, William Faulkner yearned for writers to return to writing about the human heart — "the only thing worth writing about". I surely hope this book meets your test, Bill, as it is bound to do if heartbreak and grief get points. Although it is wishfully both entertaining and informative, the objective is not to idolize the principal subject nor his ideas. The basic purpose is to expose government tyranny and oppression as it exists in the United States today.

Before the story starts, the reader should be cognizant of certain Gordon Kahl characteristics. First, he believed in the literal reading of the Constitution regarding an individual's right to bear arms and to protect his family and property. This is not uncommon among farmers and cattlemen of the West.

Next, and contrary to scores of news reports of his memberships, he belonged to absolutely no organizations in 1983. He was not even an official member of the small denominational Heaton Bible Church which he attended and supported in Heaton, ND. He was more a single voice than a "joiner".

Lastly, he believed that when physically attacked, he had the right to defend himself and his friends or family in the vicinity. This is dramatically illustrated in a letter he wrote the night of a shootout with lawmen near Medina: "...When you come under attack by anyone, it becomes a matter of survival. I was forced to kill an American P-51 pilot one day over Burma, when he mistook us for Japs. I let him shoot first. He missed and I didn't! I felt bad, but I knew I had no choice." Gordon was in a similar predicament when he killed either one or two marshals and wounded three other lawmen in Medina, North Dakota on February 13, 1983, after being cornered and assaulted by them. Had he been a violent person with a propensity for rage, he could have killed them all. He used minimal force in self defense. He was a veritable one-man army, with nerves of steel.

No intention exists of making a folk hero of Gordon Wendell Kahl. What is intended is to reveal the truth about the man, which is quite different information from the myriad Kahl news stories, virtually all of which are laced with inaccuracies. Much of the bad press about him is derived from verbal support he received from various crackpots, hate groups, cultists, and quasi-underground organizations. Ideas will accept support from whatever quarter. Unjustified derogatory comments and reports by government officials also were a primary source of such publicity. The lack of proper research, indifference to responsibility, and socialist values of the media in general are also to be faulted.

Those who knew him well invariably had a good impression of Gordon. One neighbor said, "I don't think he would tell a lie if his life depended on it." He was even-tempered and very soft-spoken. He exuded an air of quiet self-assurance and confidence. He had a good sense of humor. One could say he was paranoid about government agents, were it not for two things: (1) His fears and predictions about what was to happen to himself and his property became actual events. (Paranoia is a false fear.) (2) He was certified sane, i.e. found deeply religious and without psychosis by a prison psychiatrist in 1977. Most of us merely assume our sanity. He would not go into debt for any purpose. Therefore, he was not dunned nor needed to heed such business signs as: "We have no regular credit manager; if you want credit, go to Hel'n Waite". He had a lifelong reputation of kindness to his family and those in need of help. He worked long and hard, an expert mechanic, good electrician, and an energetic grain farmer. He was unswerving in his religious beliefs and in his devotion to stand for individual freedom. He paid his local taxes without objection and never caused trouble for others. He possessed an impeccable morality - by and large a very good citizen and accepted as such by the community.

Gordon Kahl had all the personal characteristics to which Boy Scouts aspire. His bravery was so great that an observer would conclude that he was devoid of fear. Gordon once told a neighbor's children about a time in World War II when his crew was grounded in Calcutta, India, waiting for a dust storm to subside. While there, he and his buddy came upon a snake charmer. After watching for a while, and just for the fun of it, Gordon reached into the bag, pulled out the cobra, spat into its eye, and put it back. Gordon had a philosophy that one would not die until it was his time to go. He was not devoid of fear; fear was simply not apparent. As one former government official observed empathetically, "He is a man who hurts just like the rest of us."

Gordon's honesty was beyond question. In one instance, a grain buyer made a check out to Kahl only, at the same time acknowledging that it was supposed to be made out jointly to the lien holder (FHA) on the grain. "I know you always pay your debts," he explained.

Another incident showing such integrity happened on a stormy, cold North Dakota afternoon when Gordon parked his car to go into a Carrington hardware store to buy some nails. His wife and two-year-old child remained in the car. They had come to town mainly to get a couple of sacks of briquet coal for their furnace, all they could afford. The family's only income at the time was a $33 per month pension for Gordon's 30 percent disability for war wounds. He carried shrapnel in his hip and other scars. As his wife tells of the event, "We waited over two hours in the car in 30-degrees-below-zero weather, a long time even with the heater going. When he finally came, I said, 'Where were you?' He responded, 'As I was coming to the car, I looked down and saw a billfold, so I looked into it. It had money in it and a driver's license, so I've been looking all over for the person, so I could return it to her. She had been working in one of the stores, had just gotten her check that morning and cashed it on her way to lunch at a cafe. She had lost it on her way back to work.' She was so happy Gordon returned it that she couldn't believe it. She wanted to give him a dollar as reward, but he wouldn't take it, even though we were broke. That dollar would have bought us ten pounds of sugar and three loaves of bread. Gordon always believed in the golden rule. At other times over the years, when we were really down and out financially, his reputation as the best mechanic in the area caused people to bring their ailing cars to him to fix. Sometimes he wouldn't even charge them anything, when we really needed the money!"

Gordon's patriot friends say that Kahl and his beliefs would be in good company were he to have been born 200 years ago. Thomas Jefferson, Madison, Morris, Henry, Adams and the other founding fathers would have welcomed him in their midst. He believed "...that life was not so dear ... as to be purchased at the price of chains of slavery." He knew he would face disaster, but he was determined to be true to his convictions. He repeatedly predicted not only that which was to happen to him and his home, but also the month in which this would occur - February, income tax season. He inexplicably let down his evasive guard in 1983. Perhaps he was born two centuries late.

Things are different now, many conclude. In some places senior citizens are prohibited from saying grace over their government-furnished meals. Newspapers are not particularly interested in telling the truth, if slant will sell papers better. For example, the New York Times did not print the story written by its magazine reporter, who traveled the country at great expense, concerning Kahl's death in Arkansas. Children are generally treated as property of the State rather than the responsibility of parents. "Satan" Claus is becoming the object of Christmas, as nativity scenes and such are becoming increasingly prohibited and the season is returning to its original paganism! Kahl mourned this in spite of the fact that he did not celebrate religious holidays in his later years. Kahl believed the excerpt from Chronicles, "If my people, who are called by my name, will humble themselves and pray, and seek my face, and turn from their wicked ways, then I will hear from heaven, forgive their sins, and heal their land." Gordon Kahl intensely loved his country and hated the evils he perceived being done to it with a "perfect hatred". He realized fully that no great civilization ever fell primarily from foreign aggression. The culprit was always moral degeneration, apathy, and decadence of the people.

Kahl had apprehension about certain elitist power groups. Some of his disdain was directed towards the descendents of Khazars and others whom he thought were parasites on the populace. His observation in Italy of supply ships being returned to America full of war refugees, who obtained instantaneous citizenship, did little to deter his suspicions. Kahl estimated some five and a half million such immigrants, based on census data. Centuries ago, when the Catholic Pope prohibited members from charging "usury" on loans, these people became the goldsmiths and then the bankers. One such person, Paul M. Warburg, came to America and lobbied heavily to establish a central bank for the United States. As a direct result, the Federal Reserve Act was passed in 1913, and Warburg became the initial Board of Directors (FED) Chairman. "Warburg's aliens have taken over our nation," Kahl would proclaim. Warburg's successors, pursuing a "tight money policy" in 1929 and thereafter, did much to precipitate and prolong the great depression. Gordon believed the Rockefellers and many others changed their names and beliefs in order to help effect the scam. He believed the Bolshevik revolution and the spread of Communism was financed and contrived by these forces, as well as was most of the other international turmoil. In the United States, the FED controls the supply of money, which it has changed from a system backed by gold and silver to that of fiduciary paper or credit, much more "flexible". One international financier, M. Rothschild, is quoted as saying, "Give me control of your money system; I don't care what your form of government is. I will maintain control," implying that the real power resides in the money changers. Thus, many constitutionalists, including Kahl, cried for the repeal of the Federal Reserve Act and a return to money with intrinsic value controlled by Congress, not by an independent bank which is never even audited. Thus, Kahl would conclude, our beloved Christian republic has been transformed into "Corporate America". He was leery.

Gordon and his family became aware during his saga that a judge has ultimate power. "I'm the law in my courtroom," almost any judge will tell you, truthfully. What he is really saying is that American courts have largely been transformed into courts of equity or "Roman Law" rather than courts of law. Thus, the judge can say with impunity, "Don't mention the Constitution or Jesus Christ in this court." Judicial discretion, a tendency of appellate judges to support lower courts, and a reluctance of the legislative branch to inhibit the judicial - these are some of the reasons for the situation. Only juries stand between this judicial tyranny and the citizen, and jurors are typically so uninformed and respectful of judicial authority that they are typically manipulated and intimidated into doing the will of the judge or government attorney.

Joan Kahl learned that power is an awesome thing; seductive, corrupting, and desired. Power is force just as law is force. A law is no better than its administration, its application. When power is misused, it can be devastating to individuals like Gordon and his son. The story strongly suggests that actions which are "legal" are not necessarily actions which are right. Laws and force are sometimes brought to bear where the circumstances do not justify them. Persons possessing legitimate power are sometimes mesmerized by a feeling of their own importance and omniscience. Their judgement is sometimes affected adversely and their power is often misused. Gordon Kahl strongly felt that an objective or end, however altruistic and noble, does not call for the use of inappropriate means to reach that goal or accomplish that mission. If one is to wield power over another, he should assure himself that he is acting within the will of God for the benefit of mankind. Otherwise, it is tyranny - pure and simple! The Nuremberg trials, after World War II, established once and for all that "I was just following orders!" is not an acceptable excuse for abuse of power, even though these "trials" were primarily rigged forums of victors.

We must all remember what a minority of farmers and shopkeepers did for us all in the 1770s. Out of the disdained colonies arose a group of intellectuals on a par with any in London or Paris, never happening before or since. In part, it was a black tie affair. Mostly, they were young men in their thirties. This group of freethinking and undisciplined traitors sought no less than to do battle with the greatest power on earth. This sedition was in the name of freedom and justice. The odds seemed insurmountable, and the task appeared impossible to the rational mind. Nevertheless, they prevailed, and right won the day, providing us with our tremendous Republic. "...if we can hold it," said Ben Franklin. Let's try to do just that! DeTouqueville said that we could, that is, until voters learn that they can vote themselves largesse from the public treasury.

After researching material for this book, the authors made certain observations about Gordon Kahl. From temporary disgrace, he will emerge for decades as a mountain rising from the prairie in the hearts of men, who, to view its summit, will have to raise their eyes toward heaven. He was the Air Corps' counterpart of the Infantry's Audie Murphy. Although not awarded the Congressional Medal, neither was Colin Kelly. He was a lone voice without guile, crying in the wilderness. His insight in the wisdom of such matters as avoiding personal debt is akin to that of those who abolished the manorial system of serfdom. He is North Dakota's Achilles without acclaim. He was God's child without hypocrisy. He was Good fighting Evil as he saw it, as watchful as a loyal sentry. He was liberty personified, opposing socialism and government oppression. Perhaps one can judge him best by all the love and esteem in which his family held him.

A pollster running a political survey asked a housewife, "What is the greatest problem in the country, ignorance or apathy?"

"I don't know and I don't care!" she replied.

The single hope is that the reader, after reading this book, would not provide such an answer.

—The Authors

January 1, 1986

PROTESTER

He didn't protest love,
He didn't protest neighborliness, human kindness,
helping those in need,
Being close to the soil, to each other, in a mutual
reverence for
Life and Liberty.
He protested Government, and the government that
was formed to serve us all
Declared war on one independent farmer.

—Maureen Murphy

I Scarlet?

Scarlet? No, I'm not Scarlet. She's my sister. Older than I am. She and Larry are getting married come June. As for me, I'm a Texan - born and reared a Thompson in name, but really a Kahl. You may call me "Little Dolly" if you like. Dolly is Grandpa's sister. You wouldn't know about me, I reckon, 'less you have read about my mother's death in Odessa last year, or maybe about Grandpa's adventures in infamy. He was plain murdered! It was over two years ago, in June, 1983. I was fifteen years old then.

As for my mother, born Linda Kahl, the police said it was suicide, no question about it. Really, I don't know one way or the other, but some peculiar questions remain unanswered. She was shot in the heart, and the family's pistol was found in the front car seat next to her, about four miles out of town. She had divorced our father, so that she could marry this certain guy. He later left her for another woman. This must have crushed her emotionally. But it happens to plenty of women, though, and they don't generally go out and shoot themselves. I just don't know; kinda confused about it all.

It seemed to Grandma that the police would at least have checked the fingerprints on the typewriter, as she had typed a farewell note. Maybe a woman is vain enough not to shoot herself in the head in a suicide attempt, but a chest shot is risky, is it not? Then, too, Grandma said any farewell note should be handwritten.

Well, Aunt Lorna, Mom's sister there in Odessa, thinks it was suicide, because she opines that Mom would sometimes go into extreme states of depression, from those of exhilaration. Grandma had just received a letter from Mom, joyously planning a family reunion at Christmas.

As far as I'm concerned, they murdered her, just as they did my Grandpa, Gordon Kahl, the year before in Arkansas. Not only that, they then threw Uncle Yorie, her younger brother, into prison for life for no reason at all. With domestic problems and all this grief heaped on to boot, the blame rests squarely on the federal government so far as Grandma and I are concerned, no matter who actually pulled the trigger.

Mom's death was a real loss to us all. It was just the last of a whole series of unnecessary tragedies to the Kahl family these past few years. Maybe Mom didn't go to church all that often, but she had the same deep belief in God that Grandpa and the others in the family held so dear. No particular denomination was preferred, just the close walk with Christ derived from being in the Lamb's Book of Life.

Anyway, after Mom died, Scarlet and I moved up here to North Dakota with Grandma at the old home place. This was during the summer of '84. The preacher, neighbors, and kin had restored the house after the Federals literally demolished the windows, furnishings and interior in February of '83. More about that later. Scarlet had already finished high school, but I still had two more years to go. Boy, I'll be glad when school starts. It's a real bore out here on this North Dakota prairie. One good thing, I don't have to attend that Bowden School. It's the pits - even though some say we live in that District.

My Granddad thought I was something special, and my, how all the family loved and admired that man! In a way I'm glad he doesn't have to suffer persecution any more for his beliefs. Many say he ran the course, kept the faith, and fought the good fight. He now deserves the peace of his heavenly reward. He was so kind. Surely he has plenty of stars in his crown of glory!

Most people who have heard of Grandpa Gordon and don't know him think he is a murderer and outlaw. This story is for them. It's the gospel truth the best as I can determine it. Of course, there's no way I can tell the whole story. That would take several books as big as Sears Roebuck catalogs. The story is so fantastic that no one would believe it if it were just made up. No one would believe that Uncle Sam has sunk to such a despicable level. Let the reader judge for himself. I'm going to tell it as it was told to me.

In order for you to understand my grandfather better and get a gist of the story, take a gander at this portion of a letter he wrote in the evening after the Medina "shootout" in 1983:

"I, Gordon Kahl, a Christian patriot, and in consideration of the events which have taken place within the last few hours, and knowing to what lengths the enemies of Christ, who I consider my enemies, will go to separate my spirit from its body, wish to put down on paper a record of the events which have just taken place, so that the world will know what happened.

"I feel that the awesome power which will be unleashed to silence forever my testimony will, if not checked by the power of my God, who is the God of Abraham, and Isaac and Jacob, cut short my time to leave to the world; therefore, I'm going to make this record and leave it in the hands of those who I know will bring it to light, even though I may, in the meantime, be extinguished.

"While urgency or human weakness tells me to run, my spirit says write, so this I am going to do, and if my God continues to protect me, I shall write first, and flee from the hands of my enemies later.

"We had just finished our meeting in Medina concerning how we could best implement the proceedings of the third Continental Congress, which was to restore the power and prestige of the U.S. Constitution up to and including the ten articles of the Bill of Rights, and put our nation back under Christian Common Law, which is another way of saying God's Law, as laid down by the inspiration of God, through his prophets and preserved for us in the Scriptures, when word was received from someone, whose identity I am not able to give, that we were to be ambushed on our return to our homes.

"I realize now that we did not take this warning as seriously as we should have. The reason for this was because it had happened so many times before, when nothing happened. I see now that the many false alarms were to cause us to lower our guard.

"As we pondered what to do, someone suggested that we take two cars instead of one. Consequently, I went with Dave Broer; and my son Yorie, Scotty Faul, my wife Joan, and Vernon Wegener were in our station wagon. At this time none of us really expected any trouble, but just to be on the safe side, my son Yorie, myself, and Scotty prepared to defend ourselves, in the event that an attack upon us should take place.

"As we came over one of the hills just north of Medina, I saw on the top of the next hill what looked like two cars parked on it. About this time they turned on their red lights, and I knew that the attack was underway.

"We were just coming to an approach and I told Dave to pull in on it and stop. Our other car pulled in just beyond us and stopped, also.

"I looked back in time to see another vehicle coming from behind with its red light on.

"I picked up my mini-14, and got out and got myself and my weapon ready as the vehicle coming from behind skidded to a stop about 20 feet away. The doors flew open on it and the two men who were in the front seat aimed their guns at us. My son Yorie had jumped out of the other car, and had run over to a high-line pole. The two cars which we had seen ahead of us, pulled up and stopped behind us.

"A man got out of the vehicle which had come from behind us, and ran out into the ditch on the east side of the road.

"During this time there was a lot of screaming and hollering going on, but nothing else, so it appeared to be an impasse.

"About this time a shot rang out, and the driver of the car, who I believe at this time must have been supposedly in command, turned around and stood up so he was looking at his man in the east ditch and toward the cars which had come from the north and yelled, 'Who fired, who fired?' The other man who was with him echoed his question.

"At the time the shot rang out I heard Yorie cry out, 'I'm hit, I'm hit.'

"I took my eyes off the two men who were yelling, 'Who fired?' and looked over at Yorie. He was still standing, but I could tell he was in pain from the way he stood.

"About this time, another shot rang out, and I heard Yorie cry out again. I looked over and saw that he was hit again and laying on the ground.

"I looked back toward the two men and saw the one in the passenger side aim at me, and I was sure then that they felt the situation was no longer under their control, and the only thing to do was kill us all.

"Before he was able to fire, I loosed a round at the door behind which he was standing, and while I don't think I hit him, it caused him to duck down behind the door.

"I looked around again toward Yorie, and saw Scotty Faul running over toward him. I turned my head again in time to see the driver of the vehicle which had followed us raise up from behind his door and aim his gun at Scotty. I moved my gun over and fired at him before he could shoot. I didn't hit him either, the bullet striking somewhere near the lower left-hand corner of the windshield. He ducked down behind the dash so I could only see his head. About this time the other man raised up and aimed at me again. I shot again, striking the door and causing him to duck. This happened several times, with the two men alternating, and my shots causing them to duck each time before they could aim and fire. I don't know how many times I fired, until the man on the passenger side fell, and I was able to tell he was out of the fight. The driver must have seen this, as he moved his gun from Scotty's direction toward me.

"I fired several more shots at him, each time he raised up to shoot at me. I finally realized this could keep up 'til my 30-round clip was empty. My bullets appeared to be ricocheting off the windshield and door post. I ran around toward the side of the vehicle, firing at the door as I went to keep him down until I got around far enough to get a clear shot at him, at which time I knew he was out of the fight, also.

"I ran back where I could see the third man from this north-bound vehicle just in time to see him raise up to shoot at Scotty, who had run over to Yorie. Before he was able to pull the trigger, I fired and he fell to the ground. At this time I saw the man who was behind the front end of the green Mercury raise up and aim at Scotty. He saw me swing my gun in his direction, and he ducked down behind his car. I could see his feet or legs beneath the car, and I fired, striking him and putting him out of the fight.

"I ran over to the man in the east ditch, thinking he might still be in fighting condition. When I got nearly to him, he raised up his head and said, 'Don't shoot me again, I'm all done.' He had his hand on his shot-gun, so I took that and his pistol, which was in his holster, and threw them in the back seat of the green Mercury. I didn't see the man who had been behind the Mercury, and who I thought I'd hit in the leg, so I don't know where he'd gone to.

"A pick-up had pulled up behind the north-bound vehicle, but I didn't notice anyone in it or around it, and I assumed it was the one on top of the first hill as we came out of Medina, and which I believe belonged to the city, but as to who was driving it, I have no knowledge.

"Scotty tells me he saw one and possibly two men run out into the trees and hide, but I have no way of knowing who they were.

"I think from the reports I've heard on the radio which was in the Mercury, that the car which came from behind was the one the Marshals were in. If this is so, they weren't the ones who fired the first shots. The two men who were in the front seat were both looking in the direction of the green Mercury when they were shouting, 'Who fired?'

"Yorie's .45-auto, which he had in his shoulder holster, had either a rifle or pistol bullet imbedded in the clip, shattering the grips on both sides. Had he not been wearing it, he would have been killed instantly.

"Whether this was the first or second shot that was fired at him, I don't know. One was buckshot and the other was either a rifle or a high-powered pistol, from the way the bullet looks.

"I didn't see it, but it sounded as though Yorie's gun fired after he was hit. I think probably his finger tightened on the trigger when he was hit, but I know neither he nor Scotty fired before this, and whether either of them fired afterwards, I don't know. I know that if they did, they didn't hit anyone, as I *knew* when I hit each one of them myself.

"I saw a man in the clinic when we took Yorie in who I think must have been the man in the pickup who pulled up behind what I think was the Marshals' vehicle. He had blood on his face, and I think he was probably hit by either a bullet or bullets which glanced off the Marshals' vehicle when I was firing at them. I didn't see him, and I know I didn't shoot at him, and I know neither Yorie nor Scotty shot at him.

"Vernon Wegener was unarmed, so I know he didn't shoot at anyone, and Dave Broer didn't shoot at anyone, either. My wife had nothing to do with it, other than the fact that she had ridden along with us so she could visit with a couple of other ladies who were coming to the meeting.

"I want the world to know that I take no pleasure in the death or injury of any of these people..."

I'll show you the rest of the letter later, but for now, let's get on with the story. I'd rather tell you the story than to watch those stupid soap operas and listen to the wind howl, which I do to break the prairie monotony. Perhaps the first thing you should know is where Grandpa came from - a little genealogy.

II Roots

Dear Aunt Dolly,

Grandma wants a book written which tells what Grandpa Gordon Kahl was really like. She needs some background on the Kahl clan. As his sister, you are the best source. How about it?

Love,
Little Dolly

"Dear Little Dolly,

Our paternal ancestors came to the United States from Germany in the late 1830's. According to one version of the 'story', the younger members of a titled family left Europe because they wanted to get away from the endless wars, and hoped to settle in a land where they could live without fighting. Ironically, there were four cousins who fought in the War Between the States - two for the Union and two for the Confederacy. Part of the first families who came to America settled in southern Wisconsin, and the others went to Missouri, near St. Louis.

"Our Grandfather, Henry Kahl, was born near Mt. Horeb, Wisconsin, in the 1840s, according to his tombstone in the Heaton Cemetery. He was the oldest of three children: Henry, Sophia and Jacob. Jacob married Mary Heisher. They lived on a farm near Mt. Horeb, Wisconsin, west of Madison. This family consisted of nine children, all girls. Grandpa's sister married a Norwegian named Neuman. They moved to Emrado, North Dakota, near Grand Forks. Aunt Sophie's son, John Neuman, was 'best man' for Mother's and Dad's wedding in 1917.

"Our Aunt Nina used to correspond with some of the Wisconsin cousins, but Mother and Dad only kept in touch with 'Uncle John' and 'Aunt Mary'. Mary had a brother, August, and a sister, Elizabeth (Lizzie). They lived at home and inherited the family 'fortune' when the parents died. I had the impression that they were quite comfortable when most North Dakota farmers were 'poor' during the Depression years.

"After the death of his first wife, John Neuman married 'Lizzie', her sister. They visited North Dakota annually for many years. In the fall of 1936 or 1937, Lizzie's brother, August Heisher, bought a new car and brought his family for a visit. The women wore beautiful fur coats, and each had her hair 'colored'. I was really impressed! They spoke with a real 'thick' German accent; someone said that they spoke German in their homes.

"Our grandfather, Henry Kahl, was married very young and had six children: Will, Henry, George, John, Bermilu, and Joann. I believe his first wife died when Joann was born. His second wife had tuberculosis and only lived a short time. Grandpa must have been in his 40's when he married our grandmother, Minnie Decoe. She was only 17. This was in Pipestone, Minnesota.

"Our paternal grandmother was born in Berlin, Germany, about 1867. Her father, Fred Decoe, was Alsatian-German, and her mother, whose family name was Marquette, was French. (I believe both of Grandma Kahl's parents are buried in the Pipestone Cemetery.

"The Decoe family must have come to the U.S. in the late 1870's. Grandma had an older brother who immigrated first and reportedly found gold in the Black Hills. He convinced his father, who was a successful saloonkeeper in Berlin, that America was the land of great opportunity. Grandma also had a younger brother, Herman. Soon after the family arrived in Minnesota, the older brother's trunk arrived from the Black Hills. The brother never came, nor was he ever heard from again. The family was concerned that he was killed for his gold.

"The younger brother, Herman, returned to Germany when he was grown, and was not heard from after the war began in 1914. They assumed he died in the war.

"Our grandparents, Henry and Minnie Kahl, lived on their farm near Pipestone, Minnesota during the early years of their marriage, with Minnie helping rear her younger stepchildren. Later they moved to a farm near Brookings, South Dakota. Our father, Fred, was born in Minnesota, the oldest child. His sisters and brothers who followed in order were: Anna, Ed, Edith, Herb, Laura, Nina, Charles and Arthur. Dad was almost 21 years older than Arthur (Artie). I believe it was while the Kahls were still living in Minnesota that Grandpa invented a 'sweet milk butter churn'. Prior to this, it was necessary to skim the cream from the top of the whole milk and then let the cream sour before it could be churned into butter. After planning his churn, Grandpa Kahl carved all the parts from hardwood, then put them together into a working model and obtained his patent. Unfortunately, Le Leval had patented the 'cream separator', and his working models were already in the stores for marketing. The separator enabled the farmer to separate the cream from the whole milk, resulting in three by-products: cream, butter (churned from the cream), and skim milk, whereas Grandpa's sweet milk churn only gave them butter and sweet buttermilk.

"Our father, Fred, seems to have grown up quickly. He was large for his age, and followed along after his older half-brothers to parties and community affairs when he was still very young. As a young man, Dad had a lot of 'stomach trouble'. The family doctor finally suggested that maybe a change of climate would help. Dad took the train to a German community near Moscow, Idaho. He worked for a farm family there for several years, although he still had the same health problems. Finally, a country doctor diagnosed the condition as 'chronic appendicitis'. After surgery, there was an immediate improvement. While Dad was working in Idaho, he and three friends took out tree claims near Lake Couer D'Alene, but Dad never went back to 'prove-up' on his claim.

"It was while our father, Fred, was in Idaho that Grandpa Kahl decided to move to North Dakota. In South Dakota the Kahls had a large herd of milk cows, and most of their grain farming was for feed for the cattle and horses. They had several hired men the year around, to help with the work. Grandpa heard the stories about the wonderful wheat farms in North Dakota and how much 'easier and more profitable' wheat farming was than cattle farming. So he sold his South Dakota farm and came north! He bought the two quarters of land that became the Kahl family farm, and moved the family and all their belongings. He paid cash for the land and built the barn and granary that are still there. This must have been 1906 or 1907. They planed to build a new house the following year. For the next two years, they lost their entire grain crop from hail. So the new house was not built until 1951 - the same house Richard Blay and his 'army' destroyed on February 15, 1983!

"Our Dad returned to North Dakota in 1910 and helped his family with the farming. Grandpa Kahl's health was failing, and he needed someone to 'be in charge'. Dad did very well at it, even though he had trouble keeping his mind off one 'beautiful' girl he had met in church. She was the apple of his eye, and the feeling soon became mutual. She set her hat for him, as the saying goes. Dad and Mother began dating in 1910 and continued their courtship until their marriage, January 4, 1917.

"When the consolidated school was built in Heaton, the four country schools it replaced were closed. One of the schools was in the southeast corner of 'our' home place. Grandpa Kahl bought the building and grounds from the school district and made a house out of the school for Grandma and himself and the younger children, who were still at home. Mother and Dad moved into the 'old house' where each of the children of our family were born.

"Grandpa Kahl's health continued to decline. Finally, when his skin turned 'yellow', the doctors decided he must have cancer that had spread to his liver. He was operated on in the University of Minnesota Hospital, but did not survive. He died on November 4, 1917.

"Our maternal ancestors came from Germany, Ireland and England in the late 1700's - Laudenslagers, Flaughers, Webbs and Millers. Grandma Laudenslager's parents, the Alexander Millers, were from the Philadelphia area, but moved to Missouri, where Grandma Rose Miller was born around 1792. The family later moved to Defiance, Iowa, where Grandma Laudenslager finished high school.

"Grandma Laudenslager's parents were John Laudenslager and Helen Flaugher. Helen's father had a general store in Beaver Creek, Maryland, just south of Hagerstown, and he also owned some land to the west.

The Flaughers must have been a large, closely-knit family, and I believe they were 'Southern Sympathizers'. During the Civil War, the Union Army marched through and completely destroyed everything in the store. Grandpa Laudenslager was born in Beaver Creek in 1861. After the war, his grandfather Flaugher traded his acreage in western Maryland for 80-acre parcels of land in Iowa, one for each of his children and one for himself. The entire family moved west!

"In Grandpa Laudenslager's immediate family there were five boys and two girls. In Grandma Laudenslager's family there were four girls and one boy: Mary, Grandma Rose, then Della, Clara, and Gary.

"As a young man, Grandpa Laudenslager and his brothers, John and Shelby, rode horseback through the frontier settlements of Nebraska, Kansas, and 'Indian Territory', which later became Oklahoma. I believe they were there when the territory was opened up for settlement. Grandpa told about him and his brothers riding along a trail and being approached by two other riders, who asked the Laudenslagers who they were and where they were going. They all rode together for a while, and then the two left the trail. Grandpa said they thought their companions were Frank and Jesse James! (The Posse Comitatus shot and wounded these two, killed three others, and wounded and captured three of the Youngers southeast of Fargo, ND, when the gang attempted to rob the Northfield bank. Nowadays, people think bankers rob the farmers, instead of vice versa!)

"Grandpa and Grandma Laudenslager were married in Defiance, Iowa, on Christmas Day in 1890. I think Mother (Edna) was born in 1892, Paul (Ned) in 1894, Hazel in 1896. None of the children had middle names, because Grandma said, 'With a last name like Laudenslager, who needs a middle name?' There was a sister, Elsie, who must have been a new baby when the whole Laudenslager family came to North Dakota by covered wagon in 1898. The William Flaughers were already living on their farm west of Heaton. The Laudenslagers lived in a granary of the

Flaughers until Grandpa got his cabin built on his homestead south of Heaton.

"It was a hard summer. They broke up sod for a garden and a little feed grain, but without a drop of rain all summer long, nothing grew. There were some well-to-do ranchers, whose cattle fed off the open ranges. Naturally, these people tried hard to discourage the homesteaders from coming in and fencing off the land. Both the Hardings to the west and St. Jacques to the northeast told horror stories about people freezing and starving to death during the terribly severe winter. By the end of August, without any hope of either vegetables or livestock feed, the Laudenslagers hooked up their covered wagons and started back for Iowa. It took three weeks.

"Baby Elsie became ill and died soon after they reached Defiance.

"The rains came to North Dakota soon after they left, and the seeds that had been planted grew into vegetables and feed. So the following spring, Grandpa, Grandma and their three children returned to North Dakota by train.

"There were many hard times during those 'early days', but everyone worked hard (together). Grandma Laudenslager taught in the nearby country school for a year or two. Then another child, Lillian, arrived in 1902, and she didn't return to teaching after that.

"In 1912, Mother took the State Teacher's Examination for Certification and began teaching the country school in Southwestern Spacewell District. After teaching there for three years, she took special methods courses during the summer sessions in Valley City State Teachers College and at the University of North Dakota. She also taught at Hurdsfield and Cathay before getting married in 1917.

"Gordon was born on January 8th, 1920, after a very difficult pregnancy for mother. He was really precious; the first Laudenslager grandchild and a *boy!* Besides that, he was a really beautiful baby. Aunt Hazel stayed with the folks for the first three months after he was born, because of Mother's poor health. Mother said she and Hazel would sit and watch Gordon sleep, and admire him.

"There were many relatives nearby who liked children, so Gordon received a lot of attention. It must have been a bit of a blow for him to have to share his beautiful world when I arrived three years later, February 12, 1923. My name is Delores, but he called me 'Dolly'. I think he had a nickname for everyone. Our brother Clarence was born in 1928, Loreen (Rena) in 1930 and Elva June in 1932.

"1928 was a bad year in many ways. Dad had a good wheat crop, but before he could get it harvested, threshed and sold, the price had dropped from $1.05 a bushel to 25¢. The 'Great Depression' hit North Dakota farmers before it hit Wall Street in 1929.

"The drought of the early 30's and the terrible dust storms are very vivid memories for us Kahl children. I can remember Mother being in the garden, watching big, black clouds come up in the west. While we were hoping so much for rain, a few sprinkles and a lot of thunder, lightning, and wind maybe, would be all we received. Nevertheless, we always had plenty to eat and a warm, comfortable home - thanks to Mother's 'good-housekeeping' efforts. Dad took good care of his animals and always butchered the best of the beef, pork, chickens and turkeys to eat. We sold only the cream and eggs that we didn't need for food.

"Dad was an intellectual who truly enjoyed farming. He was a perfectionist who always looked for quality when he bought something. Each season he would 'overhaul' the machinery so that it was in 'mint' condition before he went into the field to work.

"By being selective, Dad developed a variety of Assinabin (Indian) corn that would mature early and produce a fairly large ear of corn. At one time, he sold some of his seeds to the Mill Seed Company in Bismarck.

"It must have been the spring of 1928 when Dr. Westervelt examined Dad and told him he would have to quit farming, because his blood pressure was so high. Instead of quitting, Dad sold his horses and bought a tractor. He 'remodeled' his horse machinery, so it could be used with the tractor. It wasn't long until Gordon began driving the tractor in the field.

"In 1919 Mother and Dad bought their first car, a new Buick, I think. They must have had a lot of fun. Dad's family had always had spirited driving horses, and he was in the habit of passing everyone on the road. Having the new car made it even more challenging, even when the road was narrow and Dad had to use the ditch to pass.

"At this time our folks were renting the pasture land east of us. Mother learned to drive the car by taking the cows to the pasture.

"Gordon must have been about 6 years old when he began driving the Buick. He would drive down to the house from the granary 'real fast', then stop quickly, jump out and look behind to see how much dust he had 'kicked up'.

"Both the Kahls and the Laudenslagers were interested in hunting. During those early years, the plentiful game provided the only meat for the table many times for the Laudenslagers.

"I don't remember when Dad bought Gordon his first rifle, but I'm quite sure it was the fall of 1930 when he got Gordon his first shotgun, a 16 gauge. Dad got himself a 12 gauge and the two of them hunted together. These two family heirlooms were part of the 'dangerous weapon cache' that the FBI confiscated!

"In the mid-30's the 'hunters' from Heaton usually invited Gordon to go hunting with them in the 'hills' between Heaton and Pettibone. Gordon was such a good 'shot' that he made a major contribution to their bag limit.

"In those years, the State paid a bounty on gopher tails (sometimes 2¢), and in the winter the rabbit pelts brought 5¢. I believe the gophers were a real nuisance to the farmers, especially in the corn fields. It was quite a challenge to earn enough to pay for the ammunition and have some left over. Gordon couldn't *afford* to miss. Gordon hunted the year around: gophers, crows, hawks in the spring and summer; prairie chickens, grouse, pheasants and ducks in the fall; and rabbits in the winter. There were no deer in our part of North Dakota at that time. The game Gordon provided in the fall enabled us to have a lot of delicious meals before it was time to butcher pork and beef. Gordon was always good about helping to prepare the meat for cooking.

"Our mother was very ill while she was pregnant with Elva. Toward the end, she developed a blood clot in one of her legs and needed to stay off her feet. Gordon, age 12, was wonderful help to her at that time. We had a Maytag washing machine - gasoline motor, wringer type. Gordon took care of washing the clothes that spring. As I recall, he would not hesitate to stay home from school when he was needed.

"On June 19, 1932, a Sunday morning, when I was nine, Mother's labor pains began. Gordon and I bundled up Clarence and Rena, got in the Buick, and went into town to get Mrs. Brown, who was the mid-wife. Gordon asked someone to call Dr. Westervelt to come out to the farm. We left Mrs. Brown at our place and then went on down to spend the rest of the day with Grandpa and Grandma Laudenslager. We were truly the 'big kids' looking after the 'little kids'.

"The saddest event in our early lives was the death of our sister, Rena on December 22, 1937. She took sick during the night and by the following afternoon, when she was operated on, her appendix had ruptured and peritonitis had spread throughout her body. She was buried on Christmas Eve.

"Mrs. Lillian Turner, the wife of the banker in Heaton, was also an accomplished pianist. She felt a responsibility to see to it that each child in the community had the opportunity to study music and learn to play the piano. Gordon and I both took lessons for many years. Gordon was really talented, but couldn't resist playing popular music by ear instead of practicing the classical pieces. I guess Mother got tired of fussing at him, and he quit taking lessons in the early 30's. When he was in high school he played the piano for a little dance band from Bowdon which performed for community dances.

"While Gordon was in high school he always took care of the special lighting effects for our school plays and programs. He seemed to have a special talent for electricity. It must have been in the middle 30's when Gordon (15) carved a big propeller from wood to put on the house and let the wind generate current for electricity. He installed the lights and batteries, and we had our own electric light system. During the war Gordon sent Dad 'plans' to wire the old tractor, installing a generator and battery. This gave the tractor lights and made it possible to work nights when necessary.

"Gordon was talented intellectually as well as in music and art. It was hard for him to discipline himself to do school work, which he considered unnecessary. Thus, he often got lower grades in some courses, because he refused to turn in written assignments even though he always scored high on the final exams, which at Heaton were State exams.

"Gordon graduated from high school in 1938. That winter he joined the CCC and spent 6 months or so in eastern Montana. In the fall of '39 Gordon, together with Mel, Clint and Deline Anderson, worked the fruit orchards from Washington to California and then spent the winter in Arizona. The older boys then worked in the mines there, but Gordon couldn't because he was under 21.

"Gordon began helping out in the Heaton Hardware Store the spring of 1941. He tried to enlist in the Armed Forces that fall, but was rejected because his broken nose caused breathing problems. When Gordon was three or four he was visiting Grandpa and Grandma Laudenslager while the men were working on Grandpa's new barn. Gordon was running back and forth, and ran into a board that had just been put in place and hurt himself badly. His nose swelled and was infected, but the doctor didn't realize it was broken because nobody mentioned the accident until after it was all healed up. When it finally healed and the swelling went down, it was easy to see the break. The doctor thought it would be too painful to break it again and reset it perfectly.

"After Pearl Harbor, Gordon went to the County Draft Board and asked that his name be 'pulled'. This time he was accepted in the Army Air Corps. He was assigned to pilot training, but when he found out how long it would take to get his wings, he volunteered for gunnery school.

"In January of 1944, Dad was coming home from town with a wagon full of coal. The ground was frozen and there were deep ruts. Just as he was coming through the lane, the horses jerked, Dad lost his footing, and fell head-first to the frozen ground. Several vertebrae were crushed, but the spinal cord was not pinched and the doctor only put on a neck brace. He did not stop work. In early June he suffered a severe stroke, which paralyzed his entire left side. Dad never gave up! As soon as he got out of the hospital, he began working with his hand and arm, finally regaining use of them. He worked with a cane at first, and later by just dragging his left leg. He never regained the use of his left leg, but he drove the tractor, did field work and took care of the livestock. He planned, and with the help of Gordon and Clarence, built the new house without any outside help.

"I was home in January of 1951 when Mother and Dad were working on their 1950 income tax returns. I remember Mother complaining because they had to pay more than $1,000 in taxes - at their ages! Dad said, 'Let's be thankful we have the money with which to pay the taxes - think of all those depression years when we didn't even have $1,000 in income.'

" Our grandfather, Henry Kahl, was a devout Lutheran. One of the neighbors, who knew Grandpa well, told me that he never sat down to eat without bowing his head and thanking God for the food.

"Dad used to tell about an incident while they were still living in Minnesota and 'Eddie' and 'Edie' were small. The men were stacking hay, and the children were playing on top of a completed stack. Suddenly, a prairie fire came sweeping toward them with the wind blowing the flames directly toward the stack. When it seemed that there was no way they could rescue the children, Grandpa asked all the men to get on their knees, and he led them in prayer. Suddenly, the wind changed direction and the fire stopped just in time to save the children.

"All through the 30's Mother and we children attended the Congregational Church and Sunday School in Heaton. Dad was often tired and 'slow' on Sundays, but Gordon was a faithful 'chauffeur'. He enjoyed the Sunday School class for the 'Big Boys' as long as Mrs. Senter, the minister's wife, taught the class. After her death, there never was anyone who reached the young people the way she did.

"Until 1940, Mother's immediate family all lived within a two mile radius of the homestead. 'Ned' married Elizabeth Ankruin and Lillian married Johnny Ankruin in a double ceremony in November 1923. Hazel married Jack James in April of 1936. There was always a family get-together for each holiday and for each family birthday. Good food was an important part of every celebration.

"Grandma Laudenslager always had Christmas dinner with either roast goose or roast turkey, and for dessert, there was homemade mincemeat pie. As soon as the dishes were finished, out came huge platters of homemade candy: chocolate fudge, divinity, caramels, and penuche, as well as popcorn balls and bowls of unshelled mixed nuts. While we were all stuffing ourselves with these goodies, Grandma would cook a batch of taffy and we would have a 'taffy-pull'. Even the little children were permitted to pull taffy.

"Grandpa Laudenslager liked to play cards, so everyone interested would gather around the big table and play 'Hearts' or some other game where the number of players was unlimited.

"By five o'clock the card game would have to end so that the tables could be used for another meal - sandwiches, fruit jello, pickles (several kinds) and cake. Then, if the weather was bad, we would bundle up, get on the 'stone boat' and cover up, heads and all, with fur robes. Our spirited horses would cover the mile or so 'home' in no time. What a wonderful time we had!

"We often celebrated July 4th at Grandpa Laudenslager's. They would cut ice in the spring, put it down an old, dry well and cover it with lots of straw. The ice would still be frozen by July 4th, and it would be used to make ice cream by first cooking a custard and then adding the measuring cream and milk. She said she 'couldn't *think* of eating raw eggs, even if they were frozen in ice cream!'

"Grandpa Laudenslager suffered several strokes during the thirties. He died in 1940. Grandma Laudenslager died from cancer in 1944.

"Dad's family was more widely separated. Charles and Herb married and moved to Cleveland, North Dakota. Annie and her family were living in Jamestown, North Dakota in the twenties and early thirties, and Eddie lived near Cando. The rest of the family moved to Oregon in the mid-twenties. There are 'Kahl cousins' in Washington, Oregon and California. Grandma Kahl used to spend some time each year with each North Dakota family. She was the kindest, 'best hearted' person one could ever find. In the spring of 1932, she went to Oregon and lived with our Aunt Nina most of the time. She died in 1954.

"These are some of the 'facts' of our family background, to the best of my knowledge."

His love and mine,
Delores Kahl Everest"

Talking about all that food made me hungry. A teenager must eat, you know. I think I'll get a sandwich, and then tell about North Dakota farming in bygone days a bit.

III The League

You can't really understand where Gordon was coming from with his ideas without knowing a bit about North Dakota farmers in bygone days.

Ray Sorenson tells us a little about this in his diary. He was a young farmer in the Cosby area, engaged to marry another farmer's daughter, Inga.

Grain prices were good in 1914, but were disastrously depressed during 1915, when the marriage was to occur. Farmers tried to hold onto their wheat until prices rose again. Inga's family was so concerned with threatened mortgage foreclosure that the wedding was postponed. A banker named Forsythe indeed did foreclose and evict them that year. Ray writes that the capricious banker 'stole' the property. The family moved to town, where Inga's father was like a fish out of water and had difficulty in making a living. Many farmers had to mortgage their farms to meet expenses.

Farmers had more problems than just market price fluctuations. Ray asserts railroad shipment prices were exorbitant, interest rates were excessive, short weights often were a fact, and singular local grain buyers depressed prices further to the farmer. Eastern industrialists and bankers were blamed for much of the farmers' plight.

On the one hand, farmers would help one another in threshing their grain, sometimes in a race with the falling snow. On the other hand, farmers were stubborn individualists - walking contradictions. Discussion of forming a League during 1915 amounted to little more than talk. The old timers in Divide County can tell you about all this. Weather conditions for field work were sometimes harsh. Following a bright display of the aurora borealis, gale winds would often roar southward down the prairie. A person could - and still can - get lost in a blizzard only a few feet from shelter, and freeze to death.

Ray saw Inga less frequently after she moved to town. Ray and certain others turned their efforts towards organizing farmers into the League; 40,000 were recruited during

1916, but solicitation was no easy task. Ray once wrestled a farmer to decide whether or not he would join. Ray lost, but declared, "You are the real loser!" Ray kept the bargain and didn't bother that farmer any more. Inga became upset because Ray was forever away on recruitment. Wildwood was the center of the organizing efforts.

The newspapers and businessmen were vitriolic in their opposition to the League across the state. Inga opined to Ray, "These people you are fighting don't quit. If you win, you'll be fighting them the rest of your life."

The League put up Frazier as a farmer candidate for governor. On election eve, a blizzard blanketed the state, making movement to the polls difficult for farmers. Early election results indicated Frazier had lost badly. When later returns from rural areas came in, Frazier became governor elect.

Help was months away, however. Banker Forsythe foreclosed on Ray, so he and another fellow moved out near the Montana border. Elevators would not accept the grain of certain fomentors.

During the next six years, the League was of much help in ameliorating the farmer's problems. The problem of "buying at retail and selling at wholesale" has never been solved, however. Ray wrote, "You struggle for a good life, but you never get it!"

My grandpa, Gordon Kahl, understood all this only too well. Farmers in the 1980's faced similar problems. Grandpa had quit dealing with a local elevator because of being allegedly short-weighted. High interest rates and low grain prices were causing foreclosures. But my grandpa had long ago perceived an additional problem. Under the well-intentioned guise of helping the farmers, Uncle Sam was indirectly destroying them with "carrot and stick" techniques. Grandpa Gordon's was a singular voice, ignored by others, just like Ray's in early 1915.

I'm getting ahead of myself, but the movie, "Northern Lights", made about Ray Sorenson in the late 70's, tells the story. Ya' think they'll make a movie about Gordon someday? I wonder. It would surely be better than a lot of the yuck I see on TV.

IV Wartime

Joan, that's Grandma, Gordon's wife, told me no "give-away" programs existed at the time World War II started. Her dad worked on a WPA project for forty bucks a month, helping to build a dam south of Heaton. Coffee, carried in a tin pail, was warmed over an open fire for lunch. It was hard work. Everyone around here worked there, except the Kahls. Grandpa's dad was too "proud" to take anything like that. They, including Gordon, were very independent and self-sustaining people.

Grandma Joan had met Grandpa when he was managing the Heaton Lumber Company in 1941. She was in high school, living with Margaret Wilson, her older sister, married to Lynn Wilson. Judging from Margaret's accounts, Joan and Gordon became quite fond of each other that year.

With December came Pearl Harbor, and Grandpa hinted to Grandma Joan that he felt he had to enlist to help save his country, which saddened my grandma, of course. She says, "He felt the same way again in 1968 from internal threats and did so until the day he died, trying his best during both periods."

He flunked his physical when he tried to enlist - bad heart, Grandma says. They told him to get a lot of exercise outdoors and to eat properly, then try again. He asked the draft board to 'pull' his name, and this time he was accepted by the Army Air Corps on February 1, 1942. Deciding pilot's training would take too long, he volunteered for gunnery training.

During basic training, Grandpa Gordon showed a propensity for hitting what he shot at. He was an "expert", tops with the carbine (rhymes with combine), bunching bullseyes at 300 yards. He was one in many thousands who was also "expert" with the .45 pistol. This weapon was developed during the Spanish-American War to "stop" charging Philippinos at close range. The barrels in them were loose, not highly accurate. These feats influenced his selection for aerial Gunnery School at Harlingen, Texas.

He was also trained as a flight engineer, and learned to fly at some point, being awarded wings.

Grandpa Gordon's talents were immediately applied against the Axis powers as a turret or tail gunner and flight engineer on B-25J bombers. He flew 57 combat missions, 255 combat hours. His base airfields included Kurmitoly, Moran, Pauda, and Fenny. This staff-sergeant was a hazel-eyed, brown-haired, 139 pounds of flying terror for the enemy. He shot down ten enemy planes. He was an Ace.

My grandpa was highly decorated for heroism. He received a Presidential Unit Citation and nine battle stars, one each for Egypt, Tunisia, Sicily, Balkans, Naples, Rome/Arno, Air Offense Europe, India/Burma, and China. His four bronze Stars were for Egypt/Libya, Naples/Foggia, Rome/Arno and Tunisia. He was awarded a Silver Star medal. He received two coveted Air Medals for "coolness and courage under enemy fire" in Burma and China. (This is equivalent to the Flying Cross, awarded to officers.) Finally, he received his second Purple Heart. That last honor was for spilling blood in combat for his country. Enemy shrapnel finally got him. After 22 months overseas, he was then returned to the States, carrying some of the shrapnel inside him, in November, 1944.

Unknown to the Washington office, the North Dakota office of the Veterans Administration was later to deny him a military funeral, illegally. However, volunteer veterans from Harvey rendered a military burial anyway. The Washington office later apologized to Joan.

After he returned to the U.S., my grandparents were married on January 6, 1945, by a Presbyterian minister. Grandma was a Catholic, but not Grandpa. They wanted to be married by a priest, but my grandpa was told that he *must* take six weeks of instruction. He had only a 3-day delay enroute to Santa Ana, California. That incident soured them both on the Catholic Church, permanently.

Grandma Joan stayed with her oldest sister, Mary Spud, in Minnesota for a while. She then joined my granddad in Greenville, South Carolina, in April. He served as a flight instructor there until he was discharged on September 7, 1945. She fitted well in their large colonial southern home, which they rented, as she could charm the rings off a racoon's tail.

Grandma worked in Greenville as a dental assistant. This was a happy time for them, sort of their delayed honeymoon. Upon her arrival, Grandpa Gordon bought an old '36 Ford. Being a good mechanic, he fixed it up. He insisted she learn to drive and to shoot. Then he went to Sears and bought her a 20-gauge double-barrel shotgun. They went out onto White Horse Road, and Grandma learned to drive and to shoot. Grandma was a good conversationalist, but sometimes when she started talking, no one could get a paddle in the water.

That gun, which had so much sentimental value to Grandma, was later taken from her. She says it was *stolen* from the vacant house by the FBI on February 15, 1983, part of Yorie's gun collection. She and Grandpa hunted extensively together during their first three years of marriage.

When discharged, they returned to Heaton.

V Family

I'm just passing on what was told to me, like I said.

Grandpa paid down a thousand dollars to his Uncle Ned for 160 acres of land a short distance from the Kahl homestead. They lived with his parents over the winter, and then bought Ned's little house at auction in April.

He then decided to attend college in Fargo, going for an EE degree that autumn. He quickly became dissatisfied. His English teacher was a Communist. They clashed. After a semester he asked, "When do I start on electrical engineering?" He was told that in his fourth year he would put a steam engine together. At this point, he quit.

Grandpa had put a steam engine together when he was 6 years old. At that age, suffering from sinus and hay fever, he was often kept home from school. His dad brought an old steam engine from the granary and put it on cardboard in the living room. Grandpa was slow, but a perfectionist in these endeavors at that age.

Moving to Bowdon from Fargo, Grandpa worked for International Harvester dealer James Kuntz as his mechanic. Linda (my mother) was born there in October, 1947. Their Springer Spaniel, Clinker, had pups about the same time, and would run from the puppies to the baby and back, to whomever was fussing. She was a good hunting dog, too.

The spring of '48 found them back on their little farm. Grandpa decided to try a farm school in Sykeston. He could learn and get paid monthly on the G.I. Bill, too! Learning that to meet requirements for the school he'd have to go into debt about $60,000 for dairy barns and such, he came home disgusted. He began to wonder, "Why such stipulations, if the government was trying to help the farmers?"

He and his dad farmed jointly. Grandpa Gordon signed up for the farm program for a few short years. He received a small check for "not planting", but felt he was short-ended. He decided to get out, and the Agriculture Soil Conservation people told him he couldn't. He did anyway.

So after a couple of years, they told him he could farm as he pleased if he would just only sign his name as a participant. He was the "one percent" of the county who would not, even for a payment. Since then, he has often chided his neighbors about their "welfare checks" humorously. He never borrowed or accepted money from government agencies, after sensing that something was askance in the government. Gordon was curious to know what was wrong!

Typically, they farmed during the warm months and traveled to a warmer climate to work for wages during the winters. At first it was California and then Texas, since it was less congested there. They tried to be self-sufficient as much as possible. He was suspicious of market foods, especially those with chemical additives. Grandpa used mouthwash, but not fluoride dentifrices; his teeth gradually yellowed, even though he never smoked nor drank. A big garden and baby chicks in the spring and canning of meat and vegetables during the summer was the rule. Grandma Joan often expressed joy over the years of the peace and tranquility of living in the country. "It was so nice," she'd say. A second daughter, Lorna Marlane, arrived on June 7, 1951.

Grandpa and Grandma searched for the "right" church for years. They tried the Congregational Church for a while, where his mother attended, but it supported the World Council of Churches, and, as did his dad, Grandpa rejected some of its teachings. They tried other churches, but Grandpa Gordon's analytical insight caused them to be unacceptable. They became Mormons in 1955, only to resign a few years later, when Gordon learned the close semblance of the Temple rituals to those of the Masonic Lodge, which he believed to be Satanic. On June 7, 1958, a third daughter came along. For religious guidance, my grandparents depended mostly on self-study of the Bible, KJV.

Fourteen months after Lonnie, Yorie was born on August 12. Was Grandpa Gordon proud!

"You can't raise a boy with three girls," Grandpa Gordon informed their mother, Grandma Joan. So, in

October of 1960, here came Frederick Von Kahl. (He attempted to restore the Vonkahl family name, but abandoned the idea. "Von" was a middle name in America.)

Gordon was becoming increasingly concerned over political ideas about that time, according to Grandma. He and several others in the area attended meetings in Bismarck, Jamestown, and Minot. He and Grandma Joan joined the Christian Constitution party a few years later, long after having concluded that the government no longer acknowledged the Constitution. Clarence S. Martin, M.D., of Medina sponsored the Party.

Their youngest child, Loreen Marjorie, was born in 1963. The family was *always* poor financially, but was rich in friends and affections.

They were in California when John Kennedy was assassinated. Grandpa Gordon innately surmised "hanky-panky". The following summer, they addended a meeting at Fessenden, the county seat for Heaton, where Austin Flett spoke. He was one of the two or three originators of the tax protest movement. I'm told he was a personal friend of the slain President Kennedy's father, Joe. After Flett's many futile efforts to talk with President Kennedy, Joe finally obtained an appointment for him. (They tell me that the late Mr. Flett never filed an income tax return, and made speeches denouncing the "voluntary" tax.) During their confab, John told Flett that the "higher ups" - hmm (?) - wanted him to do something he absolutely refused to do, because it *was terrible.* John refused to specify just what it was. Three days earlier, speaking at Columbia University, Kennedy said, "The high office of the President has been used to foment a plot to destroy the American people's freedom, and before I leave office, I must inform the citizen of his plight." Ten days later, John was assassinated, murdered, in Dallas. Grandpa had concluded that the federal dollars "were being used to destroy us, not to help us." By 1968, Gordon decided he would no longer participate in the IRS system, "an evil organization". He would never again file, must less pay to the "enemies of Christ". Up to then, he had been paying more income tax than many much larger farmers in the area. Some paid no tax.

He wrote IRS a letter of discontinuance in 1968 and followed in the footsteps of Austin Flett. All this worried Grandma Joan, who had four little children to feed. She knew the problems facing her if he were jailed.

My granddad received a letter from the IRS, telling him to report to the tax court in Washington, D.C. He wrote them back declining their "invitation". Subsequent letters from the IRS were simply ignored. Grandma continued to worry!

They returned to Texas in the fall of 1968, continuing their pattern of returning to Heaton in the spring for several years thereafter. Grandpa joined the John Birch Society for a short while. About 1972, the general dislike of the IRS became more pervasive and vocal in Texas. Meetings became more frequent to discuss the problem. Grandpa never spoke at any of them, but attended them all.

VI Posse

Around the Crane/Odessa area where they lived, many of the meetings concerned the public schools during 1973. This drew Kahl family interest, as they had four children in school. Some parents took their children out of the "corrupt" schools, but not my family. Yorie and Fred did quit high school, though; it had something to do with their Civics class. Grandpa was managing a steaming operation in the oil fields. Since he had taught the boys how to operate the steamers, they went right to work. The tax meetings continued.

A group in Odessa had learned of the Sheriff's Posse Comitatus, so they started having meetings and selected Grandpa to be the Texas coordinator. Posses were nothing new in Texas, being frequent in the wild-west days. Grandpa explained to me that Posse Comitatus simply means "power of the county". Old English common law defines the Posse as all able-bodied males between the ages of 15 and 45. The "Reave of the Shire", a highly-respected person selected by the people, eventually became known as "the Sheriff". In the U.S., the sheriff is the executive of the county, and the only elected law enforcement office in the U.S. other than constables. Thus, the Posse is a local affair only, not a state or national organization. They are usually formed by the sheriff, when needed, but some believe the federal Posse Comitatus Act, enacted about 1878, authorized the sheriff only be notified that the law is being violated. Violations of the supreme law - that is the Constitution - is what concerns the modern Posse. Grandpa pondered, "Who, other than indignant groups of citizens, is to protest lawlessness of government bodies and officials? Who else is to oppose unjust and illegal and oppressive laws?"

The Posse Comitatus movement contended that our entry into the war was contrived. When Gordon Kahl came to the same conclusion years later, he blamed FDR as the culprit who led us into war. Unfortunately, the Posse Comitatus movement had been started by Mike Beach, in

Oregon. The "Silvershirts" had protested the country's entering the war. Naturally, Beach was branded as a traitor, and the Posse got a bad name.

The Posse Comitatus started its recent thrust in 1969, in opposition to Viet Nam protestors in Oregon. One report was that a brigadier general headed the new awakening. In 1983, Jim Wickstrom of Tigerton, Wisconsin, weak on facts but full of a desire to be helpful, claimed to be "national director of counter-insurgency" for Posse Comitatus and became so vocal during the Gordon Kahl manhunt that he became a federal target and victim. LaVerne Donald Hollenbeck of Portland, Oregon, is identified as the "commander-in-chief". Such "national" tags may be used to encourage formation of citizens groups or for communication and education, but no legitimate authority exists over local groups. About this time, the Justice Department, prompted by "Federal Agents", branded Posse Comitatus officially as "domestic terrorists". The FBI overtly denies that it investigates any "organization", as the right of free speech and assembly - even for Communists - is protected by the Constitution. No one has been able to identify any Posse members in Arkansas, even though Hollenbeck says they exist. The Posse Comitatus is viewed by the Federals as militant tax protestors. They say, "If a tax is illegal, why shouldn't it be protested?"

The Posse Comitatus concept was established upon the Magna Charta provisions where the people have the power. In California, however, one Posse leader caused the group to get a "black eye" to its reputation. The group was assisting farmers in keeping Caesar Chavez's labor union organizers from coming onto the property and disrupting work in October, 1975. The courts had specified at which non-work times during the day membership solicitations could be made. Only two entrances existed for the farm. The Posse was armed. The organizers repeatedly rushed the cable-barricaded lane, and then stopped three feet short, backing off. Many law enforcement officers were also at the scene. Francis Gillings was the leader of the group. He was a diabetic, prone to neglect towards taking his insulin and eating correctly. He had helped establish

Posses throughout the U.S. Gillings became chemically, and, thus, mentally unbalanced, even though a friend was bringing him fresh fruit to restore his sugar balance. "Ole Betsy," his single shot shotgun, "will go a long way. Pull back!" he exclaimed, insanely, ignoring wise counsel. His gun discharged. This generated hostile national publicity for the Posse. The United Farmworkers Union was endorsed by the Catholic Church, the AFL-CIO, and minority rights organizations, according to the newspaper report I have.

Government officials are properly concerned that anarchists do not displace a government of law at any time or at any place. The vigilantes - Constitutionalists - are concerned that government does not violate the rights of the people. Both viewpoints have plenty of merit.

Grandpa explained that patriots insist upon strict adherence to the law, while anarchists disregard the law.

The townspeople were discussing the issue one day when I went into the store. A semantics game of sorts wages between government bureaucrats and the modern-day patriots. With the amazing and overwhelming support of the mass media, "Patriots", instead of being called "reactionaries" are branded right-wing radicals. Instead of the populace relying on the Posse Comitatus as their protection against government oppression and tyranny, it is viewed disparagingly. "Some of this is reinforced by self-appointed spokesmen, making wild, unfounded statements or violating the law by unnecessarily procuring automatic weapons and other illegal weapons, unartfully challenging the law's validity," one speaker commented. A man named Snell foolishly killed a highway patrolman near Mena, Arkansas, when stopped with firearms in his van. He reportedly had been harrassed after the Medina shootout. He was an admitted "survivalist". The dialogue continued, "As a spinoff of such anomalies, anyone who stores a cache of food these days and owns firearms is branded a 'survivalist' in a demeaning way. Truth is, we all want to survive!

"The government would be wise to recognize the defensive posture of these patriotic fundamentalist citizens. Even though potential enemies and a Russian invasion may be figments of their imagination, they plan no aggressive action. All parties realize that a comparison with Federal firepower is that of a B-B gun against a Sherman Tank," old man Dunn explained.

"Nevertheless, some of these frightened citizenry listen to Abe Lincoln literally when he says, 'This country, with its institutions, belongs to the people who inhabit it. Whenever they shall grow weary of it, they can exercise the existing right of amending it, or their revolutionary right to dismember or overthrow it!'

"Gun control laws diminish this last possibility, as they are increasingly tightened. The IRS is going to start recording gun transactions, says the TV."

I finished my shopping and left, thinking about the conversation. When I arrived home, I rummaged through my notes.

"The press is considered the natural adversary of government," according to one reporter. Jefferson said, "If I had to choose between government and newspapers, I would choose newspapers." But it seems the press - Constitutionalists would say the "establishment press" - is now more like a PR agent for those in power. The Northern Lights Glimmer puts it well:

> John Swinton, one of the best-loved newspaper men in the United States, the dean of his profession, when asked for a toast before the New York Press Club, is quoted as saying:
>
> "There is no such thing, at this date of the world's history, in America, as an independent press. You know it, and I know it. There is not one of you who dares to write your honest opinions, and if you did, you know beforehand that it would never appear in print. I am paid weekly for keeping my honest opinion out of the paper I am connected with. Others of you are paid similar salaries for similar things, and any of you who would be so foolish as to write honest opinions would be out on the streets looking for another job. If I allowed my honest opinions to appear in one issue of my paper, before twenty-four hours my occupation would be gone. The

business of the journalists is to destroy the truth: to lie outright; to pervert, to vilify; to fawn at the feet of mammon; and to sell his country and his race for his daily bread. You know it, and I know it, and what folly is this toasting an independent press. We are the tools and vassals of 'rich men' behind the scenes. We are the jumping jacks. They pull the strings, we dance. Our talents, our possibilities and our lives are all the property of other men. We are intellectual prostitutes."

A sad commentary on the fourth estate, I'd say! The price of liberty is eternal vigilance! As Rev. Martin Niemoller said, "In Germany the Nazis came for the Communists, and I didn't speak up because I was not a Communist. Then they came for the Jews, and I did not speak up because I am not a Jew. Then they came for the trade unionists, and I didn't speak up because I wasn't a trade unionist. They came for the Catholics, and I was a Protestant, so I didn't speak up. Then they came for me ... by that time there was no one to speak up for anyone."

I'm sure everyone was just "following orders". Alexander Solzhenitsyn made similar statements about Russia

Hey, supper's about ready. I wonder if Scarlet and Larry will get back from town in time?

VII IRS

Grandpa Gordon appeared on TV one night, along with another Posse member, W.M. Reinhardt. He explained what the Posse really was like, and protested federal direct taxes on individuals. Grandma says that the next day, 250 men in Dallas just quit paying into the IRS.

The predictable response from McCanless, IRS District Director, was to tell his agents, "I want you to go stomp on those bastards." (IRS Special Agents carry guns, and usually travel in pairs to confront a person.) The IRS can get anyone! Congressmen are scared to death of them. It is an unbridled agency, out of control. Rep. George Hansen of Idaho wrote a book, *To Harass Our People,* attacking IRS abuses. The IRS then attacked him, underhandedly. Of course, he's no longer in Congress, but continues his battle with the IRS. His book cover reads, "Law-breaking government at all levels jails ministers - makes fugitives of women and children - rigs juries, conducts illegal wire taps and spends billions to send innocent citizens to jail."

So the IRS started in on Grandpa again. In Heaton, he received a summons to report to court in December, 1976 at Midland, Texas. Grandma says he could have "skipped" out that time, too, but naively thought the Constitution would protect him. He and Grandma drove down. My grandpa was put under bond, restricting him to the district. Grandma returned here to her beloved Heaton homestead alone, to care for her children.

At year's end Grandma went back for the trial, which ended February 12, 1977. Although convicted, Grandpa then went back to Heaton with Grandma until April. Then Grandma and her youngest, Aunt Loreen, worked for relatives at a truck stop, while my granddad was undergoing psychiatric evaluation at Springfield, Missouri, by court order. Grandpa was released on June 30 and came home. He continued attending tax protest meetings, never speaking. The crowds were growing in size, noticeably larger.

Grandpa was charged by an "information", not an indictment, illegally unsupported by an affidavit of probable cause, of willfully failing to file tax returns for 1973 and 1974, under Title 26, which is not a part of the Criminal Code, Title 18. The U.S. Code indicates on the title page that Title 26, Internal Revenue Code, has not been enacted into law. My grandpa's primary defense was that he was a victim of selective prosecution and that his religious beliefs prohibited him from filing returns. His attorney, Buford Terrell, did not emphasize Grandpa's belief that the Constitution protected him from being required to file. He was found guilty on both counts on April 4, 1977. The case was appealed to the 5th Circuit Court, where the decision was affirmed on November 16, 1978. It was published in 583 F2nd 1351 (1978).

The Appeals Court found that the IRS had a policy of selective prosecution, and cited that the 14th Amendment would be violated if based on an improper motive, but that Kahl had not presented a "colorable" case. The Court also determined that no statute requiring him to file need be cited in the information, that he should have objected to absence of affidavit during the trial, that it was not an "infamous crime" requiring a grand jury, that his religious belief of the law's invalidity did not negate willfulness, and that requiring him to provide copies of his returns during probation was proper, not involuntary servitude. The conviction was upheld. Grandpa worked as an accountant while in prison.

On count one, Grandpa was sentenced to Federal Prison Camp at Leavenworth, Kansas. Upon his arrival a female staff member indicated to him that he should not have been sent there; a tax misdemeanor didn't belong there. She assured him he would go elsewhere when she got it straightened out. After not hearing from her, he sought her out. Her response was that she had been told emphatically to keep her nose out of this case if she liked her job, according to Grandpa. He was there from February 1 until August 8, 1979.

Now mark this! My grandpa didn't plead "not guilty" as the records show. He entered no plea at all. His Special Appearance Notice said that he appears specially and not generally and ... "I object to the jurisdiction of this court over the subject matter and over my person, and therefore refuse to plead ..." He challenged the court's jurisdiction! It was ignored, as was his choice of counsel.

The tree which was to bear the poisonous fruit in future years was the sentence on count two. It was destined to cause misery and death to many, and to cost taxpayers a huge sum. The sentence was:

> "One year imprisonment and $2,000, execution suspended and Kahl placed on probation for 5 years with supervision. Probation to begin upon his release from confinement under Count 1. Probation under terms and conditions of Probation of 12/26/72 and on the following special conditions: Defendant is to divorce himself from organizations advocating willful disobedience of any local, state, or federal laws, and refrain from public displays of any nature connected with these organizations during this probationary period. The defendant will furnish the probation office with a copy of his income tax return at the appropriate time for filing."

Another man, W. M. Reinhardt, also appeared on the 30 minute telecast that fateful night. The judge termed the two cases to be companions. Reinhardt was sentenced to a prison in Safford, Arizona. Before much time elapsed, he had a heart attack in the prison. Fellow prisoners pleaded with the guards to get medical help, and gave Reinhardt mouth-to-mouth rescusitation, to no avail. After a few hours he died. Gordon fervently believed that the authorities induced the heart attack by some drug or other. Had the illness not have been induced, they would have given him treatment! He also genuinely suspected the same fate faced him were he to return to prison a second time.

Grandpa's psychiatric examination indicated that he was deeply religious and without psychosis, but that he did have some schizoid features. Who doesn't? (A clinical psychologist remarked that in the context used, this meant he was inclined to be a loner, rather than social mixer.) He had an intense belief held for ten years that the IRS is a sinful, evil organizat ion against his religion. He had a deep personal commitment, and wrote the IRS, telling them so. At the sentencing his attorney argued, "We on the defense faced a difficult decision, because no one can say where one man's religion stops and another man's insanity begins.

"I do feel that in this case this man has such a strong commitment that his actions were totally governed; he was a man without choice in it, and I would show, also, that it was not his activities in breaking the law that brought him before this court.

"He did not pay taxes from 1969 forward. He wrote the Internal Revenue Service and said, 'I can't pay them. It's sinful to pay them.' He is here because he appeared on television for 30 minutes.

"Jerry Stamps of the IRS testified that given another man with the same factual situation, earning wages of under $10,000 and *not* appearing on television, that person would not be prosecuted."

The Court: "Mr. Kahl, may I hear from you, sir?"

"I don't think I can add too much to it, Your Honor. That pretty well covers it. I felt I had a choice to make. I realized I could be cast into prison here or I could spend an eternity in the 'Lake of Fire'. It seemed to me that the choice of the two would have to be whatever punishment I had to receive here. That's all I have to say."

Judge D. W. Suttle expressly denied that the sentence in any way infringed on Gordon's first amendment rights of free speech. The judge displayed symptoms of senility. For example, in court he once stated that he was departing for a long vacation on that day, and shortly thereafter told the clerk to make an appointment for him with someone for Monday.

Following his release from prison, Gordon was on good terms with probation officer John Noah, who visited his home in North Dakota. He completed the monthly forms until Holliday took over his case. This Holliday did not have the sap and spunk of the infamous 'Doc' Holliday of the Old West, who shotgunned a Clanton gang member in the gunfight at the O.K. Corral at Tombstone, as you will soon learn.

After his probation file was transferred to Bismarck from

Fargo, Gordon concluded that since he could not in good conscience comply with the income tax return portion of the probation requirements, it was useless to comply with any of them. When a U.S. Marshal asked him why he didn't send the monthly reports in, Grandpa retorted, "Why should I? They would send me back to prison anyway, so why fool with it?" Judge Suttle, in attempting to coerce Grandpa, had in fact delivered a life sentence to him for a misdemeanor.

It is ironic to note a 1985 case in the 1st Circuit Court of Appeals. In Aitken, the Court said:

> "In determining whether failure to file income taxes is willful, it is one's subjective state of mind that must be judged.
>
> "We draw from all these cases the rather clear inference that willfulness in criminal tax prosecutions is subjective.
>
> "Whether the defendant's beliefs about the legality of his actions were right or wrong, reasonable or unreasonable, is irrelevant to willfulness; the only issue is whether those beliefs were in fact held. 755 F2d 188

Grandpa contended that the court might well have added that if the beliefs were anchored to a decision of the Supreme Court, the beliefs would be buttressed further. The amazing fact is that the decision followed the U.S. Attorney's admonition to the tribunal, "Washington says they can't afford to lose this case." Anyway, the current trend toward more acquittals is a tad late to help Gordon.

Grandpa felt that the modern day minutemen do not contest the government's right to tax for proper government functions, while at the same time being concerned that government is much too big and expensive. Arthur Godfrey once said that he was proud to pay taxes in the U.S., but he would be just as proud for half the money. Protesters like him say that they are called illegal tax protesters because they protest illegal taxes. They contend that Federal Reserve Bank fiat paper notes are not dollars, as dollars are measured by precious metals. A dollar is a unit of measure, like an inch. The federal government is prohibited from directly taxing individuals; such must be apportioned to the states in ratio to their population.

Amendment 16 was never properly ratified, a fraud by Secretary Knox. Even if it were valid, it pertained only to corporations. Wages (compensation) are a *quid-pro-quo* exchange for labor, so no gain or profit exists that can be taxed; wages are an income *source*, not taxable. It is not a proper government function to plunder those who work in order to give it to those who don't work; benevolence requires volunteerism. Tax returns require a waiver of 4th and 5th amendment rights of testifying against oneself and are an invasion of privacy. "Income" is profit or gain. The IRS is a private corporation, not part of the government, and it mistreats people. No statute requires a person to file a return. The tax is voluntary. These, and many other arguments of Kahl and other patriots are rooted in the Constitution. Courts generally consider the arguments all frivolous, but then maybe they have a vested interest in seeing to it that the government troughs are full. Many of these growing numbers of protesters stand ready to go to jail, if need be, like my Grandpa Kahl, for their ideals.

A Penthouse magazine article in April '84 by J. Cummings and E. Volkman was entitled "No Deposit, No Return". Part of it concerned Gordon Kahl. They quote an IRS official: "The Service likes to pretend that they've got the thing under control, but to tell the truth, they're scared s---less. They know there is no way to beat a widescale, well organized tax protest movement, whose members in effect look you straight in the eye and say, 'Look, you want to put me in jail? Okay, go ahead. I ain't gonna pay you one red cent anyway.' ... What do you do? Shoot them?" They shot Grandpa, so who knows? In contrast, I think most Americans are so terrorized by the awesome arsenal of weapons wielded by the IRS and are so worried about their own personal problems that they are not about to challenge Uncle Sam. Regardless of their beliefs, they quietly submit - some to "it's the law" propaganda, others to cowardice or pragmatism. I decided to note such comments and put it with the data I was collecting.

Seems to me they'd tax consumption or something, rather than destroy people's incentive to work, and abolish that horrible IRS. Former IRS Commissioner T. Coleman

Andrews said, "I believe that a better way to raise revenue ... must be found, because ... the present system is leading us right back to the very tyranny for which those who established this land of freedom risked their lives, their fortunes, and their sacred honor to forever free themselves." Grandpa knew all this.

On the average, about 120 persons are jailed each year on income tax charges of all types, a little over two per state. IRS makes a lot of noise with each case, seeking maximum publicity.

A poll of jurors in the Aitken case indicated that the tax protester's exoneration was 90 percent attributed to the District Judge's instructions to the jury concerning "willfulness". It's a good bet that when convictions occur, which is more often than not, jury instructions are again the key item. For this reason, the consensus among the Constitutionalists is that their only hope is to educate potential jurors to the principle of "jury nullification". One document used to do this is the "Handbook for Jurors". This explains a principle which trial judges take great pains to hide: juries have a right to try the law as well as determine factual guilt or innocence. Let me quote the portion I underlined:

"You - as a juror - armed merely with the knowledge of what a COMMON LAW JURY really is ... if you feel the statute involved in any criminal case being tried by you is unfair, or that it infringes upon the defendant's natural God-given inalienable, or Constitutional rights, you must affirm that the offending statute is really no law at all and that the violation of it is no crime at all - for no man is bound to obey an injust command. Which means if the defendant has disobeyed some man-made criminal statute and the statute itself is unjust, that defendant has committed no crime. Jurors - having ruled then on the justice of the law involved and finding it opposed in whole or in part to their own natural concept of what is basically right - are bound to hold for the acquittal of said defendant.

"The charge to the jury in the first jury trial before the Supreme Court of the U.S. illustrates the TRUE POWER OF THE JURY. In the February term of 1794, the Supreme

Court conducted a jury trial in the case of the State of Georgia vs. Brailsford, et al, (3 Dall. 1) ... it is presumed that juries are the best judges of facts; it is, on the other hand, presumed that the courts are the best judges of law. But still both objects *are within your power of decision.*" (Emphasis added) "... you have a right to take upon yourselves to judge both and to determine the law as well as the fact in controversy." It goes on to explain that the juror is *the* "judge" in a criminal matter, and should not be persuaded against his conscience or better judgement to vote "guilty" by fellow jurors. As jurors, you have the prerogative of nullification if circumstances seem to warrant.

Grandpa did not think he was legitimately on "probation" after the first year following prison. "How can you be on probation for a longer period than your sentence? Where does the Constitution give the federal government the right to put any citizen on probation? The federal government has only those powers delineated in the Constitution, and this is not one of them. "It's usurpation, cut and dried," Grandpa contended. Certainly Judge Suttle knew he was sentencing Grandpa to an impossibility - to do acts contrary to his conscience.

Grandpa was perturbed that he was tried under Title 26, Section 7203 of the Internal Revenue Code, but was sentenced under Title 18, the Criminal Code, for tax evasion, or something for which he was not tried. He said, "If you have enough money you can fight them, if you can find the rare lawyer who will take them on. I need a Christian lawyer who will fight for my First Amendment religious rights, but any lawyer who prevails in doing this will soon be disbarred. It has happened many times."

Grandpa ordinarily didn't have enough money even to "pay attention".

Really, I'm not a philosopher like Li'l Orphan Annie. These big words and ideas I sometimes use are fed to me by Gordon's friends. I have a hard enough time just gettin' by in high school. But I guess by now you're beginning to get the gist of the story.

VIII Memories

By talking to Grandma, I learned some interesting things about my grandpa.

The federal agents were not finished in their pursuit of Grandpa after his release from prison. Not by a long shot!

Grandpa must have been elated, indeed, as he approached Heaton in the summer of '79, following his release. The big sky covering the endless fields of grain, gently undulating from the prairie breeze, is a magnificent sight in August. His memories recollected then were those God gave him, so that he may have bouquets in life's autumn. The cute little prairie dogs along the roadside appeared as old friends, as did the birds of prey, effortlessly circling over the fields.

"Been gone a while," a neighbor said.

"Yeah, I've been visiting one of your kinfolks down in Kansas, Uncle Sam," Gordon responded wryly, which was his nature. "I'll never go back, though."

Heaton is in central North Dakota, two miles north of Highway 52, and three miles from the homestead. A grain elevator, "prairie cathedral", is the predominant building, but like many others, has not operated for several years. A service station that stays open part-time and a post office are the only businesses. The tavern building has been converted into the Heaton Bible Church.

Grandpa got a taste of federal operations here back in 1952. He applied for a mail carrier's job and scored 95 on the exam. The next highest score was 69. The kicker was that neither of them got the job, awarded to the third man down the list.

The Kahls were not the kind to go to social functions much. They preferred to stay home, but company was welcome. With Grandpa on the piano, and his brother-in-law on strings, song and dance time was fun for all.

Gordon later expressed how his thoughts went back to bygone days during those peaceful days at summer's end:

His reverie included the joyful trip made to Montana with their friend and physician, Clarence Martin, and his wife in 1977.

He remembered his love for hunting and conservation. Smugly grinning to himself, he recalled that when others were just talking about ecology, he was planting habitat around his fields for the wildlife. He possessed a reverence for life which few can comprehend, very likely stemming from the war years when he was wounded at least twice.

I imagine he conjured visions of his childhood. Given his dry sense of humor, I remember him telling stories on himself when he was in grade school.

"You may not believe it," he would begin, "but I've been short all my life. I was four years old before my legs were long enough to walk. When I started school, the teacher marked me only half-present. She told the class to rise, then told me directly to stand up. 'But I am standing.' She'd reply, 'Then stand on a book.' When she said it was my turn to read aloud, I told her I'd like to, but I'm standing on my book..."

His years of "farming together" with his neighbor, Arley Brakel, were fond recollections, as were his labors for Herman Widicker, a large-scale farmer and a church elder near Bowdon. These were dear family friends. He felt sincere appreciation for these families in helping the Kahls over financial tight spots and in assisting with the children.

After Gordon's death, Herman Widicker wrote this about Gordon:

"It was right after World War II that we got to know Gordon Kahl. He came to Bowdon and worked in the International machine shop as a mechanic. He was a top mechanic, and did quite a bit of work for me. He always had a pleasant attitude, and we became good friends.

"We became better acquainted after he started farming a few years later. We would exchange work and machinery, and this went on for a number of years. He loved the out-of-doors and believed in wildlife conservation.

"He told of a time in the Army when they were camped in North Africa during the war in a make-shift base where they did not have any electricity. (He loved to visit and reminisce.) Gordon used his ingenuity by finding an old motor and a generator on the base. He hooked the two up, and the camp then had electricity while they were there. He liked to work with electricity.

"One time Gordon was working on a piece of machinery in the yard when a little four-year-old girl came riding around with her tricycle. She circled him and the machine several times, coming a little closer each time. He warned her to stay away, but finally she cut the corner too close and knocked down the props where he was working. Thereupon, he took command of her, warmed her bottom, and she came into the house and told her mother, 'That Gordon is sure snoopy.' Arlie smiled.

"Gordon was always willing to do a favor for his friends and neighbors. He was honest, kind, and a wonderful Christian."

One pleasant memory was when Yorie was 6 years old. Gordon was combining grain, Joan was driving the grain truck, but left it and Yorie in the field while she attended to some matters at the house. When rain threatened, she observed the truck apparently with no driver, coming slowly towards the house. Upon its arrival, it stopped, and she ran to it. There was Yorie, barely able to see over the dash. "I did it just like Dad showed me!" he blurted. Joan nearly went into shock! Yorie idolized his dad. In actions and beliefs, Yorie was a mirror image of his father.

Grandpa's thoughts were often on his children and six grandchildren. Linda had us two girls - Thompsons. Yorie and Janice had three children, but were just getting their family started then. Loreen married Charles Dyck, son of Peter Dyck, who preached at Grandpa's funeral. Fred married Claudette; they live in Texas, as do Lorna and Phil Adkins.

He pondered the long hours he had spent over the years, sometimes at it all night, studying the Bible, the Constitution, and the government. There were no regrets. He had the peace of God, which surpasses all understanding. He realized his battle was not really with flesh and blood, but with the powers and principalities of the air, as Paul the apostle had taught.

One Sunday afternoon I heard Grandpa prophetically explain to Grandma that the Federals - the alien sons of Satan - would get him sooner or later. If he had to leave in order to prevent this, she should not expect to ever see him again. His final assurance was, "But don't worry!"

IX Coloquy

You're searching to find out what happened, aren't you? I guess looking for answers is a good way to find them. The newspaper reporter then came in from the porch. Do you wanta' ask Grandma some questions? Go ahead. Her name is Joan, and she's in the kitchen.

"Sure, I'll talk with you," said Mrs. Kahl.

Q. Did Gordon contact his probation supervisor?

A. He just ignored the probation, since he didn't think it was legal. The probation officer did come to the house once. Seems that his name was Bob Holliday from Bismarck. I served him coffee and cake, and we were nice to him. Gordon left no doubt, however, that he would not go back to prison for income tax matters.

"You must sign one of these forms and send it in," Bob informed him.

"Give me the whole stack," Gordon retorted, "I'll sign them all now. I'm not going to fill them out anyway, just sign them."

"Can't do that," Holliday responded, and departed.

Q. When did he come back?

A. He never did. He would stick the forms in the mail box, but Gordon just threw them away. We were as nice to him as we could be, but he had a terrible fear of Gordon, which he later spread to others. This caused retired Marshal Bud Warren to remark later, "Here was a U.S. probation officer, a federal agent, authorized to carry a firearm and use it in self-defense, authorized to make arrests, supported by the Department of Justice and the courts, acting like a scared kid."

Q. Did you stay in North Dakota that winter?

A. Yes, we did. Everything was relatively quiet and peaceful until the next summer, 1980.

Q. What happened then?

A. The probation officer must have reported Gordon for not furnishing a copy of his '79 tax return. He probably didn't bother to check and see if Gordon had income sufficient to require him to file, being as he was in prison most of '79. This would have been around May 20. Then, on July 2, the Court in Texas wrote an "Order for Issuance of Summons", with a show-cause hearing set for noon, August 20.

The summons was sent to North Dakota on July 15, and Deputy Marshal Dean, of Minot, served the summons. Gordon firmly told the marshal at the time that he was not going to appear. The summons was quickly returned to the court in Texas, with the refusal notation. Gordon's signature had been forged on the summons document.

On July 21, 1980, the government's attorney down there filed a "Motion for Revocation of Probation". It charged that he had not furnished the probation office with a copy of his '79 tax return. That previous week, the Terrells had written the court, saying they were no longer Gordon's attorneys.

One day during this time, a deputy sheriff from Fessenden came out to the Widickers looking for Gordon. Two marshals were with him. Herman told them, "Leave Gordon alone; he isn't hurting anyone!"

A few days later they came to the house. The sheriff came this time. Gordon told them that he would like to "educate them" and also politely told them not to come back otherwise. They were not interested in talking and hurried off - the sheriff couldn't leave quickly enough!

Gordon always said he'd never go looking for them, but if "they" came looking for him he wouldn't back off. He said they had no jurisdiction over him.

Q. Whatever came of that application to revoke parole?

A. The government withdrew it the next month! The court issued an order - by Judge Burton this time, not Suttle - allowing the U.S. Attorney to withdraw the motion. This was on September 21. I think Reverend Dyck and Martha Geier may have used some influence to get this done. In any event, the Kahl case should have been over and done with at that point! This was just the beginning of the government's cat and mouse game with Gordon.

Q. He never did anything to rile them after that?

A. Of course not! He always carried his rifle with him, but he was an avid hunter, and had done that for years, just like a lot of other men. He didn't carry it on the streets or into stores, though.

Q. Where did the probation go from there?

A. The following year, the court issued an "Order for Issuance of Arrest Warrant to Show Cause Why Probation Should Not Be Revoked". Maybe the empty Kahl folder in the hands of the probation officer was getting to be an embarrassment to the cowardly Bob Holliday, and he requested the revocation.

However, those who know how IRS operates don't think it was that simple. The warrant was issued on March 30. Just before filing time, the IRS likes to make a big publicity splash, and arresting a tax protester would help terrorize any who are tempted not to file, or who are wavering. Criminal tax prosecutions are much more frequent during the first quarter of any year. Just check the newspapers and see for yourself!

The warrant issued may not have been valid - it was not issued "TO" anyone. A notation at the bottom of the form says it can be issued "To: Any U.S. Marshal" or "TO: Any FBI Agent". The space was not completed, left blank, so maybe no one was officially authorized to arrest Gordon. Notification of the warrant was sent to Marshal Harold Warren in Fargo, North Dakota, for execution. According to the stamped date, the warrant signed by a *deputy* clerk was not received by the North Dakota district until June 26, 1982, sixteen months later. Prior to that, they had facsimilies. This warrant was returned by others to the Court after Gordon was killed - marked UNEXECUTED, in June, 1983, a yellowed document.

Q. Did action pick up after that?

A. I should say so. For instance, we were in Harvey on Mother's Day in May, 1981. We heard by the grapevine that the Harvey and Fessenden police were spreading word that a SWAT team was coming out to our farm and blow us away.

So on May 11, Gordon decided to go away, alone. I learned later how destructive a SWAT team can be! He wouldn't tell me where he was going, explaining, "If you don't know where I'm going, you won't have to lie to them when they ask."

I couldn't believe they would do that to us, but Gordon said seriously, "Nothing is beneath those people.If they are really going to do it to get me, I don't want to endanger you and Loreen."

They could have arrested Gordon any day! He had not been in hiding. He was often on the streets and in the stores, unarmed. What's more, the federals knew every move he made, knew his habits and all about him!

After he left, federal agents soon checked-out our farm and determined that he was not here.

Q. You've got a lot of grit for a girl, but didn't that put quite a burden on you?

A. Yes. I was doing the best I could, with mowing yards, weeding the garden and taking care of the chickens. Then one day in mid-July, when I was having all kinds of trouble with the water system, the kitchen door opened and in walked Gordon. I was *so happy* he came home, and just in time to fix the water system! Gordon could fix anything mechanical, and he was *so* courteous and considerate.

During the following weeks we gathered our garden, gave much of it away, and canned the vegetables and chickens for the winter.

Q. There's nothing so strong as a woman's apron strings to tie a man down. One more question: any comments?

A. Yes, I have. Gordon always thought he was so alone, especially up here. If he had known of the thousands of Christian, patriotic supporters he had all over this country, it would have made it so much easier on him. I just wish he had known!

X Keystone Kops

I began to collect data and discuss events which would tell the real story of my mentor. I did not want our family and friends to remember Grandpa from a few tidbits of bad publicity.

A magazine reporter, who seemed to be enamored with my company, spent a quiet afternoon absorbing the summer sunshine and relating events. His song-song voice seemed to keep time with the swaying creaking of the yard swing.

He told me about his interview with a North Dakota U.S. Marshal.

Harold "Bud" Warren was the marshal in Fargo at the time the warrant was issued. He was an appointee of President Carter.

"Deputy marshals are under Civil Service," my admirer explained to me. Upon receiving the warrant in early April, 1981, Warren's days as marshal were numbered, since President Carter left office in January.

Being only two years away from retirement at the time, this posed a problem. He accepted the appointment, presuming Carter would be re-elected. His civil service status was forfeited when he accepted the marshal's position.

Part of Bud's problem in Fargo was because he was a Democrat, but not the kind Will Rogers had in mind when he said, "I pretend to be a Democrat because they're funny and I try to be." Bud's tenure had been polemic up to then. The two Republican federal judges had initiated a secret investigation of him as Chief Marshal, with the charge being general mismanagement. Warren sued them, and a federal judge in Washington ruled the case; no specific accusations were in evidence, and no wrong-doing could be found. One of the problems was that Bud ran the office "by the book" as an agency of the Justice Department, and within the executive branch of the federal government; not as an adjunct to the federal courts within the judicial branch, as perhaps the federal judges would have preferred. He insisted that the deputy marshals perform only the law enforcement duties clearly specified for them to do, not court bailiffs or "court jesters".

Bud Warren, though soft-spoken, makes a striking presence. He impresses one as having the physique of a 250-pound Chicago Bears linebacker, and equally as fearless and confident. His actions in the Kahl matter proved that his wisdom matched his other good traits. He tended to follow Andrew Jackson's admonition: "Take time to deliberate, but when the time for action arrives, go in."

Here's what Marshal Warren has to say:

"I received the warrant in early April and surmised it was comparable to a DUI charge. Nothing urgent: time was on our side. The Assistant Probation Officer in Bismarck called me, saying that he had initiated the warrant from Texas because Kahl had not mailed in his monthly reports. 'I'm so scared of him I won't go out there anymore!' he blurted, adding, 'The probation violation of Gordon Kahl is a very touchy situation. You had better use a lot of caution when you try to apprehend him.'

" 'Allright, I'll send it to Minot and let them investigate it.'

"They checked into the matter. They reported that citizens were of the opinion that Gordon Kahl 'would shoot you if you try to serve it.'

"I decided to handle it myself. To obtain all the pertinent information, I called the probation office, and then I called the Sheriff, who said, 'I don't have any trouble with him, but I understand he can be dangerous.' Gordon had let it be known that he was not about to be arrested and returned to Texas peaceably. So I called Gordon Kahl to get to the bottom of it:

" 'I sent a couple of fellows out, Dean and Wigglesworth, and they got run off!'

'No, they didn't get run off. They were nicely told they were not going to be welcome, and they took that very seriously and went back to Minot. They were all wind and no weather.'

'I'd like to come out and talk with you.'

'I don't think we have anything to talk about.'

'Well, we've got a warrant for probation violation. People are very sensitive about discussing the situation concerning you, because they're afraid of what might happen. We could talk about that!'

'You don't have to worry about violence; there will be no violence. I wouldn't hurt anybody. I wouldn't even shoot a jack rabbit unless it was to feed my dog,' Gordon responded.

'I'd like to come out and talk, maybe tonight.'

'OK, but we have church in Heaton tonight. How about tomorrow? You'll have to come alone and come unarmed.'

'That's no problem.'

'And it'll have to be where I say.'

'OK, no problem.'

'We'll meet at a neighbor's house, and I'll have some friends along.'

'Fine. I have no problem with that.' "

Grandpa would as lief visit a bull buffalo, but he was always good for his word.

"Having a mug shot, I decided to drive out that same day to survey the area. I picked up Pete, a friend in Jamestown, formerly a sheriff, to go with me.

"In Heaton, three or four cars were parked in front of a building. Leaning against the corner of the building was this little guy wearing a baseball cap with an I-H monogram pulled down over one eye. He had a big smile, watching us go by. I thought, 'This can't be the man.' I had a big, tough-looking guy in mind.

"Pete asked, 'Do you see him?'

'I seen a man that fits the picture.'

"We went back by, but by then Kahl was in his car. If I hadn't been so astounded by his meek appearance, I could have arrested him before he went to his car.

"I said, 'There's no way now we will be able to take Gordon Kahl tonight, as he carries a rifle in his car, and I think he has made us.'

"We then encountered the preacher down the street at the service station, who asked, 'Any problems?'

'No, no problems. We're state engineers looking for a place for the crew to eat and whatever.'

"He just smiled and chuckled.

"The next morning, after Kahl had verified no construction project was existent, he called me.

'Were you here last night?'

'Yes.'

'I didn't know it was you, but I knew it was law enforcement officers.'

'We didn't have a deal last night, our deal is for tonight.'

'Lucky you didn't try it!'

'You mean after you got in the car?'

'Yeah, I had my mini-14 along.'

"We discussed mini-14's for the remainder of the conversation.

"That night I met the minister in Carrington, and we drove up to the neighbor's house. Both sides recorded the discussion at Bud Brakel's. The crux of the meeting was that Gordon was determined not to go back to Texas and face that judge. He would voluntarily appear in court, maybe, if his case were moved to North Dakota.

'That should be no problem,' I explained with relief. 'Federal courts are everywhere, and this is where they claim you violated parole. I'll get on it immediately.'

"I suggested an attorney Gordon might contact, formerly with IRS, who should be unique in expertise. This attorney had represented one of my female employees in a discrimination charge against me, the charge being originated by a federal judge. I informed Kahl that his attorney should contact the federal judge in Bismarck. This judge and I had personal and political differences, but I thought him to be a compassionate man. I surmised if he could get the 'feeling of this case' everything would work out all right.

"Meanwhile, the probation office had put out word that Kahl was a very dangerous man. Gordon's attorney - not the one I recommended, as this didn't work out - contacted the judge, who wouldn't see him because of the reports.

"I approached the U.S. Attorney in Fargo, explaining that, in my estimation, Gordon was not dangerous. The attorney responded positively, seeing no problem. Two days later, the attorney said, 'I don't know what's going on, but these probation people are scared to death of this case.

They just want to get rid of it! Sorry!'

"I called Gordon and told him about the report.

"He responded, 'That's true. They were out here a couple of times and we were as nice to them as we could be. Last time it was Holliday, and my wife served him refreshments. I made it perfectly clear that I hadn't violated anything, and that they intended to take me to Texas whether I filed monthly reports or not, so why send them in? That probation officer won't even come into the yard anymore, and we treated him with the utmost respect.'

"The situation thus waxed ridiculous. The Justice Department, the IRS, and the federal judiciary - the whole works - all afraid of this little man. I laughed to myself.

"Leaving my family here in Fargo in 1967, I had spent six to eight years on the east coast, working with organized crime. I was one of seven marshals in the nation selected to establish the witness security, internal investigation and court security systems. I lived with a man for 18 months who had killed 27 people. Contrast him to Kahl. I lived with a Mafia Godfather in the New England states. At first, I protected others from him and then him from others. These people would kill for next to no reason at all. Then I came out here and saw all the pusillanimity, and I couldn't believe it was happening.

"Gordon did have an abnormal mental quirk, I have concluded. He had some unconventional beliefs, but to him they were the *only* beliefs. He had a rigid, closed mind in certain matters.

"Somewhat disgusted, I called Gordon Kahl and let him know what transpired, and that we had to resolve this thing.

"I had no doubt that I would do my duty and arrest Gordon. I had brought in a security specialist for the State. We inquired into Gordon's personal and routine habits and needs, such as his shopping and mail habits. We decided for the security agent, a stranger, to be shopping in a certain grocery store which Gordon frequented on a regular basis. I would remain out of sight until we were ready to take him, simply handcuff him with, at most, a mild scuffle. He did not take his rifle into stores. Management of the store was apprised of the plan. Newspapers had picked up on the story of Kahl's warrant, so I knew some action was needed. About a month had passed since receiving the warrant, but I still had no sense of urgency. Gordon trusted me and had told me as much.

"Before the plan could be implemented, I made a trip to Washington regarding my negotiations to revert to a deputy marshal. If they didn't accept my deal, that would let Kenneth Muir come in now as a temporary judicial appointee, selected by Paul Benson. It would require several months for them to oust me via the Senate confirmation route and federal courts.

"The bargain was completed on that trip. I was to become deputy marshal assigned to Grand Forks. I briefed Muir on the Kahl case. His response, which was to be the same many times thereafter: 'When you were marshal, you did it your way. Now that I'm marshal, we'll do things my way. We're going after Kahl.' The store plan was discarded.

"One of Muir's attempts in which I was ordered to participate was for four of us to pretend that we were a road survey crew. When Kahl drove by, we were to radio the message to Muir in a vehicle a mile or two ahead. 'Then we'll take him,' Ken said. I protested that we would be on foot, with Kahl in a car, and we would only have side arms. 'How are we going to take him?' He replied with his standard spiel of how we do things his way now. I told him, 'Kahl can smell you a mile away; he doesn't even have to see you. Even if he didn't, he'd know something was amiss when he did observe us. You've got your head up your ass.'

"We went out to the road before daylight, unusual for a road crew, and paced up and down until one or two o'clock, when Muir discontinued the effort. Kahl didn't come by. We looked ridiculous out there.

"Another Muir plan, which was never executed, was to pretend we were hunters during deer hunting season, and arrest Kahl while he was hunting.

"And later, of course, was the foolish roadblock, resulting in the shootout at Medina."

I interrupted, "Would you like some lemonade?"

The reporter continued the monologue as he sipped the cool, tangy beverage.

"Marshal Warren had mentioned that a kibitzing pastor, who escorted the marshal to the meeting mentioned earlier, made an interesting comment to the group while there.

'As an observer, I definitely feel that Mr. Kahl, here, has not had proper due process of law. I feel there is a need for him to get proper Constitutional protection. The thing that disturbs me about this whole matter is that evidently Gordon's position on religious grounds has not been considered. The second thing is that it has not only been not considered but rejected by the one judge, who told Gordon he didn't want to hear anything about Jesus Christ or the Constitution. These were his two defenses, his religious beliefs and the greatest document ever written,just thrown out of court. No judge in the land has authority to throw both of them out of court, and I would think these citizens gathered here tonight have a right to be very disturbed about that happening in the United States of America. I have a tendency to believe this happened to Gordon because it is not an isolated case; it has happened many more times, where the judges make their ruling, not on the Constitution at all. They make it on political expediency many times, on the political climate and on administrative laws. We are so entangled in administrative laws we don't get anywhere within a mile of the Constitution. Gordon feels he has been pushed over the brink ... let's see if we can avert some tragedy. If he is sincere in his religious beliefs, he should be protected by the citizens or else my religion will be next.'

"After the conversation, I sat thinking. When the two deputy marshals visited Herman Widicker earlier in 1981, looking for Gordon, Herman told them 'not to get lippy around here,' as they acted 'snotty' with the tone of their questioning, rubbing him the wrong way. The AP subsequently reported the events this way:

'Two marshals went to the Bowdon, ND, farm of Herman Widicker, where they had information Kahl had been employed off and on previously. Evans said the report on file reflects they were met by four armed people in the driveway who blocked their entrance.'

"I surmised that since the probable cause that Gordon Kahl was on the premises wasn't strong enough, that they backed off at that point," Evans said.

Widicker's wife, Janice, said she remembers her husband telling her about two marshals coming to their farm looking for Kahl, but he said the armed reception Evans described didn't happen. "That's ridiculous," she said.

Mrs. Widicker said she was in their farm home when her husband and son were outside working on some machinery when the two marshals drove into their yard. Mrs. Widicker said her husband told her that the two men, without identifying themselves, belligerently demanded to see Kahl.

(Ron Evans succeeded Kenneth Muir as marshal in February, 1983.)

The remainder of this story is sad and tragic - four people killed, five injured, and numerous people jailed. The primary reason for this is because of the actions and words of public employees, supposedly our servants. Their lies, deceits and concealment of facts has since brought misery to scores of people and has cost taxpayers untold thousands.

According to former marshal Bud Warren, authorities in Washington subsequently instructed Ken Muir to discontinue efforts to apprehend Kahl, as "It was not worth the trouble and the risk." In Washington, government is only narrowly understood, according to George Will, columnist. Muir disregarded these instructions, which came from Deputy Director John Twomey. He ordered Muir to "put the file away." Twomey later denied calling off the pursuit, but Joan said, "Some bureaucrats would rather lie on credit than tell the truth for cash." Warren later swore in court that Muir had detailed the directive to him.

My goodness, how's a body to know which government officials to believe? Maybe a test is whether or not they have an axe to grind or something to cover up. I think Orwell called it "New Speak".

This was only one of many reports I stored in my memory.

XI Airplane

Uncle Freddie and his wife, Claudette, came to visit on Labor Day weekend, 1981. I wasn't here then, but they told me about it. Yorie, who owned a two-seater Cessna 172 airplane, was away working in the oil fields at Minot. Fred and Grandpa decided to go for a spin in the plane. After flying around for a few minutes, they landed on a farm to let a thunderhead pass.

Upon takeoff, which required rapid elevation to clear a tree line, the airplane went into a spin and crashed. Freddie was not hurt, but Gordon broke three ribs and had a cut on his head, requiring several stitches.

When they had been gone about an hour, Dennis Unterseher called and told Joan about the crash. He owned the farm where Gordon had landed. "An ambulance has taken Gordon to the hospital at Harvey," he said. Grandma and Claudette rushed to Harvey, only to learn that the ambulance had taken him to Carrington. The Kahl's family physician in years past, Dr. Voglewede, tended to him. Grandma stayed with him during the night.

The FAA eventually investigated the damaged airplane, which Yorie towed back to the farm and later sold. They concluded that the plane had run out of gas. When Grandma suggested to the two investigators that it was perhaps sabotage, they only looked at each other without replying. With my granddad's experience as a flight engineer, it would have been extremely out of character for him to fly on a low tank of fuel.

An acquaintance said Grandpa related this account: "Freddie passed out in the front seat when I was attempting to clear the tree line with all flaps down. I also alternately passed out and regained consciousness, being able to get some air from my side window. The plane went into a spin and I came to just in time to avoid an awful crash. I think they tied a spray can of ether to the flap cables so that when I pulled cables back to lower the flaps, the contents discharged."

Yorie writes this version: "After I pulled the plane back home, the FAA said it had run out of gas. However, I know for a fact it was completely full when they started flying. I filled it. They told me that they flew it only for approximately 15 minutes and set it down to let a thundershower pass. Then they took off, and as they neared the end of the field, Dad pulled the flaps, which is what we commonly did to quickly force the plane almost straight up to clear any obstacles. At the point the flaps were pulled, the engine immediately lost power, but continued to run at not much more than an idle.

"Along in this period of time, Dad told me he would pass out and then come to several times. The last he remembered was waking up in a spin, leveling off just off the ground, and did not remember hitting the road.

"My brother at that time told me he didn't remember anything; however, he has more recently told me he vaguely remembers the spin. I just don't know.

"What I do know is that several days later, after my first contact with the FAA in Fargo, someone came out to the farm where I had the plane tied down. They removed the cowling and did *something* to the plane. I found out about it immediately and called the FAA the same day and asked him if he had been out to inspect the plane. His response, best as I can recall, was 'No, we'll probably be out Thursday.' And I believe this was on Monday.

"At any rate, I went down to the farm and, sure enough, the cowling was off. At the time I was concerned for Dad, and it didn't snap to me what had happened."

"I did, however, find out that 'whoever' took the cowling off were wearing three piece suits and drove a small, brownish car. They weren't mechanics! They never came back.

"Later, Dad had an opportunity to talk to an ex-CIA agent who specialized in sabotage of aircraft. He told Dad that they have a device of some sort, that when the flaps are used gas is released from a CO^2 cartridge-type container and either kills or puts to sleep the pilot and/or crews. He said that is why you see so many unexplained plane crashes on landing. He said there are also numerous other devices that can be used."

Yorie's .45 calibre IDS Army pistol was always stored in the cockpit, along with ammo and his pilot's folder. These were removed by authorities at the crash scene and given to Sheriff Curt Pellett of Wells County for safe-keeping. Yorie's attempts to recover the pistol during the next eight months resulted in verbal confrontations between them, and was used in Yorie's federal trial later as a tool of character assassination.

On November 19, 1981, Yorie, with Scott Faul, attempted to retrieve the property. Pellett gave him all except the pistol, on which he erroneously perceived the serial number to be altered. During the winter, Yorie's youngest sister, Loreen, attempted to get the pistol, explaining the family was out of state. She was refused, ostensibly because she did not own the gun. On May 25 Faul and Yorie again visited the sheriff. After much haranguing over pistol permits, the Constitution, and so forth, Yorie obtained the pistol.

The sheriff had sent the weapon to the federal laboratory, which tested the numbers with acid, damaging the finish. The lab instructed the sheriff to return the pistol to its owner. He didn't. Yorie went after it again, and sharp words were exchanged over the damage to the pistol. For a while thereafter, the sheriff wore his sidearm when off duty, because the frustrated Yorie had told him during this fours hours of heated discussion it was only a sin to shed "innocent blood", not his.

After Gordon was admitted to the hospital in Carrington, Foster County Sheriff James Dunn notified the marshal's office in Fargo of the fact. The marshal's office wanted Dunn to "Watch Kahl all night," but Dunn refused. "I'm a one-man department ... I need my sleep ... and I have other duties to attend to. There are 12 deputy marshals in this state. Why should I sit here and wait? It took them 15 hours to get here. They should have told me they weren't coming. When I talked to them, all I got was the run around."

Dunn said when the marshal did arrive, he wasn't sure the warrant was valid and tried making phone calls to confirm the warrant's validity.

In the meantime, Grandma had heard that the marshals were coming to get Grandpa. Between 7 and 8:00 a.m., Grandpa's I.V.s were removed, and he and Grandma quietly left the hospital and went to a friend's house.

Chief deputy marshal Ron Evans claimed Dunn could have arrested Kahl. Dunn retorted that he had no warrant and that such statements were made by someone trying to pass the buck.

Grandpa continued to live with friends in the vicinity while his ribs and gashed head were healing.

At first it was confusing to me, being three different states involved in this story. After a while, though, I reckon I got it all sorted out so that it makes sense. By that I mean one can understand what happened. You can decide for yourself if anything the government did in this whole sordid affair makes sense. To me, their logic smacks of "Alice Through the Looking Glass". I'll be a little like Lewis Carroll now, I guess! The time has come, the walrus said, to speak of many things ... of silver bars and cockle shells, of green beans and kings.

XII Arkansas

Grandpa recovered in fine fashion.

Grandma suggested a trip to visit her sister in Iowa and then return to the farm, which they did. Their daughter, Lonnie, went with them. The two weeks were considered by all to be a good trip. During the trip, they passed through three road blocks, so Grandma concluded that they were not looking for Grandpa.

Upon arriving back on the farm near the end of September, they finished winter preparations, canning garden vegetables and chickens, as was usual.

My grandparents decided to go away for the winter, as they had done so many times. Grandma suggested they go somewhere away from so many people, where they could be alone, yet in a warmer climate. Arkansas was selected, the Mt. Ida area. To assure privacy, an alias was used. She insists this was for no other reason than they "just wanted to be alone." Nevertheless, it was a little distasteful for her.

Grandma and Grandpa moved into a large house, and was it secluded! They were delightfully alone for a while. Then "drifters" started coming to the house and staying for a visit. Before long, Grandma decided that this was not so nice as back in Heaton, where they both preferred to be; yet the peacefulness of Arkansas was appealing.

Grandpa reasoned with Joan that these "guests" would soon leave and they would again be to themselves, but Grandma felt differently.

In the middle of May, 1982, Grandma returned to North Dakota, overtly because her youngest daughter was graduating from a Christian school in Harvey soon. Yorie brought her north. Her nephew had rented the Heaton house until August, so she got a job at the Carrington hospital as housekeeper and lived in Carrington.

In October Grandpa came home. Yorie and Janice returned, also, with their two children, Katie and Wendy. They moved into the farm and Grandpa and Grandma rented an apartment in Carrington, where they lived openly until that fateful Sunday, February 13, the unlucky date of the Medina shootout. One could get Trikadecophobia from that date.

During his stay in Arkansas, Grandpa made certain acquaintances who were to be of assistance to him later, after he became "the most wanted man in America".

Some of these people were in the Identity Church. This denomination shared some of Kahl's beliefs, and had other rather unconventional beliefs of their own based on their interpretation of the scriptures. These included that the chosen people were white, that America is the Israel of prophecy, that people who did not accept Jesus as the Christ could not possibly be God's elect and will not be saved, and that armed confrontations could be expected during the last days, and so forth.

It's merely speculation on my part, but I feel that Grandpa's stay in Arkansas reinforced his beliefs that his beloved Republic had become Corporate America controlled by international financiers. I think he also became more convinced that they planned to destroy him. The endemic Spartacus said, "They may get this old body, but it's mostly used up anyway. They'll never make a slave of me!"

Grandpa and Grandma had discussed this possibility more than once. My granddad felt certain they would "get" him sooner or later, and Joan was not to expect ever to see him again. To Grandma, "get him" was somewhat vague. She supposed one day a marshal or a couple of agents would either lead him away in custody or kill him.

Grandpa had never been extended the courtesy of being told that the decision had been made to "put away his file" by the Washington headquarters of the Marshals' Service. Grandma said that such decisions aren't made, surely, without coordination with other divisions of the Department of Justice, including the courts. Yet, they just left him in a sort of limbo, not knowing.

Earlier, about June 30, Deputy Marshal Robert Cheshire, about 31 years old, of Bismarck, solicited Marshal Kenneth Muir of Fargo for permission to apprehend Gordon Kahl. Cheshire assured Muir "it would be done by the book," with bulletproof vests and other safety precautions being followed. As on at least one other occasion, this request was denied. Even though each of the four USMS offices in the state had a copy of the old warrant, it is difficult to understand why a young married man with small children would seek such a risky adventure. Certainly, Cheshire didn't realize he would be dealing with an expert marksman who would spit in the eye of a cobra. Most likely, he immaturely sought esteem enhancing hero status by doing that which others had failed to do. Another speculation is that perhaps he was goaded by the probation office there in Bismarck or by the IRS. Anyway, Cheshire was hilarious after skidding his RAM Charger to a stop a few months later, cornering the Kahls and others just north of Medina, after he shouted, "You're going to die!" He and another officer laughed at that time. Who knows whether those were guffaws of nervous fear or of merriment!

If the Justice Department had recently been passive in the Gordon Kahl case, the IRS had not. In November, about a month after Grandpa's return from Arkansas, the IRS had scheduled a sale of the homestead land for back taxes. The newspaper accounts say it was for 80 acres of the land, but Grandma claims the entire 400 acres was on the block, including the house. The IRS claimed back taxes of $38,000, including fines and penalties. No one else knows how they conjured that figure, but it does go to show that if someone fails to file a tax return voluntarily, they have the *de facto* if not the legal power to collect any tax they compute, without putting people in prison or shooting them.

The property had been registered to the Gospel Doctrine Church of Jesus Christ, in which Grandpa represented himself to be a Bishop. Grandpa had no objection to local taxes, and he paid taxes on the property regularly. The church was evidently not registered with or else not approved by the IRS as a charity organization. The IRS is the self-appointed agency to determine what is or is not a church or legitimate charity in the United States. Therefore, not being able to find any such church building, the IRS determined it to be simply a tax dodge, which may or may not be true. It was the only church to which Grandpa belonged. He often attended the Heaton Bible Church and the nearby Seventh Day Adventist Church.

The foreclosure auction was on November 8, and Deputy Marshal Wigglesworth was there with the objective of serving the warrant on Gordon. The marshals still had not learned that Gordon would never place himself in a vulnerable position or one in which trouble might develop. But they knew he was back in North Dakota, living openly in Carrington with Grandma. Scott Faul, a friend of Uncle Yorie's, made photographs of persons at the auction, after obtaining permission from the judge, for a patriot newspaper. Deputy Marshal Wigglesworth was one person photographed, although his identify was unknown at the time. Faul thought he was a farmer. The IRS had notified the Minot marshal's office of the impending sale. For whatever reason, no one would bid on the land, so the IRS purchased it. Gordon had earlier told Joan, "If anyone comes out and starts working our land, we shall just invite him to leave."

Gordon was acting as one might who assumed that he had an allodial title, a Federal Land Patent, which he did not. This is a deed, rather simple and inexpensive to obtain, based on homesteading. In short, it prevents the land from being taken for financial obligations, although the idea has not been tested in the courts to finality. Grandpa had roots in the soil, though, for sure.

Grandma's brother subsequently paid the IRS the tax assessment and took title to the land. He plans on returning the title to Grandpa's heirs, once he has farmed the land until the rent value equates the value of his investment. As you know, Grandma, Scarlet and I are now living here in the house.

It beats me! If they wanted to arrest Grandpa, they could have done it any day right there in Carrington. Joan and Grandpa lived openly right there, and the federals knew it. They didn't slip around or avoid anyone. It's really perplexing!

Fact is, Grandpa had presumed the old warrant matter had become a thing of the past. According to Grandma, three and a half years had passed since he was released from prison, over five years since he was convicted of the misdemeanor. As 1983 approached, he had heard nothing about the warrant since leaving the hospital fifteen months earlier. Nevertheless, he remained somewhat cautious, ever believing the federal government was determined to exterminate him sooner or later, as he had been a thorn in their side for so long - just confounding them.

Before long, Grandpa was to be back in Arkansas, fleeing the persistent federal pursuers.

XIII APB

My Granddad, as Grandma said, along with many others in the movement urging return to Constitutional government, believed that front men, agents of a one-world conspiracy, had stolen his country. She said, "He was as certain of this as if clones from outer space had surreptitiously replaced the elected officials who were to represent and serve the American people. The proof to him was quite evident: They had, en masse, rejected their oath to uphold the Constitution. To illustrate, he might well have pointed to the second amendment: The right of the people to bear arms shall not be infringed. Or, Article I, Section 10: ...only gold and silver coins shall be made legal tender. Or, Amendment 16, income tax, never legally enacted or ratified and invalid, being almost identical to the second plank of the Communist Manifesto. Instead of government officials and employees being servants of the people, they had set themselves up as rulers. In their view, Gordon thought, Liberty was a statue in New York harbor rather then an inalienable God-given right and blessing. Gordon considered the subservient people who were so duped as being those who were born free but taxed to death - paying tithes to Babylon. He believed people had the *right* to use public highways and byways, with driver's licenses being unconstitutional titles of nobility."

He was once stopped in Texas while driving his grandchildren to school. He told the officer that he had no driver's license. When asked

"Where do you live?"

"Anywhere," Gordon answered.

"Not in town?"

"No."

The officer shrugged his arms in exasperation, walked back to his vehicle, and drove away.

Grandma rambled on. "If one were to brand Gordon an anarchist, picking and choosing which statutes and ordinances to obey, what does one call those who disregard the supreme law - the Constitution - which Gordon so revered? To him the laws which contradict the Constitution are null and void, with the real lawbreakers being those who, in Judge Paul Benson's words, 'enlarge' the Constitution. 'The people are sovereign,' Gordon would say, 'with only limited sovereignty being granted to the government.' Nowadays, it would seem to him, things are topsy-turvey, with government over the people rather than the people properly being over the government. I ask you, for example, what would happen if an off-duty marshal went to a farm house to buy eggs, and the housewife came out with a rifle at port arms and told him to leave because he was trespassing? What would happen to him if he pulled out his gun and shot her dead?' 'Some people are more equal than others,' says the pig in Orwell's *Animal Farm.*"

"My granddad didn't smoke, drink, cuss nor lie! Let's compare him to federal agents - mercenaries - who receive pay for assuming hazards as a built-in increment of compensation for their fat sinecures and retirement. Why do we need a whole army of marshals? There are probably 3,000 now, compared with a modest 600 a few years ago. Just maybe Grandpa knew what he was talking about, and just maybe they wanted to shut him up for good! Something triggered action from all fronts against him all of a sudden; it was more than just coincidence, surely.

A meeting of farmers was scheduled for Wishek on February 20, following an earlier one at Zeeland. Word was spread in advance that any attendees at Zeeland could forget abut getting FmHA loans. Forty attended anyway, and stayed late. Over a thousand, maybe sixteen hundred, farmers were then facing foreclosures in North Dakota. Patriots from out of state were to speak. Could the Caesars have thought, "Make an example of a vulnerable farmer and stop the meeting?" After the shootout on the 13th, the meeting was cancelled.

On Thursday, February 10, 1983, the following All-Points-Bulletin was issued and broadcast on the statewide police network. TV stations and other media covered the story, also. Ward County Sheriff Art Anderson apparently issued the APB from Minot which was both stupid and thoroughly inaccurate:

> "(Rusty Kouba)...seen leaving Carrington approximately 11:30 CST 2/10/83 enroute to Minot. The subjects are heavily armed with AR-15 rifles and other weapons. A Gordon Kahl may be with these subjects. U.S. Marshal's Office has a warrant for subject Gordon Kahl. Vehicle believed to be a white '75 Oldsmobile station wagon, North Dakota license 1906. If this vehicle is located, do not try to apprehend, but notify State Radio and Ward County Sheriff's Office immediately."

Truth is, Grandpa and Kouba did not know one another, had never met, though Yorie knew him.

State authorities refuse to disclose precisely who requested the APB.

The automobile in question belonged to Scott Faul. He's about 29, whose wife, Shauna, and five children were using the car in Harvey at the time. He was told about the APB in a jesting manner by a friend, George Berman, at a pool hall the next evening, who had heard it broadcast. Scott let it pass as being some kind of absurd error, which in fact it was. The car had not been to Carrington or near Mr. Kouba.

Albert "Rusty" Kouba was a tax protester in North Dakota. Scott was a friend of Kouba's, I'm pretty sure. A landmark state court decision went against Kouba in 1978 concerning taxes.

Deputy Marshal Carl Wigglesworth had supervised the sale of some of Kouba's property for taxes on Monday, February 7. "I received some calls on it," he said later. This auction was in Jamestown with the help of Stutsman County, and was peaceable. Knowing that Sheriff Anderson was to do the same in Minot shortly, the deputy marshal called the sheriff on Thursday from Carrington. Among other things unknown, Wigglesworth informed the Sheriff of an outstanding warrant for Gordon Kahl and obtained Muir's authorization for the APB portion concerning Gordon Kahl. Whatever transpired evidently frightened the Sheriff into calling for an APB on that Thursday.

I guess you could ask a lot of questions about the contents and the reason for the APB. I can't answer them, but any experienced lawman knows there are always young policemen who would unwisely try to apprehend anyone mentioned in an APB. I guess you could pass the whole thing off as a comedy of errors by the keystone kops, were it not that the APB was the portent of a terrible tragedy commencing three days later.

The upcoming man-made tragedy was one of the worst in North Dakota history, perhaps only surpassed in 1920 when Henry Layer killed a farmhand and seven members of the Jacob Wolf family at Turtle Creek because their dog had injured some of his cattle, and only the baby survived.

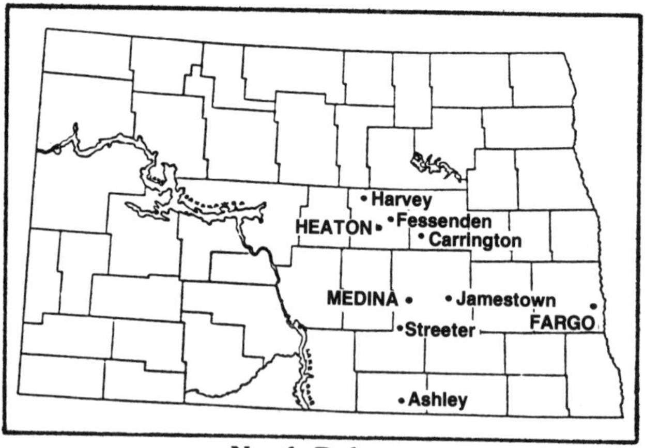

North Dakota

Regarding Robert Cheshire, present circumstances make it imperative that the whole nine yards be rolled out regarding this deputy marshal. As I tell this story, five persons languish in Federal prisons as a direct or indirect result of his actions. He was the primary instigator of the shootout debacle on February 13, 1983.

In 1980 or 1981, the following narrative report on Deputy Cheshire was written by an unidentified superior:

As of July, 1978, this employee was tentatively assigned to this district by the personnel section, USMS. He completed the USMS training academy some 3 months later, then returned to the Bismarck Field Office.

For the next 6 months and up to the last annual performance rating period of March, 1979, this DUSM trainee performed in a satisfactory manner, reflecting promise and potential toward being a creditable Deputy Marshal.

Shortly thereafter, this employee's attitude toward a senior and later designated Deputy in charge of this field office, was one of resistance to guidance, direction and supervision. This resistance is considered a bad reflection of this individual as a DUSM trainee. Further consideration is directed toward this employee's same resistance demonstrated toward this district's supervisory and management staff, this being the basis for the decision made by myself and the CDUSM equally, to designate a field office deputy in charge as the only alternative to a forced transfer of this employee. This designation was to no avail and only seemed to infuriate this individual, in fact this problem was a partial cause of the involvement of the Judiciary in demanding an inquiry of this district by the USMS Director's Office.

Additionally, two more recent unfavorable incidents involving this same employee are noted. The first taking place in January 1980, during a field trip of serving process. During the field trip this employee overtook a farm truck loaded with gravel traveling on an interstate highway. Supposedly the wind was causing portions of the truckload to be blown from the truck box to the highway and at passing vehicles. This employee saw fit to interrupt his assignment, and notifying the highway patrol by radio, he stopped and delayed the truck until the highway patrol arrived. A traffic citation was issued and a court date set, the traffic citation was later dismissed. The foregoing type of traffic in this area is as common as day and night and can be observed frequently.

(The following letter was received from the farm truck family:

I wish to thank you for your efforts concerning our little problem with the deputy. The case was dismissed for "lack of witnesses" on the side of the state.

I'm sure that you are aware that a study of history shows that free societies have always lost their freedoms because of unrestrained federal police forces, rather than because of the so-called criminal elements.

You re-affirm my faith in this great land of ours. May the time never come when the American citizen will have to live in fear of uncontrolled federal enforcement agencies.

Thank you, L.& N.R.)

The second incident resulted when this employee attempted to serve a civil process on an individual who was an agent for the FmHA. The agent, not appreciating being served in connection with his employment, in essence was not being cooperative. To compound the problem, this employee became overly determined to serve the individual, causing the local BIA law enforcement, the local Sheriff's Department and the FmHA agent's wife, coincidentally being a Deputy Sheriff, all becoming involved in one manner or the other to effect service of a civil process, thereafter requiring a staff meeting between the District-FmHA and U.S. Marshal to partially resolve this matter. As of this time the possibility of a civil law suit by the FmHA agent's wife "Deputy Sheriff" against the USMS is under consideration.

(On February 5, 1980, the following letter was written to one of Cheshire's superiors:

Dear Sir:

I would like to bring to your attention what I feel were improper acts by one of your representatives, Robert Cheshire. On January 30, 1980 your agent asked if I would be in town on Friday, February 1, I said I thought in the p.m. No definite time was established.

On Friday, February 1, 1980 at 1:45 p.m. your agent arrived in the FmHA office in Fort Yates. I informed him through my secretary I was tied up but would be able to see him at 4:00 p.m. He felt I should drop whatever I was doing to visit with him. I did not. He was very persistent and disrupted my staff on several occasions.

At some point he left and went to the Courthouse. I understand he alerted the entire Sioux County and Standing Rock Police force to be on the lookout for someone or something. What was his reason for this? I had informed him I could see him at 4:00. What a waste of manpower!

At 2:30 he arrived at the Courthouse to see Sheriff Miles Utter. He was then informed that my wife was an employee of the Court-house. He then proceeded to badger and threaten her. He asked her to go home so he could serve the dwelling. As she had a medical appointment, she declined. He spoke in a loud voice, in public, and clearly attempted to intimidate her. He did not identify himself.

When my wife said she would not go home he said they would get an arrest warrant and put me in jail if we did not cooperate. He also stated this delay would have a direct bearing on the case. All this time he was writing in his notebook. If this is not intimidation, I don't know what is. Why did he have to do this when it was only a short time until our 4:00 p.m. appointment?

It kind of sends shivers up one's back when a Federal Marshal acts in this fashion. As a result of this my wife was late for her medical appointment and has been mentally on edge....

Cordially, E.T.L.)

These two avoidable incidents resulted in embarrassment to this office, creating unnecessary and unjustified time and expense to consult and reduce this problem to an acceptable level between participants and agencies.

It was my decision to have this employee transferred to an office that would provide immediate close and direct supervision. In my opinion this is the only realistic salvation available for this employee. I will initiate this endeavor as soon as practicable.

An additional detrimental aspect of this employee's performance is one of carrying agency "in house" matters to other agencies, staff, and managers that should remain within the confines of our own agency.

Gordon - 1942

Kahl house after repairs

Gordon and sister, Delores

XIV Prelude

Sunday, February 13, 1983, dawned a beautiful, unseasonably warm day in North Dakota.

Marshal Kenneth Muir and his wife attended church in Fargo that morning. Because of his own indiscretion - pride goeth before destruction - he was to die later that day. Upon leaving for Medina in mid-afternoon, his wife's last words were, "Don't try to be a hero!" He was an expert shot with a handgun.

Marshall Muir had been the subject of an USMS internal investigation in recent weeks. This pertained to possible irregularities in using government resources for his private picture framing business, among other items. This matter was never made public after his death. Hushed up! Inspector William J. DePasquale had been making the investigation of the serious matters.

On Friday, February 11, Mr. Muir had received a call from an efficient State Crime Bureau official, Milton Lennick, who was aware of the APB, and who said, "I don't know what you intend to do about these people, but you had better be very careful in your determination of what you are going to do!" Muir just chuckled and replied, "I'm the marshal and I can handle anything that comes up." Maybe he thought, "If I can become a hero of sorts regarding this Gordon Kahl matter ..."

Deputy Wigglesworth, who accompanied Muir to Medina, was in the middle of baking a cake when he was called away.

Deputy Marshal Robert Cheshire was at home with his wife and family in Bismarck.

Stutsman County Deputy Sheriff Bradley Kapp was in Medina, a sleepy town of 500 on I-94 between Jamestown and Bismarck. That afternoon, he telephoned State Radio Dispatcher Debra Parsons to verify the Kahl's vehicle identify, a '75 Oldsmobile station wagon, parked at the Medina Clinic. She then verified the APB. "I know where this Gordon Kahl is right now," he told her. At his request, she contacted Cheshire, who in turn called Kapp. This was around three o'clock. Within forty minutes, four federal marshals were enroute to Medina. Hopson rode with Cheshire in his RAM Charger from Bismarck. While enroute, Cheshire told Hopson to remove his badge and put it in his pocket, which they both did.

Cheshire had immediately phoned Muir at Fargo after the radio confab. Muir was then on the spot. He had to instantly decide whether to go after Kahl or to obey his "put away the file" orders from Washington. If he turned Cheshire down this time, if he did not continue his pursuit, it would take away from his position and damage his authority. His ego was at stake. The decision was without hesitation. They would meet at Medina and "do things his way."

Muir phoned Deputy Warren at his home, explained the plan, and asked if he would like to go along.

"No, not necessarily so," responded Bud, having an option.

"Well, OK then, if that's the way it is, OK!" Muir angrily retorted, and slammed the receiver down.

Queried by his wife, Warren sadly said, "They'll be dead before the day's over. I don't know who, but someone is going to die."

Bud is of the opinion that his career would have ended had he gone along. He would either have sheltered Kahl at the scene and run him off and been arrested the next day for impeding federal officials, or he would have killed Gordon and been charged with excessive force during a misdemeanor arrest, or he might have been killed by a gunshot in the back. Nevertheless, he would have gone if ordered.

At 5:15, shortly before the marshals met up, Cheshire radioed his location and said, "...and the *subjects* are in the vehicles and do have weapons..." Hm-m, *subjects!* He then immediately radioed, "Cleveland, could you get ahold of Wells County SO and also Carrington SO and tell them to stand by with some marked units in case we need them right away?"

"10-4, stand by."

"Cancel that," Muir interjected, "We don't want to go

any further than we're going right now." No more sheriffs wanted.

"10-4," said Cheshire. "Cleveland copied."

You figure out that puzzle, I can't - too many witnesses or what? Maybe Muir was crawfishing a little, having second thoughts about a confrontation momentarily? I learned all this from radio scanner reports.

Complying with the marshal's desire, Deputy Sheriff Brad Kapp had kept my grandpa's automobile under surveillance from a southerly direction, remaining in his pickup, about a block away, using binoculars. He slid down in the driver's seat with his transceiver as the meeting broke up and some attendees came outside. He was to get into the RAM Charger within a few minutes, assisting the marshals, at their request. Earlier he had rebuffed Darrell Graf's request to call the whole thing off, one reason being that the marshals were already on their way. Similarly, he ignored Graf's advice not to participate.

Medina Police Chief Darrel Graf, who also provided contract police protection for Missile, North Dakota, was requested to join the marshals. He declined, sensing the great potential for trouble, which he thought to be unnecessary. "It was like a tornado coming up, and I couldn't do a thing about it," he later remarked. Graf was admittedly scared of the developments.

Graf had been attending meetings concerning farm foreclosure problems and a proposed Constitutional Township. These had been held during the past several weeks at Ashley and at the Medina Clinic, hosted by Dr. Clarence Martin, who was concerned about "British Israelism." Such a meeting was held starting at 2:00 p.m. on the 13th at the clinic. Graf did not attend, saying later that he had not been notified. Not so! Just as Kahl and some others were armed at the earlier meetings, so was Graf, who once brought a Colt AR15 weapon in a guitar case. He later said it was for a joke. Graf had learned of the APB and had notified Dr. Martin of the assertion that a federal warrant of some sort was outstanding for Kahl, incorrectly presuming Dr. Martin might want to disassociate himself from such a person. He also notified another regular attendee, David Broer, including his incorrect conjecture that Kouba and Kahl had threatened the Minot sheriff. Broer, a well-educated paralegal, had helped him with some legal problems.

Sensing that trouble was likely that Sunday evening, Graf contacted and assembled several voluntary ambulance and medical rescue personnel at the fire hall, located on the highway leading north out of town. "At least I hope we can save Dave's life," he commented, referring to Broer, with whom he had talked on the telephone twice during the past hour.

Officer Steve Schnabel, who worked for Graf, was still dressed in his camouflaged military fatigues when he responded to Muir's request for assistance. He had been attending a weekend National Guard drill. Graf told him, "I wouldn't send anybody into an area I wouldn't go," and Graf was not going, but he did not prohibit Schnabel from doing so.

Muir and Wigglesworth, in Muir's car, and Schnabel, in his green Mercury police car, set up a roadblock by a grain elevator near the fire station. Graf requested that they move further north on Road 68, to prevent danger to the townspeople. They moved to a point about a mile north of town, after being assured the lakes on each side of the road would prevent any evasion or escape route. The two vehicles were parked in a "V" heading south, at that point. The plan was for the RAM Charger to follow from behind Grandpa's car. Cheshire and Hopson were in the front seat of the Charger, Kapp in the back.

In an unrelated event, a car caught fire near the fire hall, and some of the emergency personnel went to it and extinguished the blaze. They were there when the shooting started.

About the same time, a little green sports car passed the fire station heading north. Graf chased it down quickly. Mark and Carol Lanenca had been visiting relatives and were enroute home. They were told "Get the hell out of here. There's going to be a shootout, and this time the police are in the wrong." They retreated a distance and waited.

Graf then became agitated because of the situation, later explaining, "Just standing there and letting everything go to hell around you!"

Stanley Hennum drove his city pickup over the hill towards the roadblock scene, and then returned, backing a ways and then turning the vehicle around, after Kapp told him to "Get the hell out of here!" He had not known about the roadblock.

Stanley had been performing his twice-a-day duties of greasing the sewer station, one on each side of the Reardon Farm. When he arrived at the fire station, he asked Graf about what was going on. Darrell replied, "They have a tax evader down there, and they're going to shoot him!"

Graf instructed the dispatcher to call the Reardons, who lived in the trailer home near the roadblock. He did so, informing them to go to the back room and stay down.

The time was approaching 6:00 p.m., but it was yet broad daylight on the prairie.

Grandma and Grandpa were delighted with the beautiful Sunday morning, nicest day of the winter. They had planned on attending church in Heaton, but Grandpa said, "It's such a nice day, and since weather permits, maybe I had better get the Rambler in good running order at the farm, so that if we move back there you'll have a car to drive to work." The afternoon was reserved for the Township meeting in Medina. Joan went to church, and Gordon worked on the car nearby.

Scott Faul was at his farm near Harvey, some 40 miles from Heaton, with his charming wife, Shauna, and their five children. He was intensely concerned about farm foreclosures and interested in other Constitutional issues, and planned to attend the Township meeting in Medina that day. One thing puzzled him, causing some wonder. "Why hadn't the court rescheduled his hearing date?" This concerned his taking the children out of public school and enrolling them in a private school. This was after the school sought to provide his first grader with sex training that fall "before even teaching him the ABC's." Sheriff Curt Pellett had served a warrant on him for truancy the evening prior to court date. On that day, the sheriff and deputy were already there when he arrived home, and they had gone to the barn when Shauna had not answered the door. Ignoring their shouts, Scott went into the house to check on his family, answering the door then with his mini-14 at ready, port arms. Knowing that the state sometimes removed children from parental custody, he didn't want them bothering his wife and children without a court hearing. Pellett claims Scott pointed the rifle at his midsection; Scott denies this. The officers left after they stuck the warrant in the door - or threw it on the floor - depending on whose version is correct. Scott called the lame duck judge, got a continuance because of the short notice. Nothing was ever heard about it again. He and the sheriff had argued earlier about Yorie's pistol. Whatever the reason, Scott and Shauna had a minor disagreement on that Sunday morning, and Scott had departed for the Medina meeting without kissing her goodbye and telling her he loved her, as he usually did.

Scott went to Uncle Yorie's first, as planned. Yorie was undecided as to whether to go to the meeting or not. His wife, Janice, would be left with their two children, and was expecting another in late spring. Since Scott's vehicle was low on fuel, Grandpa suggested they all go in his station wagon. "Hey, we might kill some rabbits on the way," Scott said to Yorie. "Go back and get your rifle." Yorie did this, and got his pistol, too. They did kill a jack rabbit while enroute, which both of them went to fetch from a field. (Hunting was so second nature to them that they later had trouble remembering who actually shot the rabbit.) The meeting had started when they arrived shortly after 2:00 p.m. Bible verses were being read.

Grandpa and Dr. Martin immediately engaged in a heated discussion over eligibility for membership in the Township. Grandpa desired a more restricted membership than did Clarence Martin and his following. Several attendees, including Scott, Yorie, Grandpa, and David Broer, had weapons at the meeting, as was usual. When asked by one attendee to explain the guns, my granddad said, "We need to assert our Constitutional rights more actively." Bearing arms was one way to do this. The Township, which emphasized political ideals more than a geographical area, was an attempt to foster individual rights.

Dave Broer and his wife, Joni, were paralegals who had moved to Streeter, North Dakota from Oregon. He drove to the meeting in his small AMC Hornet station wagon, accompanied by his friend Vernon Wegener, a former Streeter policeman. As usual, Broer brought along his small shotgun, which had a fold-down stock, loaded with birdshot.

About fifteen persons attended Dr. Martin's meeting at the clinic on the east side of town, including Len Martin of Ashley, and Mouritz Enquest and Russell Larson of Oakes. Two women were there, one of whom had brought Joan a box of potatoes from Gackle. The women sat together at the meeting, visiting but not participating.

The meeting did not go well, as Doctor Martin and Grandpa could not reconcile their differences concerning religious and racial composition of the township. Scott and Yorie backed Gordon; the others, including Joan passively, were generally sympathetic to Doctor Martin's views. David Broer was neutral, and assumed his traditional role as conciliator or mediator. The meeting broke shortly after five o'clock when Grandpa walked out to the north side of the clinic saying, "Anyone else coming?" Yorie and Joan followed, with Joan saying, "Well, I guess I had better go, too." Then Scott left, saying, "If I want a ride, I'd better go."

Shortly, Broer said, "Hey, I want to catch those guys before they leave," and followed them out. Grandpa asked Dave whether or not they could continue the township discussion on another day. Dave explained that Sunday evening was his only available time, but maybe he could drive home with Grandpa for further discussion on the way. Wegener, who had come with David, was given alternative rides home, but chose to go with David and the group.

Grandma took her seat in the front passenger seat of their Chrysler, where she remained. The others spied a man in a pickup watching them; Yorie pointed at him. Everyone but Joan returned inside, where Dr. Martin identified the man as Bradley Kapp. He had attended an earlier meeting. Several wanted to go to the pickup and confront Kapp as to what his purpose was. Dave suggested they not do it, and Grandpa concurred. Instead, Dave called Darrell Graf concerning the APB he had mentioned earlier. Graf said, "The APB was for Rusty Kouba and another man." After a brief discussion following the call, someone suggested calling him back to get a check on the vehicle involved.

Dave called Graf again, this time motioning for Yorie and Scott to listen on the extension. The license number was 1906, Scott's Oldsmobile. This puzzled and upset Scott; he was shocked. "That's my car!" he said, and explained how his wife was using it during the week to do laundry at her sister's and such. Some of the others were a little disconcerted, also. The concern was about Scott, not Grandpa. Graf had been careful not to mention Kahl's name, knowing what was coming down!

Scott was also concerned that his wife and children might go visiting in the Olds and be apprehended. His apprehension was increased by his recent reading of a man (John Singer) in another state (Utah) being shot down in the back at his mailbox after he had taken his children out of public school. Scott was scared. I say again, conversations in the clinic centered on Faul and the APB, not on Gordon Kahl.

Grandpa, Scott and Yorie came back out and got into the car. Scott asked Grandpa to drive to the south side of the clinic, as he wanted to talk with a couple of people, especially Len Martin.

About this time, someone drove up in a dark colored station wagon and told Grandpa, "I think you're being set up!" He then drove off.

Grandpa got the potatoes from the pickup and put them in the station wagon.

The men went inside the clinic. While there, Yorie insisted that Gordon and himself switch coats. Yorie took

Grandpa's bright blue cap and coat, giving him his brown coat and a brown stocking cap Yorie borrowed from Len Martin. Grandpa and Len shook hands. It was agreed that Gordon would ride with Dave in the small AMC and the others would follow in the Kahl Chrysler with Yorie driving. Scott was seated behind Yorie, and Wegener was behind Grandma.

In the event of any trouble, Dave Broer planned to serve as peacemaker. However, they did not really expect trouble. Warnings had been received before. Earlier, Grandma had expressed a desire to stay at the clinic if there was going to be any trouble. Grandpa reassured her that there would be no trouble.

The two cars headed north out of town. Yorie noticed the RAM Charger was following them, and commented on it. Their conversation mainly concerned what distance to stay from the front vehicle, except for that.

As Grandpa and Broer topped Cheese Factory hill just past the elevator, they noticed two vehicles in the road about a mile ahead. The one in their lane, which they learned later was Schnabel's green Mercury police car, turned on its red flasher light. The two station wagons turned left into the Reardons' driveway entrance and stopped, side by side. While Yorie was trying to explain to his dad, through rolled-down windows, the fact that a four-wheel drive was following, Broer backed out to head back south. His small car was mostly in the southbound lane, heading generally south. "Anything to avoid trouble or confrontation," Grandpa and Dave were surely thinking.

XV Countdown

The RAM Charger topped the hill with a roar at high peed. Cheshire slammed on the brakes and skidded to a stop, catty-cornered across the road as he turned left to block the southbound lane. The marshals were opening the doors before the Charger stopped. Their weapons were already pointed out the windows. As they were skidding, Gordon prepared to get out of the Hornet and stand in the V of the door with his mini-Ruger 14. A red flasher light on the dash soon came on in the cab of the RAM Charger. Yorie and Scott had not dismounted at this point.

"YOU'RE GOING TO DIE!" one of the marshals yelled, and then Cheshire and Kapp chuckled.

"Throw down your weapons or WE'RE GOING TO BLOW YOUR GODDAMN HEADS OFF! WE'RE GOING TO BLOW YOUR FUCKIN' HEADS OFF!" Cheshire screamed. Ironically, his was the only head eventually blown off. Hopson also yelled the same threat.

Scott turned to Yorie, "What the hell's going on?"

"I don't know!" Yorie responded fearfully, leaving the driver's seat with his mini-14. He side-stepped in a half-moon route around the 4-foot ditch southward to a telephone pole, the only cover he could find, constantly facing the RAM. At this point, he was nearly ten yards from the Charger. He pointed his rifle at Cheshire, who was already aiming his rifle at Yorie.

"I don't think I can miss," Cheshire blurted. "This is an automatic." Yorie did not respond, but his heart was beating so hard that it seemed to want to leap out of his throat, to burst his chest.

"Hey, how about you lay down your weapons and back off," Grandpa exclaimed. "Let's talk this over."

The countdown stalemate was to continue for another eight minutes - a Mexican standoff. Police scanner reports helped to record events.

Hopson immediately stood outside the passenger side of the RAM with his shotgun pointing. Realizing the opened door was little additional protection to his flak jacket, he went to the east ditch, across the road. He radioed Muir: Time -

5:46: (Jim Hopson) Come in ... they got three carbines ... Ken, let's call in more units.
(Ken Muir) We're here. (Muir's vehicle was way up the road to the north.)
(Bob Cheshire) Is that a 10-4, Ken?
(Ken) Tell them to drop 'em.
(Bob) We're doing that. They're not doing it. Let's call in some more units. 10-4?
(Ken) 10-4. We got 'em coming. (Highway patrolmen)

5:47: (Bob) You're cutting out. Let's go on in. Permission to call in more units, Ken? Ken, can I call in more units? ... 26. Come on! We need them closer. Pull them in closer. We're looking right in the faces of these guys. Let's go! You guys reading us? We got one behind a telephone pole. We got one in a station wagon, and one in the Hornet. Copy?
(Steve Schnabel) 10-4.

5:48: (Jim) Hey, you guys ... bring yourselves up here. We're standing looking these guns right in the face. Come up behind them. You've only got one pointing in your direction. We've got two pointing in our direction. Get in the damn car and move this way! (Muir and Schnabel then moved their cars southward in tandem; timorously and cautiously stopping some 75 yards north of the driveway. Hopson was obviously upset that they didn't come in closer, which they did after the following transmissions.)

5:52 (Ken) Is the subject here? Is he one of these guys?
(Bob) Apparently he's in the...ah...station wagon.
(Ken) He's still there? Okay.
(Bob) Ken, apparently he's changed clothes. This SO (Kapp) said he thinks he's in there, but he's not sure. (Muir had earlier been told that Gordon was wearing a bright blue jacket and cap.)

5:52 (Ken) Is anybody ... are you in contact with one of those guys there at all?

(Bob) We are talking to one of the guys. The guy is a driver and owner here ... and is the one looking out toward you.

(Ken) Can we talk to these people at all?

5:53: (Bob) I don't know. Hang on ... somebody's moving ... Ken, I think it would help a little bit if you guys would get in a little closer. We're right down the barrel with these guys. (Wegener had backed up the station wagon a few feet.)

(Ken) Yeah, we'll come in. (The two road-blocker vehicles then moved.)

5:54: (Ken) What's this guy that's ... ah ... got the gun ... what's he saying? I mean, is he saying anything? What's his problem?

(For the third time Gordon said, "Lay down your guns and back off." According to witnesses, this time he added, "It's not worth someone getting killed over," a statement the government later tried to attribute to Hopson.)

(Bob) They're not saying anything. The only one we're talking to, Ken, is the passenger (Gordon) in this small sedan right here.

Bradley Kapp exited the unmarked RAM Charger with a 12-gauge pump shotgun loaded with double-ought buckshot. His attention from the vehicle rear was focused on Yorie, at the pole. When Hopson went to the ditch, Kapp moved up and replaced him behind the passenger door of the vehicle. With his red beard and shoulder-length frizzled hair, he did not give the impression of one who is a federal marshal. "They all looked like farmers to me," Yorie was to later relate, referring to the fact that none were in uniform. Hopson, however, wore a cap with an embroidered marshal's emblem on it. Who was looking? No badges were evident. Nevertheless, the Kahl contingent suspected they were lawmen.

Wegener remained motionless in his seat in the back of the Kahl Chrysler. He was unarmed. When the station wagon tended to go forward slightly, he got out, walked around to the driver's seat, and backed the vehicle for a short distance, remaining in the seat - or the floorboard - thereafter, next to Grandma.

Dave Broer remained in his driver's seat, hands folded, with his birdshot-loaded shotgun untouched by his side. Hopson made his way northward down the east ditch until even with the Hornet, and ordered Dave to come into the ditch with him. Dave shook his head - negative, but then opened the door slightly, turned and put his feet on the pavement. There he remained until a shot was fired. When the incident was over, Broer told Wegener, who had taken his seat in the Hornet, to hand Gordon his property, a pistol and some ammunition. Wegener did. During the countdown, David later said that he thought he was going to die. Even so, he did not try to defend himself.

After placing his feet on the ground, Broer asked Hopson, "Am I under arrest?" Hopson's answer: "No!" Hopson then came out of the ditch and went to the rear of the Kahl Chrysler, which was headed into the driveway. He slammed his shotgun across the top rear of the station wagon. "There goes one of your buddies," he shouted, referring to Scott Faul's departing the scene. After the first shot, Broer got on the ground, palms on the pavement - praying.

Grandma Joan Kahl, during the entire incident, was on the floorboard facing the front passenger seat, praying. Hobson told her to get out and get in the ditch, but she ignored him. He later said, "Maybe it's a good thing she didn't, as I got hurt and she didn't." As time passed, her prayers increased in fervor, with a touch of hysteria, calling on the name over all names - Jesus!

Seeing Yorie leave the vehicle and the RAM Charger stop, Scott Faul got out, loaded his rifle and stood west of the rear door with his mini-14, which Yorie had sold to him. He remained there two or three minutes, halfway pointing his weapon at those aiming at him, 20 or 30 feet away, but he usually held the piece at a ready position. After some time, Scott asked, "What do you want?" "We want him," was the answer, along with a weapon barrel gesture toward Yorie and Grandpa.

At this point, two or three minutes of the countdown had elapsed. Scott's heart tried to leap out his throat, he was so frightened. "My head was pounding with each heartbeat." He began to backpedal westerly, towards the entrance of the mobile home. Then, seeing the trees to the north of the mobile home, which served as a windbreaker, he trotted quickly around the east end of the trailer to a small tree on the north side. He was looking back and forth as he traversed the distance, half turning at times with trepidation. He feared being shot in the back.

"Everything was racing through my mind," Scott averred, "all my children and my wife and .. I wanted to get away from the situation that I was apparently in. When I got almost to the trees, somebody started yelling at me from a ways north, seventy-five to a hundred yards distance."

This would be Deputy Wigglesworth. He was the passenger in the Muir vehicle as it halted some 75 yards north of the driveway. Scott was making his departure about this time, observed by all: Some of the lawmen may have suspected that Scott was trying to outflank them, to form an askermishers line of sorts rather than get away from trouble. Why Muir, armed only with a pistol, stopped out of pistol range north of the impasse is explained only by the fact that discretion is the better part of valor!

Wigglesworth said, "Ken, we've got one running away. I'm going to cut him off!" Saying this, he dismounted with his AR and went north along the road a few steps, then followed a path to the west, crossing the ditch and a barbwire fence. After going about fifty yards west, he broke through the ice in knee-deep water. He then went further north a few feet to dry ground, to a knoll farther from Scott, and assumed a prone firing position. Scott and Wigglesworth each say when they saw the other, he had a weapon pointing at that time. Scott, feeling trapped and terrified, moved around in the pine trees, whose trunks averaged about four or five inches thick. He could see movement in the house. In fact, Mr. Reardon was loading a gun at that time, unknown by those outside.

Wigglesworth was yelling, "United States Marshal. Put your weapon down and move back to the highway," but

Scott maintained he couldn't tell what the guy was yelling at that distance - 75 to 100 yards away. He was just yelling! Realizing the sparse pines provided little cover, Scott moved back to the corner of the trailer, the northeast corner, nearest the road, for protection from Wigglesworth. For some strange reason, Wigglesworth did not observe this nor did he ever see Scott again that day. He presumed, incorrectly, that Scott ran westward into the "woods' and remained there. A search conducted later proved this not to be so. Wigglesworth, following the firefight in which he inexplicably did not participate, later crawled back to the highway, continuing to fear the imaginary "threat" in the "woods". Combat records show that a certain proportion of troops freeze, get buck fever, when confronted with an adversary. Wigglesworth may have retreated somewhat from his position as Scott was unable to observe him from the trailer, though he tried to.

After strong prompting from Hopson, Muir and Schnabel moved their vehicles closer to the driveway and dismounted to the driver's side of each vehicle. One must wonder why they did not come up to the driveway?

Inside the trailer were Mr. and Mrs. Reardon, their two small children, her sister and Jeff, the sister's husband. Jeff was running to and fro, excited, observing what he could out the window. Most all of them peeked out the windows from time to time. Jeff wanted a gun, but Mr. Reardon thought it was wisest for himself alone to be armed. He loaded a shotgun, but never fired it nor left the house, which they had locked following the telephone call from the fire house.

When Hopson came from the east ditch to the Kahl station wagon, Yorie yelled to Gordon, "Watch out behind you!"

Cheshire resumed his redundant scream, "I'm going to blow your goddamn heads off. I'm going to ..." he repeated this five or six times, according to Yorie and others.

Now, at this juncture, Yorie told me no one had been told he was under arrest. No identification nor warrant had been shown. The red lights flashing were an indication of law enforcement. Whether or not the marshals had communicated the fact that they indeed were U.S. Marshals to Scott, Yorie and Gordon is problematic. Grandpa was probably satisfied that they were marshals; Yorie and Scott probably suspected as much, but were uncertain.

Marshal Muir decided that the time for talk had ended. Nine minutes was enough; it was now time for action - force! The misdemeanor arrest would now be done Muir's way!

XVI Shootout

After Yorie shouted his warning, Cheshire yelled to Muir, "Come closer!"

Powp! The flat report of Muir's pistol rang out. No one observed it. Everyone heard it. Strangely, all government witnesses were later to swear the shot came from the opposite direction, from the south, from Yorie! This mistaken impression could be for two reasons. A bullet makes a "crack" as it sails by through the sound barrier. Then, too, the .38 calibre slug struck Yorie's pistol handle in his shoulder holster, making a sound upon the impact and destruction of the grip. Muir must have been amazed in seeing his victim remain standing, wondering if he could have missed. How could he have?

Whatever possessed Ken Muir to employ such a tactic is anyone's surmise. We only know that he was a good shot and proudly confident in his ability to hit his target. However, as Deputy Marshal Warren was to point out later, this time it was not paper silhouettes, but real flesh and blood which was his target. As the government attorney later claimed, he may have had a legal right to do so! Nevertheless, anyone with an ounce of common sense wouldn't have done it. Charge it up to fear and panic, I guess.

"Who fired?" Cheshire shouted, and Hopson echoed, "Who fired?" At the same time, Yorie staggered away from the pole slightly, tottering and unable to breathe, and exclaimed, "I'm hit! I'm hit!"

Now, being hit by a .38 at that range is comparable to someone hitting you in the chest with a sledge hammer. The energy equals the mass times the velocity squared. It is no wonder that the breath was knocked out of Yorie, who perhaps thought he was mortally wounded when only badly bruised. He was in considerable pain. Perhaps Grandma's prayers from the nearby wagon guided the bullet. As Grandpa indicated in his letter, had Yorie not been wearing his holster, he would have been killed instantly.

Had Muir missed the message or forgotten it within five minutes that Gordon might have exchanged clothes and was at one of the vehicles? Why Yorie?

Three or four seconds elapsed, then all bedlam broke loose!

Yorie, from desperation or reflex, may have fired next, toward the general direction of Cheshire and the RAM Charger. Kapp says this is so. In any event, Yorie's two unaimed shots in rapid succession in all probability went awry. The government claims they struck the door of the Charger. Yorie says, "I know I didn't hit the door!"

Kapp fired his pump shotgun with 00 buckshot four times at Yorie in rapid succession over the cab of the RAM Charger. Kapp says he fired after seeing the muzzle flash of Yorie's rifle. A muzzle flash in daytime? Well, maybe at 6:00 p.m. Grandpa said that the shotgun fired first, with Yorie firing in reflex to being hit by buckshot. In any event, the shotgun and Yorie's rifle were all fired about the same time.

Kapp, who only recalls firing two or three times, says that he missed on the first shot and then hit Yorie. Must have been like a magpie diving on a wounded gelding. It seems funny to me that someone who has to pump a gun to reload it can't remember that he fired it four times. That totaled thirty-six pellets. Yorie fell face down into the mud after being struck by the buckshot, which continued to hit him and to splatter in the mud around him after he had been shot down. "It was a miracle of God," Yorie said later, "that more of the pellets did not hit me." Plenty of them did.

Muir shot three more times with his pistol, presumably at Yorie and Grandpa. The noise and consternation that his target didn't fall initially must have rattled Ken Muir, affecting his usual expert aim. No one knows where these bullets went, but one or two of them may have caused the flesh wound to Yorie's left shoulder or to his chin, which was cut.

Cheshire fired his automatic rifle three times. One of these pierced the baggage rail on top of the Chrysler wagon. Neither Schnable nor Hopson fired their shotguns, and Wigglesworth, who seems to have disappeared, apparently did not fire his automatic. Who knows for sure? Scott, standing at the corner of the trailer with bullets ricocheting from metal and whistling by, joined the melee. He fired six half-aimed shots in rapid succession with his semi-automatic towards the hood and middle of the windshield of the RAM Charger. As Scott fired, his barrel was elevated each time by the recoil. Some of the later bullets pierced the windshield. In all probability, he didn't hit anyone.

Scott then saw that Yorie was shot down. At this point, he was no longer in the fight. That is, his shooting was over. He turned rescue medic, running over to Yorie to help him, carrying his rifle along. Like the young coward in Crane's "Red Badge of Courage", this valiant effort showed extreme bravery. Love of a friend wrought utter disregard of perilous dangers. What greater love is there than one who will lay down his life for a friend?

Dave Broer was on the pavement. Wegener was on the floorboard of the Kahl car at this time, next to Joan, who continued to pray. This left only Grandpa in combat with the five lawmen. He had a semi-automatic; they had two shotguns, a pistol, and two machine guns (automatic rifles) dispersed roughly in a semi-circle around him. A facetious observer would contend that the odds were not fair. "Had there been twice the number of aggressors and double the number of weapons, augmented by a couple of fragmentation grenades, and those deployed in a complete circle, then the odds would have been more nearly even," a wag might say. The federals were never to make the mistake of being undermanned thereafter when dealing with Grandpa.

Hopson was seriously injured in the gunfight, primarily by a piece of pavement being thrown by a bullet into the side of his head. This caused him to be almost totally disabled, perhaps partially permanent. This is especially sad, because he alone of the group had no understanding of the situation. He just came along to give Cheshire support. One may question if this justified his conduct.

Kenneth Muir was killed while attempting to fire the last round remaining in his pistol. A .223 bullet passed through his arm and struck him in the middle of the chest. He died quickly.

Grandpa probably shot Muir, but this is uncertain, as Grandpa does not mention the fact in his account of the gunfight. Some believe that Muir was killed by a federal bullet, perhaps by crossfire from Cheshire. Since the bullet was so accurately placed, such an *accidental* impact is unlikely.

Kapp's trigger finger was severed by a Kahl bullet. Another of Grandpa's shots grazed a superficial cut to Kapp's head, but one that bled extensively.

Robert Cheshire received four significant wounds, the last one blowing the top of his head off, killing him instantly. One was a wound to his hand, perhaps a defensive wound. His other two wounds were potentially fatal, one in his neck and another through his left arm and into his chest. These two wounds were from bullets which are believed to have first passed through the windshield glass. It is highly probable, almost certain, that all were inflicted by Grandpa.

Later that night, he wrote of his role in the shootout. Someone later said, "Gordon was jumping around like a mud hen, dodging bullets," during the multi-second ordeal. Actually, Grandpa had few bullets to dodge. The tactical mistake of the lawmen from start to finish was the focusing of their attention on persons around the pole primarily, rather than on Grandpa, the real threat at that point.

Grandpa wrote as follows (with my additions and comments in parentheses in this iteration):

"As we came over one of the hills just north of Medina, I saw on the top of the next hill what looked like two cars parked on it. About this time, they turned on their red lights, and I knew that the attack was underway.

"We were just coming to an approach, and I told Dave to pull in on it and stop. Our other car pulled in just beyond us and stopped, also.

"I looked back in time to see another vehicle coming from behind with its red light on. (Wrong, Grandpa, the light came on after it stopped.)

"I picked up my mini-14 and got out and got myself and my weapon ready as the vehicle coming from behind skidded to a stop about 20 feet away. The doors flew open on it, and the two men who were in the front seat aimed their guns at us. My son, Yorie, had jumped out of the other car and had run over to a high-line pole. The two cars which we had seen ahead of us pulled up and stopped behind us.

"A man (Hopson) got out of the vehicle (RAM) which had come from behind us and ran out into the ditch on the east side of the road.

"During this time, there was a lot of screaming and hollering going on, but nothing else, so it appeared to be an impasse.

"About this time a shot rang out, and the driver of the car (Cheshire), who I believe at this time must have been supposedly in command, turned around and stood up so he was looking at his man in the east ditch and toward the cars which had come from the north and yelled, "Who fired? Who fired?" The other man who was with him (Hopson) echoed his question.

"At the time the shot rang out, I heard Yorie cry out, "I'm hit, I'm hit!"

"I took my eyes off the two men who were yelling "Who fired?" and looked over at Yorie. He was still standing, but I could tell he was in pain from the way he stood.

"About this time, another shot rang out, and I heard Yorie cry out again. I looked over and saw that he was hit again, and laying on the ground.

"I looked back toward the two men and saw the one in the passenger side (Kapp) aim at me, and I was sure then that they felt the situation was no longer under their control, and the only thing to do was to kill us all.

"Before he was able to fire, I loosed a round at the door behind which he was standing, and while I don't think it hit him, it caused him to duck down behind the door.

"I looked around again toward Yorie, and saw Scotty Faul running over toward him. I turned my head again in time to see the driver of the vehicle which had followed us (Cheshire) raise up from behind the door and aim at Scotty. I moved my gun over and fired at him before he could shoot. I didn't hit him, either. The bullet struck somewhere near the lower left-hand corner of the windshield. He ducked down behind the dash so I could only see his head. About this time, the other man (Kapp) raised up and aimed at me again. I shot again. The bullet struck the door and caused him to duck each time before they could aim and fire. I don't know how many times I fired, until the man on the passenger side (Kapp) fell, and I was able to tell he was out of the fight. The driver (Cheshire) must have seen this, as he moved his gun from Scotty's direction toward me.

"I fired several more shots at him each time he raised up to shoot at me. I finally realized this could keep up 'til my 30-round clip was empty. My bullets appeared to be ricocheting off the windshield and door post. I ran around toward the side of the vehicle, firing at the door as I went, to keep him down until I got around far enough to get a clear shot at him, at which time I knew he was out of the fight also.

"I ran back where I could see the third man (Hopson) from this north-bound vehicle just in time to see him raise up to shoot at Scotty, who had run over to Yorie. Before he was able to pull the trigger, I fired and he (Hopson) fell to the ground. At this time I saw the man who was behind the front end of the green Mercury (Schnable) raise up and aim at Scotty. He saw me swing my gun in his direction, and he ducked down behind the car. I could see his feet or legs beneath the car, and I fired, striking him and putting him out of the fight. (He received a flesh wound in the leg.)

"I ran over to the man in the east ditch (Schnable), thinking he might still be in fighting condition. When I got nearly to him, he raised up his head and said, 'Don't shoot me again. I'm all done.' He had his hand on his shotgun, so I took that and his pistol, which was in his holster, and threw them in the back seat of green Mercury. I didn't see the man who had been behind the Mercury, and who I thought I'd hit in the leg, so I don't know where he'd gone to. (He had gone into the ditch and was disarmed. Grandpa probably ran to Hopson and then to Schnable.)

"A pickup had pulled up behind the north-bound vehicle, but I didn't notice anyone in it or around it, and I assumed it was the pickup we saw on the top of the first hill as we came out of Medina, and which I believed belonged to the city, but as to who was driving it (Hennum), I have no knowledge.

"Scotty tells me he saw one (Wigglesworth) and possibly two men run out into the trees and hide, but I have no way of knowing who they were.

"I think from the reports I've heard on the radio which was in the Mercury that the car which came from behind was the one the marshals were in. If this is so, they weren't the ones who fired the first shots. The two men who were in the front seat were both looking in the direction of the green Mercury when they were shouting, 'Who fired?'

Yorie Von Kahl

"Yorie's .45-auto., which he had in his shoulder holster, had either a rifle or pistol bullet imbedded in the clip, shattering the grips on both sides. Had he not been wearing it, he would have been killed instantly.

"Whether this was the first or second shot that was fired at him, I don't know. One was buckshot, and the other was either a rifle or a high-powered pistol, from the way the bullet looks.

"I didn't see it, but it sounded as though Yorie's gun fired after he was hit. I think probably his finger tightened on the trigger when he was hit, but I know neither he nor Scotty fired before this, and whether either of them fired afterwards, I don't know. I know that if they did, they didn't hit anyone, as I *knew* when I hit each one of them myself..."

That is the extent of Grandpa's written account of the scene.

While Scott was running to Yorie, the injured Kapp started running north in the east ditch, according to later testimony. He held onto his dangling index finger with the same hand and onto his bleeding head with his left hand. "We lost, we lost!" Once he paused and turned briefly. This triggered Scott and Grandpa into leveling their rifles at him. He resumed his retreat, and they lowered their rifles from the man who had blasted Yorie repeatedly and had fingered the Medina group. Upon arriving at the firehouse, he implored Chief Graf, "Look what they've done to me. I want you to go down there and kill all those mother fuckers." Graf ignored him and sent the ambulance to the scene. I wonder why Kapp kept pumping lead into Yorie after he was sprawled head-east on his belly in the mud?

As Scott was running to Yorie, Grandpa was in the middle of the road, after disarming Schnable. Grandpa asked Broer, lying on the pavement, if he was hurt. He wasn't. Grandpa went by the RAM Charger, headed toward Yorie, when he was startled. According to Scott, the scare came from Cheshire reaching for his rifle. Grandpa quickly reacted, shooting for the second time into the cab at short range, exploding Cheshire's head. Cheshire slid out of the cab onto the pavement. The shooting was ended. Grandpa had fired a total of 13 shots in the fracas.

Hopson laid on the pavement, injured; Muir and Cheshire were on the pavement, dead. When Cheshire was first injured, Kapp asked him if he was hit. "Yes, but not bad," he answered, probably referring to his neck wound or hand wound, and broadcast on the radio, "Officers hit! Officers hit!" The time was 5:56 p.m. Shortly thereafter, following more shooting, Cheshire said, "I'm hit bad." The shooting had lasted about 15 or 20 seconds, according to court transcripts of testimony.

Scott turned Yorie over, near the pole; blood was everywhere. Yorie said, "I'm going to die, I'm not going to make it!" He handed Scott his .45 saying, "They shot it. You take this. I'm not going to need it anymore." Meanwhile, Grandma, in the station wagon asked loudly, "Is Yorie hurt?" Someone answered her affirmatively. Scott told Yorie, "Hang on, I'm going to take you to the doctor. You've got to just hang on!"

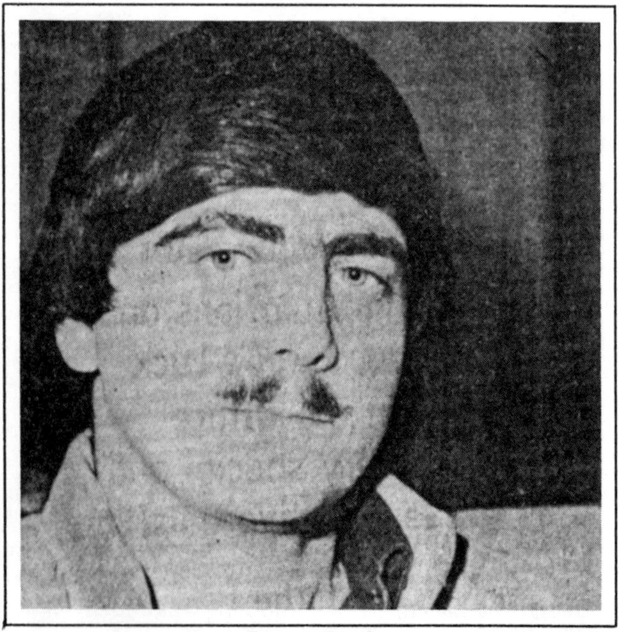

Scott Faul

Scott got Yorie to his feet and moved toward the station wagon. Yorie collapsed or slumped down, saying that he couldn't go on and needed to rest. He was all bloody. Grandpa came from the RAM and helped with Yorie.

Noticing that the other vehicles had the Kahl wagon blocked, they put Yorie in the front seat of the Mercury police car. Scott drove it to Dr. Martin's at a high speed, and was waved through by Chief Graf at the fire station.

Grandpa, driving his station wagon, was close behind, followed by Dave Broer and Wegener. Rescue personnel were arriving at the scene, and took Schnable and Hopson to the clinic. Wigglesworth crawled back to the road and took charge at the scene of the shootout, being ever cautious of his imagined "man in the woods". Mr. Reardon came out of his house, later recalling, "One of the deputy's bullets came within four feet of my little 4-year-old boy!" (The Kahl group never shot in that direction; the Marshals did.) Some of the rescue personnel assisted Doc Martin in tending to the wounded at the clinic.

Graf established a command post at his home to coordinate law enforcement activities. He evacuated the Reardons to a relative's house in Medina. The shootout scene was cordoned-off.

Now, to be sure, the shootout account is as accurate as I could tell it, based on all the information I could collect. Where probabilities were involved, I told the most plausible version. If you were to listen to the government's version, especially their earlier ones, you would hardly recognize it as the same encounter. They had Yorie firing first and Scotty "executing" Cheshire.

My lawyer friend drew some definite conclusions. Everyone, especially Grandpa, underestimated his prowess with a rifle and its efficacy. Grandpa shot about 13 times, with 7 or 8 of them inflicting bodily injuries. The .223 calibre lead bullets with copper jackets tend to disintegrate when striking an object. Grandpa's decades of carrying a rifle essentially gave him a third arm. His accuracy was almost beyond belief! As Louis L'Amour wrote, "There's a little cowboy in all of us."

The government became outraged over Grandpa's "assault on the law". Grandma and her church friends feel the fallacy in this is that lawmen, acting as "hoods" even though technically legal, are not society's law. In their first week of law enforcement training, officers learn not to attempt arrest when peers or family are nearby, which might cause him to resist in order to save face.

They are taught not to endanger bystanders nor to arrest one when armed friends are observing. Grandpa lived openly and could have been arrested most any day on the streets of Carrington while unarmed and alone. Within a few hours, Grandpa was to become the government's "most wanted" man.

Grandpa was forced to kill in self-defense, but was later killed himself for not doing that which, according to IRS Commissioner Roscoe Eggers, Jr., millions of other Americans do not do - file voluntary income tax returns. At least that's what some of Grandpa's friends told me. Or, was this the real reason? Many think not.

Maybe it seems that I'm stringing incongruities and absurdities together in a wandering and sometimes purposeless way, as they say Mark Twain did, but really, I'm doing the best I can to relate the real story.

Gordon - 1941

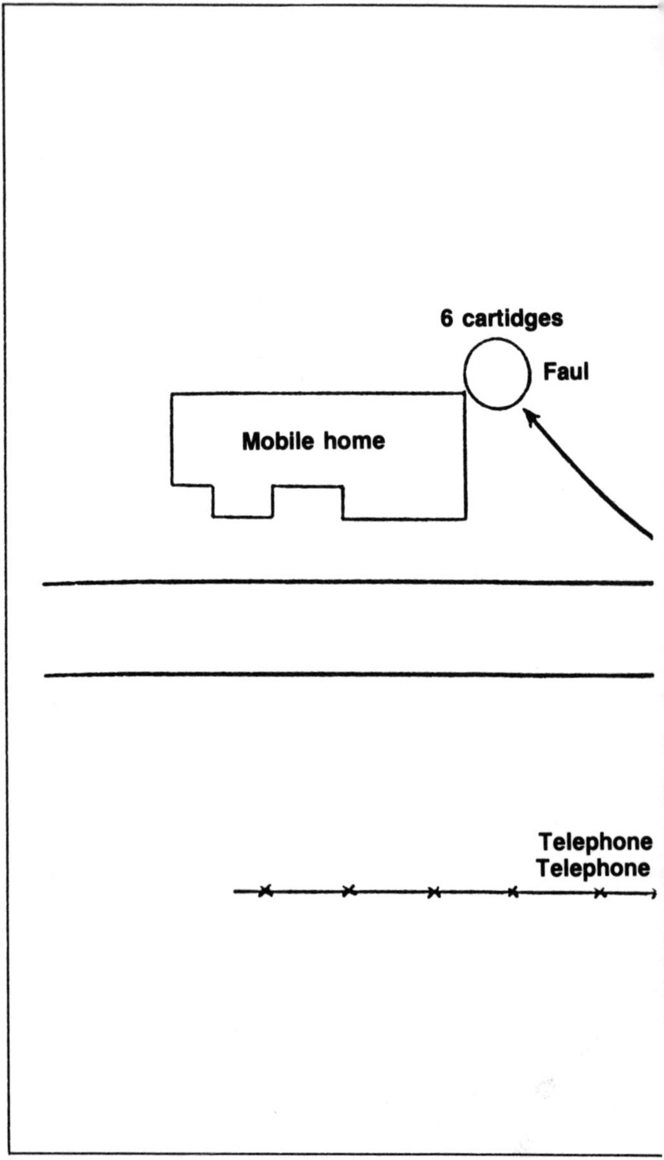
6 cartidges
Faul
Mobile home
Telephone
Telephone

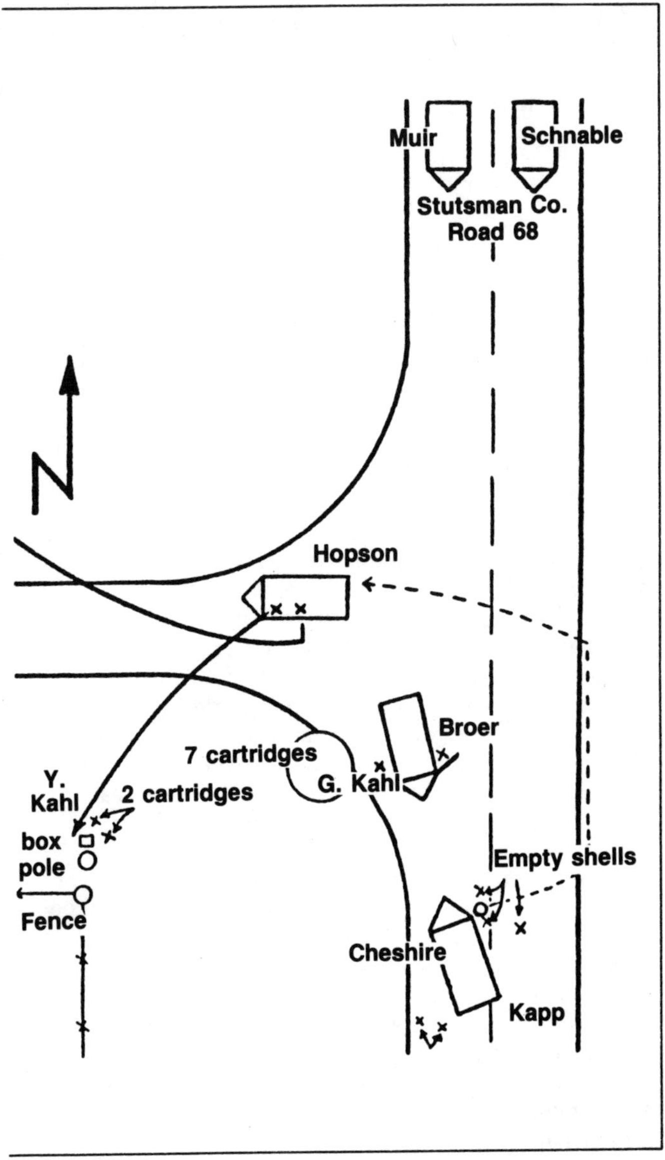

Muir
Schnable
Stutsman Co.
Road 68
Hopson
Broer
7 cartridges
Y.
Kahl
2 cartridges
G. Kahl
box
pole
Empty shells
Fence
Cheshire
Kapp

XVII Roundup

The phone rang.

"Hello."

"Hello. Is that you, Little Dolly?"

"Yes. Is Yorie OK?"

"I'm with him now," Grandma replied. It looks bad, but Dr. Martin and the others are doing their best. Don't worry. I'll call again tomorrow and tell you all about it, but Yorie needs me now. Bye."

Dr. Martin had returned to the clinic by the time Yorie arrived. A very white Yorie was laid out on the examining table. Dr. Martin had extensive experience with gunshot wounds in the military. Yorie had two minor wounds, one grazing his chin and one through his upper arm. His two major wounds were through the right kidney and a chest wound, higher up. He was given a drug to inhibit arterial bleeding and Stadol shots for pain. Dr. Martin then called Dr. Kostick in Jamestown, alerting him for surgery. Then, intravenous blood transfusions were started.

"This fella's not going to make it - too much internal bleeding," Dr. Martin had said, initially, but at the same time he was encouraged by the vital signs. It looked bad.

"Mom, I'm not going to make it," moaned Yorie. "Will you take care of Janice and the kids?"

"You are going to make it!" responded Grandma, not quite believing it. "Yes, I'll look after Janice and the children!" Joan was herself again, after blacking out during the ride to the clinic.

"Take my boots off," said Yorie, and Joan did.

Hopson had been treated by others at the clinic, and indicated that he was not in much pain. Dr. Martin accompanied the two seriously injured patients to Jamestown in the ambulance. While enroute, Yorie mumbled, "Doc, I did what I had to do!"

Hopson was treated and evacuated by helicopter to a hospital in Bismarck. Hopson was the other passenger in the ambulance. His pulse was continuously monitored by Dr. Martin during the trip.

Yorie's kidney and gall bladder were removed in surgery, plus the small intestine being resected. The large intestine perforations were sewed and a liver injury treated. He remained critical for an extended period. It was a close call. He was under arrest and his hospital room was guarded. Grandma called again to let us know what all was going on.

Hopson was the other passenger in the ambulance. His pulse was continuously monitored during the trip by Dr. Martin. Hopson was then treated and evacuated by helicopter to a hospital in Bismarck.

Later I found out that three months later Hopson still required assistance in walking and could not remember many of the details of that day. "I was a whole man when I went to Medina that day," he later said. Such a statement pricked the heartstrings of the jurors, as it would anyone with compassion. It also helped thwart justice, some say.

I should tell you what happened at the Medina Clinic, as Scott told it later.

At the clinic, where the injured were being treated, tension was overwhelming. Kapp exclaimed to Scott Faul, "Boy, you are in big trouble now!" The rescue team had taken him there soon after Yorie had arrived.

Scott didn't answer, but the statement filled him with fear. He didn't know but what lawmen were coming there to kill him! The statement puzzled him, as he didn't know exactly what was meant.

Grandpa came into the clinic, brandishing two mini-14s. Mrs. Martin, the doctor's wife, shouted, "Get those guns out of here!"

Grandpa and Scott then left the clinic, driving in the City's green Mercury police car. Grandpa drove to Heaton on back roads, parking the car in a clump of trees in the middle of a field, about a mile southeast of the farm house. While enroute, Scott asked, "What am I going to do? What's happened?"

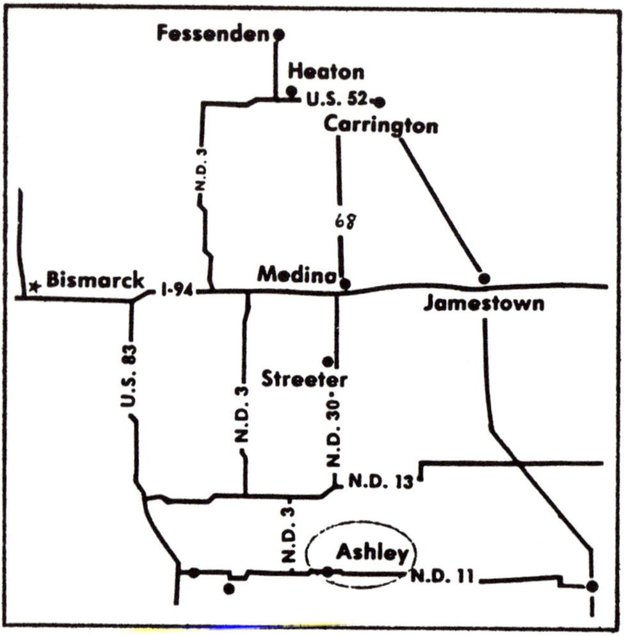

S.E. North Dakota

"Scotty, I don't know," Grandpa responded. They rode quietly for most of the distance, but over the silence hovered a cloud of fear and sadness. They walked to the house where Grandpa discarded Len's stocking cap and picked up some items of clothing. My grandpa got $5,000 at the house, which he had been paid for a recent land lease. They left in the AMC Rambler, which Grandpa had repaired earlier in the day. Scott left his car at the farm, and they traveled some 40 miles on back roads to within five miles of Scott's home near Harvey. The car was then parked inside a deserted farm building, and the two remained there for the night and until the next evening. That night, on brown paper, Grandpa wrote the letter describing the events of the day, along with remarks explaining some of his beliefs. A later writer philosophized,

"Born in blood this nation was. Reborn it now shall be." (Louis R. Bean, Jr.)

Scotty wanted time to think and sort things out. Before leaving, he put his rifle on the rafters and left Yorie's pistol in the Rambler.

"Where can I go?" Scott asked.

"I don't even know where I'm going," Grandpa replied.

Scott decided that he wanted to go home, partly because of the little spat with his wife the day before. "Oh, Lord, in our extremities, what gargantuan problems our minds muster from trivia," he thought. He wanted to talk to her and then turn himself in. The love that cures, panacea to both the giver and receiver, was apparent. Grandpa gave Scott the letter he had written and insisted on driving him closer to Scott's home. Both he and Scott were bewildered how Scott had gotten involved in such a situation.

Fear of being shot held them back from going directly to Scott's house. Instead, Gordon dropped him off at a neighbor's. Scott saw Arlie Rohler's lighted barn and began walking toward it.

"Oh, my God, Scott!" Mrs. Rohler exclaimed, as she ran out to meet him. She put her arm around him. He explained that he was concerned about his family.

Arlie came from the barn and spotted them. Scott explained that he probably should turn himself in, knowing from his portable scanner that the police were looking for him. When Scott asked about his wife, Arlie told him that he thought they locked her up. Scott left his .45 and shotgun in the shop, and they went into the house. Scott called attorney Ted Seibel, asking if it could be arranged for him to be turned in safely. After another call, Seibel came after Scott, taking him to the sheriff in Fessenden. He was later taken to Jamestown and then to Fargo.

Dave Broer and Vernon Wegener left the shootout scene in Dave's car. They, too, were waved through by Chief Graf. They went to Streeter, using back roads. "So, that was why Darrell was not at the meeting," said Dave enroute, referring to Graf. Mostly, though, they rode silently. Wegener thought back on how Joan started crying after she asked if Yorie was hit, and he had confirmed it. While enroute and at Dave's suggestion, they decided to call Chief Deputy Sheriff Jack Miller. Vernon knew him personally from the time when Wegener served as police officer in Streeter. They called at 6:33.

During the time the two were together, Dave indicated that he had some apprehension while lying on the pavement that Gordon might shoot him for not helping defend the group. Of course, this was pseudo fear, completely without basis, and was soon dispelled by Grandpa, but real to Dave at the time. Maybe he felt a little guilty about playing possum.

Miller and other deputies came out and talked with them. They returned at two o'clock that night and arrested them.

Wegener remained in jail until Good Friday, April 1, when his bond was reduced from a hundred to twenty thousand dollars. This day is more properly called April Fool's Day, because he pleaded guilty to forcibly impeding federal marshals in their duties. He had agreed to turn state's evidence and pleaded guilty to a minor charge with the potential of a three year sentence. Otherwise, he faced a potential sentence of 25 years plus fines, if convicted. The "cop out" affected Broer's trial later. As preview to the nature of the trial to come, Broer's attorney was prohibited from asking Wegener what kind of force he used, or how was "doing nothing" using force? Wegener pleaded guilty to a lie!

You know, if Broer had subsequently been found innocent, which in fact he was, he would have served more jail time just waiting for trial than Vernon served, who pled guilty to a felony. Wegener never went back to jail for his "felony", and I think he knew pretty well that he wouldn't all along.

But I'm really getting ahead of my story here. Let's go back to the Medina Clinic after the shootout.

The ambulance had taken Bradley Kapp to the clinic and then quickly went to the shootout scene. Rudolph Hoffman, an elderly member of the rescue team, remained at the clinic and ministered medical help to Kapp. Dr. Martin was occupied with the more seriously wounded.

During this time, Kapp said, "We could have talked it over instead of shooting!"

Hoffman interjected, "That's a heck of a thing to do, shooting people over income tax!"

Another of them said, "It's more than just a little income tax!"

Dennis Krambich, a farmer and member of the ambulance squad, was at the clinic. He had attended four of the earlier civic meetings, being concerned with farm foreclosures. He later related that he owned a number of firearms, including an AR15. He also told of a Posse Comitatus that had been organized the preceding year by the citizens of Medina to combat any threat of transient motorcyclists. He drove the ambulance that Sunday.

After Grandpa let Scotty Faul out of the car that Monday night, he was headed north. He quickly turned southward, probably on the back roads of the foggy prairie, on which entire states can be traversed. He eluded the dragnet, and presumably headed for Texas or western Arkansas - or both. Rumor has it that the Rambler was cut up and buried in Texas. Who knows? Someone does, but they're not saying.

Grandpa was the only one in the party who was not quickly arrested and originally charged with first degree murder plus numerous other charges. Originally, according to the record I saw, his bond had been set at $1,000,000 by the Texas court for his alleged misdemeanor - parole violation. If that was reasonable bail, I've gotta wonder what his bond would have been for the Medina shootout? Of course, there would have been none.

Earlier on that Monday, KXMC-TV reporters Rae Schobinger and Peggy Ulrich made a quarter hour tour of the

Kahl farmyard in their car, taking pictures after the shootout and before the Task Force assembled. These were shown on the evening news. Their question was, "If this is the most logical place for him to be, as asserted, why wasn't the law here?"

Yorie's survival of the operation was the best Valentine's greeting Grandma ever received! Much credit goes to the expertness of Dr. Kostick. Still, Yorie's survival was touch and go for a good while, compounded by the serious threat of infection. As he was coming out of the effects of anesthesia and while under heavy sedation, a suggestion was planted into his unconscious mind. The deputy sheriff guard asked him, "Did you shoot first?" Fifteen minutes later, as he was lapsing back into sleep, Yorie said weakly, "Yeah."

Grandma was at the hospital while Yorie was undergoing surgery. She was offered a sedative for shock, which she refused. Instead, she said she needed to make some telephone calls. She called her daughter, Lorna, in Odessa. In Joan's words:

"She said later I didn't even sound like myself, so I guess I was in shock. Were it not for Gordon, those ambushers would have killed us all. I called Yorie's wife, Janice, and told her that Yorie had been shot up real bad, and not believing it myself, told her he'd be okay. I also told her to call Bud and Alta Brakel, neighbors, and for them to come over and get her and the babies. I went back to the waiting room where Doc Martin and I talked a while. Doc left and I proceeded to call the Brakels myself, when two big marshals grabbed me and handcuffed me.

'You're under arrest and you're not going anywhere.'

'But my son is dying and I have to be here!'

'That doesn't matter, there are two dead marshals out there!'

"So away I went, and my whole life changed in minutes! I was taken to the sheriff's department and questioned for hours. Then they booked me, took my purse, inventoried it and threw me in a little old dingy cell! I couldn't believe what was happening to me. Early the next morning, they slipped something they called 'food' through a little slot in the door and said, 'Here is your breakfast.' I told them to take it, I wasn't hungry. He said, 'You will be before this is over.' I had not closed my eyes all night. My daughter, Lonnie Kahl, and her dear friend and mine, Pearl Duhart, stayed all night. They stayed with Yorie after Lonnie found out I was not going to be released.

"It really hurt me, because Lonnie was 'crushed' to say the least when she said, 'Mom, they can't lock you up!You didn't do anything!' But they locked me up anyway. After I didn't eat breakfast, and they picked up the tray, I just wondered what was next. To this day I'm wondering 'what next?'

"About noon they came in and said, 'You're going to Fargo,' and I said, 'Why?' They said, 'That's where all federal prisoners go.' I didn't know if I was going to be able to handle that mentally or not, and then I decided I had to. I had no other choice, so I 'braced' myself and made up my mind, 'Whatever will be, will be!' I also learned in a hurry after February 13th that I would take one day at a time, and if that didn't come, I wouldn't need it.

"I still am living that way, and I will until I die. All this time I'm worried sick over Yorie, and if he did die, would they even tell me? They were talking to me as if I were a criminal, and I didn't do anything! All the way to Fargo in handcuffs in the back seat with an officer of 'some kind'. He was pressuring me to say where Gordon was. I had no earthly idea, even *if* he were alive. No one believed me. We got to the Federal Building in Fargo about three o'clock p.m. I was put in a holding cell until about six o'clock when they took me in another room, all handcuffed with a chain around my middle, in front of the crime investigators from Washington, D.C., questioning me for several hours as to where Gordon was. I kept telling them I didn't know. At different points during the questioning

Joan Kahl

they got hateful and accused me of being a 'Christian woman' and then telling them lies! 'Yes,' I said, 'I do consider myself a Christian woman and I *am* telling the truth.' At this point, they said to each other, 'Take her away, she's no help to us,' at which time they took me to the city jail, booked me again, and there I was for 16 days, until my brother, Vic, bonded me out. During my stay in jail, I was fingerprinted four times and questioned again and again by federal marshals as to Gordon's whereabouts. I still had no idea, but I just hoped and prayed then they'd never get him, because I knew if they ever did, they would be merciless, even though it was their own doings concerning what happened in Medina on that Sunday.

"My brother, Victor, had put up my bond money, and I was to be released on a Friday evening, but I wasn't! To this day I don't know why, but I was informed I wouldn't be released until Monday. And for some 'sneaky' reason, I was taken across the state line on Friday evening to a jail in Moorehead, Minnesota. My daughter, Lorna, tried to get to talk to me after she found out I was sent to jail in Moorehead, and she was told I said I did *not* want to talk to anyone *or* see anyone. I never did make such a statement, so they (my children) tried again on Sunday, and were told the same sinister thing. Only, all this time I didn't know they had told my children these lies. On Monday I was released from jail *finally,* and I asked them for my purse. I was told that my purse had been in Fargo, but was sent back to Jamestown, and I could pick it up on my way back to Carrington at the sheriff's office or command post. We got to Jamestown - my brother, Victor, his ex-wife, Clarice, my daughter, Lorna, and myself. After waiting an hour while they're supposed to be looking for it, I was told they sent it back to Fargo, but they would have it there for me at Jamestown on my way back to Fargo next time, as I had to meet with Mr. Ramlo, my attorney, appointed by the government.

Gordon's parents, Fred and Edna Kahl

"On my next trip to Fargo, I stopped in Jamestown to pick up my purse. I was told it wasn't there yet, but they would notify me, and I could come and get it. Now, Fargo was 125 miles from Carrington, and Jamestown was 40 miles. I didn't even have gas money! Nevertheless, one day two weeks later, I got a call from Jamestown to come and get my purse. My son, Fred, and his wife took me to Jamestown to get it. I didn't dare drive alone, because my driver's license was in my purse, and I had decided by now maybe that's what they wanted me to do, to drive without a license - 'title of nobility' - and then put me back in jail, because this time they would have a reason! Anyway, we got to the sheriff's office. They told me my purse was there. It *really* was there! But the guy that had to give it to me wasn't, so I still went home empty-handed! They still had my purse, but they said, "On your way to Fargo tomorrow you can stop by at 8 o'clock and we'll see that you get your purse." The next morning I had to meet with my lawyer at 11 o'clock, so we stopped to get my purse on the way. This time they told me they were 'so sorry.' I couldn't have my purse because they were all in a meeting, and the meeting wasn't over until 10:30. I

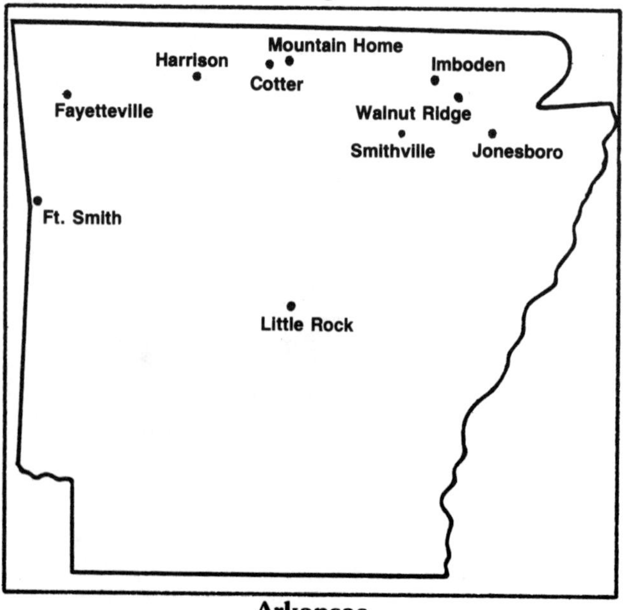

Arkansas

had to be in Fargo nearly 100 miles away by 11 o'clock. So again I left empty-handed. Now I was getting angry. A few days more of that, and I had my daughter take me to Jamestown to get my purse if I had to wait right there until I got it. Lonnie and I got to Jamestown at 8 o'clock and we had to wait until 2 o'clock p.m. before they *finally* gave me my purse. The FBI agent I talked to tried to get me to talk before he gave me my purse, but I just kept telling him I wouldn't answer any questions without my lawyer there. He finally gave up and gave me my purse.

"I was under very heavy surveillance after I got out of jail, and I didn't have any peace, with FBI agents coming to our door and wanting to talk to some of my children.

"When Yorie was in the hospital and I was in jail, the room he was in was so heavily guarded his wife couldn't even see him. These orders were given by the federal marshals. (None of us knew if he were dead or alive.) They wouldn't even tell the family how he was, or *if* he was dead or alive! Janice, his wife, kept trying to see him, and one day, when she went trying to see him, one of the marshals or FBI agents said to her, 'We've got good news for you,' and she thought she was going to get to see Yorie. He added, "You can't see Yorie anymore!' She thought for sure he had died. They treated the family cruelly with their remarks, and they certainly left a bad impression throughout the countryside in their search for Gordon."

I really love my grandma, no matter what, and she's helped me a lot with this story.

The roundup of everyone in the two cars, except for Grandpa, was quickly completed. They were charged with numerous offenses, everything from first degree murder to conspiracy, aiding a fugitive, and forceably impeding federal officers. All were charged with murder.

As for Grandpa, the biggest manhunt in North Dakota history was beginning. The media were to have a heyday! Grandpa Gordon Kahl was branded a vicious outlaw.

XVIII Manhunt

They came from everywhere. Scores of FBI agents and U.S. Marshals Service officers constituted the task force for the Kahl hunt. From McLean, Virginia, Chief Inspector Thomas C. Kupferer, head of the Fugitive Apprehension Unit, was in charge, a dark-complexioned, dark-eyed marshal, with a rumored propensity to appear anywhere in the country where shootouts occur. He has been surreptitiously nicknamed "Goat Eyes" by jingoistic critics.

Why spend tens of thousands chasing Gordon Kahl? Hundreds of fugitives are at large. One could say that vengeance and retribution for the Medina shootings were the certain reasons. Len Martin, who attended the meeting on shootout Sunday, provides another answer in his booklet, *"Why They Wanted to Get Gordon Kahl"*, published by Pro-American Press, Detroit Lakes, Minnesota. In a taped interview, Grandpa explained the real reason he was sent to prison.

"My research and exposure of the part the power-grabbing parasitic hierarchy has played, and is playing in the destruction of America, was a big part of it ... exposing the (elitist) tie was the main activity."

Why else a million-dollar bail bond for a misdemeanor? No doubt exists that Grandpa was sure in his mind that this was the main reason he would be hunted relentlessly by the "Goyum".

I previewed some material in Grandpa's library. It is obvious that Grandpa did extensive research which led to his beliefs. Examples of Gordon's sources were the 1950 World Almanac, and some Gerald L. K. Smith books, such as *"The Beseiged Patriot"*, CNC, Box 202, Eureka Springs, Arkansas 72623. He read such tracts as *"Symbol (Masonic) of Satan's Church"*, by Preacher Man, Rt. 3, Box 238-C, Waynesboro, TN 38485, which points out that the hottest places in hell are reserved for those who, in times of moral crisis, maintain their neutrality. I'm here to tell you, no one could ever accuse Grandpa of fence-straddling or hypocrisy. I am told he also had read many other books, such as *"Descent Into Slavery"* by Des Griffin, *"Tragedy and Hope"* by Dr. Carroll Quigley, and *"Empire of The City"* by E. C. Knuth.

Here are some other excerpts from Grandpa's letter: "...I would have liked nothing other than to be left alone, so I could enjoy life, liberty and the pursuit of happiness, which our forefathers willed to us.

"This was not to be, after I discovered that our nation had fallen into the hands of alien people. As Ben Franklin stated, 'They are vampires, and vampires cannot live on vampires, they must live on Christians.'

"We are engaged in a struggle to the death between the people of the kingdom of God and the kingdom of Satan. It started long ago, and is now best described as a struggle between Jacob and Esau.

"I would like to write more, but the Spirit says this must suffice for now. Should the hand of Elijah's God continue to be over me and protect me, I shall someday see this once-great nation swept clean of Christ's enemies, and restored to its former greatness. If it should be the will of our Father and the Father of our Lord Jesus Christ that this be, there will be no way that Ahab's god and his people can stand before us. Mystery Babylon with all its greatness will be destroyed. Take heart, my fellow Christian Americans, God has said that there will be a great shaking in the land. That started this evening. Let each of you who says that the Lord Jesus Christ is your personal Savior sell his garment and buy a sword, if you don't already have one.

"If you've been paying tithes to the synagogue of Satan under the 2nd plank of the Communist Manifesto to finance your own destruction, stop right now and tell Satan's tithing collectors, as I did many years ago, 'Never again will I give aid and comfort to the enemies of Christ.' To those of you who were engaged in the ambush and attack on us and were spared, thank God you have a chance to remove your support from the anti-Christs who rule our nation.

"To those of you who are or have been supporting the edicts and commands of the great whore, stop now and come out of her, as her time is getting short, and when the hour of her judgement comes, that you be not judged with her.

"I must cease now and move on. If it should be the will of the Father that I have more to do for Him, He will protect me, and no device whatever that is used against me shall succeed.

"To my wife, Joan, who has been with me for so long - I know this will be a hard and painful experience. However, remember that prophecy will be fulfilled, and you have now been a witness to some of it. Remember that I love you as much today as I did when I first saw you more than 50 years ago. Put your trust in God, and whether I live or die, He will be with you to the end of your days.

"To my son, Yorie, and my dear friend Scotty - you both displayed the qualities of first-rate soldiers of Jesus Christ. May God bless all of you."

Without a battle, there can be no victory. Prior to that tragic Sunday, the minister remarked, Grandpa had fought with words only, never with force. It was his adversaries who unilaterally employed force up to then. He had sacrified much with little observable success in the advancement of his ideas. Every battle has casualties, and as the preacher says, the victory is not necessarily to the strong. He posed such questions as, "Could it be that from the ashes of the arsoned home where Gordon's murdered, mutilated, and charred body would be removed with a pitchfork, a martyrdom and victory was to emerge? From his apparent descent into disgrace, could it be that the flame for the quest for freedom would become relighted in America? Could it be that people will turn to God and reverse the trend away from morality because of this battle, just as was the effect of Joan de Arc and Portugal's Lady of Fatima?"

The Federal Task Force came to eastern North Dakota in the name of justice, and, like some of the Christian Crusaders of old to the Holy Land, acted lawlessly and foolishly in many instances in their operations, like infidels.

A "WANTED" poster was issued and distributed to Post Offices and lawmen throughout the nation, bearing his picture. The marshals first published a poster, and then the FBI. Copy on the poster identified Grandpa as being suicidal. Refusal to be taken into custody was just the opposite, in Grandpa's thinking, deeming custody to be tantamount to an untimely death at the hands of authorities. He had said, "If I go back to prison, that'll be it." It also asserted that he used January 1, 3 and 8 (1920) as his birthday at different times. I don't know where that came from. It branded him as dangerous, which would be true only during an attempt to take him into custody.

The first order of business by the task force was an assault on the Heaton farmhouse, where Yorie and his family had been living. In her interrogations, Grandma, unable to tell them where Grandpa was, emphatically and repeatedly told them where he would not be - at the farmhouse. Shades of Brer Rabbit! They presumed Grandpa would make a final stand, holed up in the house. The green Mercury police car from Medina was spotted a mile away early Monday morning and placed under guard the day after the shootout.

A special tactical squad under FBI Agent Richard Blay was formed, but the search warrant did not arrive on Monday, so the large SWAT team was forced to postpone the operation until the following day. A personnel carrier, resembling a tank, was procured from the National Guard for the assault.

Bud Brakel, a neighbor living about a mile away, volunteered to go to the house to see if Grandpa was there. "I've known him for decades," Bud told them. "Gordon is my friend, and he wouldn't hurt me." He was not permitted to do this. In fact, he was ordered to vacate his home and sleep elsewhere. He objected, but the federals required him to do so. He submitted, having no desire to obstruct justice.

Blay suspected Grandpa of being heavily armed and of utilizing a system of imagined tunnels leading from the farmhouse in a network. He also suspected booby traps, trip wires, land mines, and fortifications inside the house. All this proved incorrect. They only found goats and chickens and a dog.

When the assault got underway on Tuesday by 100 lawmen, the first shot on the lawn was into the neck of the Kahl dog, named Brownie. The dog was injured and lost its ability to bark. Reporters asked, "Why the dog?" The explanation was that this was standard operational procedure; it might turn vicious, and they didn't want the dog barking and warning Kahl of their approach. The 18 nanny goats and 28 chickens welcomed the brigade.

Another 30 shots were tear gas cannisters being fired into the house. Tear gas is a fine powder. All window panes were broken, some 44, including the storm windows. The front door was broken down, and the interior of the house, including many non-concrete walls, was heavily damaged with axes. Mirrors and pictures were smashed, the dining room table was axed, the antique piano partly disassembled and scattered, the kitchen ruined. The place was devastated. Strangely, the two closed doors in the basement to a pantry and to utility equipment were evidently not opened, either from oversight or from fear. The tear gas did a slight amount of fire damage, and ruined all the stuffed furniture and curtains.

Since newsmen were prohibited in the farmhouse area, one reporter rented a helicopter and flew over. This raised the ire of the lawmen. A TV team tried to walk to the house from the west, but were caught. As mentioned, one TV team had already been to the house.

Len Martin's cap was retrieved by the SWAT team, and all the Kahl family's firearm collection (20-30) were confiscated, with much ammunition. These included a crossbow and some pistols, but mostly just various shotguns and hunting rifles. Their greatest damage, perhaps, was heartbreak and despair to the Kahl clan, especially to Grandma, arising from this wanton destruction. Shelter is a sensitive matter in the wintry clime.

Grandma later filed a claim against the government, which was disallowed. The task force had to return to "square one" in its pursuit of Grandpa. The next day in Fargo, Chief Deputy Marshal Ron Evans said he hoped to have Kahl in custody by sunset, but he declined to say how he might do that. He also said the suspect was holed up, but this turned out to be false.

Scott Faul had told the agents where to find his rifle, and it was retrieved. Marshal Kupferer led the press to believe that his grid and search technique was responsible for recovery of the mini-14. Most of the search team stayed at a motel in Jamestown. They consoled themselves and the press by saying, "At least we have 5 of the 6 in custody!"

Needless to say, the whole affair received national and intense statewide publicity. With some notable local exceptions, the press coverage was inaccurate and detrimental to the Medina Six. To counter this somewhat, Len Martin and some of the wives started issuing periodical news pamphlets, providing their version of the developments to patriot groups across the nation.

Reporters, interviewing Heaton residents to learn about Grandpa, wrote some Kahl quotations: "Income tax came from the second plank of the Communist Manifesto ... Communism is Satanist ... call it the ten commandments of Satan ... I'm going to try to live by God's law as long as possible. When it isn't possible anymore, we'll have to die trying. I've gone as far as I can ... World War III is going to start when they come."

Grandpa's daughter, my Aunt Loreen, told reporters she didn't believe it was necessary for authorities to use such force to enter the house.

"I knew my dad wasn't in there," she said. "I don't know where he is, and I don't want to know, either."

"This is unbelievable," remarked her sister, Lonnie. "They're hunting him like a dog."

At the assault scene, one observer commented, "Well, even if he is not in there, this can be a hell of a training exercise."

"Apparently this is exactly what it was," wrote the Bismarck *Tribune*.

Len Martin, God bless him, ran the American Christian School at Ashley, which had only a handful of students. Four days after the shootout, the task force sealed off Ashley for about four hours. Some 40 officers plus K-9 dogs searched two homes, a veterinarian's clinic and Martin's school upstairs. No probable cause existed for the search other than Blay's remark, "This was a logical place for him to be." Persons owning the properties were members of the "patriotic community".

"We've got to go back and regroup," Blay concluded.

Of course, Grandpa was probably far into the South by then.

Meanwhile, at the hospital, Yorie was beginning to show good signs of recovery. He was allowed no visitors, messages, newspapers or TV. This irritated Dr. Kostick, who wanted the support of relatives to give Yorie the correct environment for recovery. The guards would say, "I'm not allowed to talk with you, to answer your questions." Yorie asked them to get someone who could talk.

The federal agents were waiting for this opportunity, not to answer Yorie's questions, but to interrogate him. Yorie was under heavy sedation from Demerol and Thyorazine, but appeared clear-headed to the agents.

"I know you think I shot first, and I may have shot first, at the the man in the white shirt (Cheshire)." This was later to be admitted into evidence at the trial in May.

Yorie had been read his Miranda rights, but not having his attorney, nor one offered, and feeling no guilt, freely conversed with the agents. A similar ambiguous confession was given the agents, more formally, three days later. He remained under the influence of the drugs. He was arrraigned in the hospital room, at which time he noticed the Masonic rings which later disappeared.

After two weeks Yorie, having made a tremendous recovery, was transferred to jail to await trial.

Deputy Hopson was improving, also, in a Bismarck hospital.

The U.S. attorneys were busy gathering evidence for the grand jury against their five captives.

Bismarck attorney Irv Nodland, representing Scott Faul, filed an early objection with the court over the government's use of the term, "murderers", at a hearing. "A jury decides whether this is so," he objected.

"That's the charge, your honor," responded U.S. attorney Crooks to Judge Benson, a fellow Mason.

As portent and prologue of the pattern in the trial to come, the objection was overruled.

FBI Agent Dick Blay continued to labor under the mistaken assumption that Grandpa would remain in the area, because of his wife's incarceration and his son's injuries. Dr. Martin's Medina Clinic was searched eight days after the shootout, without results. The marshals were beginning to have a strong suspicion that Gordon might be in Montana. (Montana is one state in which the IRS does not ordinarily pursue tax violators criminally, as juries seldom convict, partly due to "Red" Beckman's public information efforts. Beckman is a farmer and author, whose books focus on government criminality.)

The FBI established two toll-free numbers to get leads on Grandpa. Nine federal agents were assigned to answer the calls around the clock. Numerous calls came in, but no useful information.

The Marshals Service offered the biggest award in its history for information leading to Gordon Kahl - $25,000. This was the one move which eventually was to be fruitful in finding Grandpa.

Grandma was persuaded to plead on TV with Grandpa to turn himself in. She did this only because she knew Grandpa. She knew he would know she was coerced into doing it. She knew he would pay no attention to it, even if he heard it. She knew it might cause the authorities to treat her less harshly.

After a month, the task force had been reduced to 50 officers. Blay admitted that Grandpa might have the advantage of the rural countryside, different from a city manhunt.

Blay asked one person friendly to Grandpa, "If you knew where he was, would you tell me?"

After pondering the question, he replied, "Well, he's a friend."

An Associated Press report quoted Blay in what was to be a precognitive and prophetic utterance:

"...You have someone (like Kahl) who could go to a farm in some remote area and be very happy for years and years. Unless someone happens to go to that farm and recognize him and notice him, the odds of getting any information are far more remote than they would be in a much more urban setting."

He said one solid lead - a call from someone who had seen Grandpa - would put then in "good shape."

"I'm optimistic," Blay said,"but yet I also realize that it might not necessarily be tomorrow, it may not necessarily be for several months."

Every point Blay made was to become reality.

Here is a letter from the Bismarck paper, under the banner, "Questions Raised in Medina Incident".

"Editor, Tribune:

"How come this human being named Gordon Kahl is being judged guilty before anyone hears the other side of the story? It isn't that I do not believe my government is not of the law; it is that every story has two sides, and I want to hear both before I go gunning after a 'crazy man'.

"Why arrest him with force? He didn't seem to pose any threat to those around him; wouldn't anyone in his position try to protect themselves if they knew they were going to be set up and shot like animals? I guess I pay less attention to what people say than what they do. If a man does no harm and much good in his life, I would be unlikely to be afraid of him, even if he had some pretty weird political views. After all, we are supposed to be a free people.

"I do not believe in organizations that control one's thinking to such a degree that you refuse to listen to the other side. If any organization or government demands total control over its followers, it has the potential for another Holocaust. People are what count, and human rights must come first if we are to survive.

"And Scott Faul, he's 'different' because he didn't believe in pesticides and fertilizers? My goodness, I have neighbors that don't believe in birth control or Bangs vaccinating! Should we lock them up now or wait until they go berserk?

"History tells things such as what these 'different' people are saying and doing, but 'they' were heroes then because England was the government being harassed. If a nation uses evil means to secure its goals, it is an evil nation. Notice that I said 'if'.

"My heart breaks for the families of each marshal lost. They didn't deserve to die. They were only doing their job. It is a truly senseless tragedy. May justice come to those truly respnsible.

"Where did anyone get the idea that Kahl's dog was dangerous? I hope it wasn't local gossip. Heaven help me if the law is ever after me and all they know is gossip! Or rather, heaven help my dogs!

Allan Rhoads
McClusky"

That letter had a different tone from most media coverage.

The bad press for the Medina Six was pervasive. This angered Alvin Faul, Scott's father, in regard to Scott, which, in turn, became the basis of a Tribune article. Part of his anger was from the newspaper claiming that Alvin was a lobbyist for the Farmer's Liberation Army. The FLA, reported the paper, is an underground protest movement. Regarding Scott, "I think he was drug into this by accident," Alvin said.

"It's just one of a million calls we get every day," spouted a Watertown, South Dakota police officer. Frank Williams of Sykeston had reported spotting Grandpa driving north on the interstate.

After about six weeks, an APB was released describing Gordon's green Rambler. The authorities claimed the reason this was not done earlier was to protect those who might otherwise confront Grandpa.

"Escape to Wisconsin" is that state's tourism slogan. There, persons in a truck painted in a camouflage pattern were originally questioned in the process of the Kahl hunt, by sheriff's deputies, either with or without pistols drawn, near Waukesha. One of these, David Stroede, was forced to post $634 bond for an $80 fine they said he owed Whitehall County. He then filed a $25,000 liability claim against Waukesha County, and a like claim against Whitehall County for not recording his payment when he paid it the first time.

Back in Dakota, the manhunt continued, spreading to other states, including Arkansas, as the weeks went by.

In Great Falls, Montana, Blanchard Lien was aroused by a telephone call to his motel room. He was sternly ordered to come out with his hands up. The call was repeated seconds later. When he and his wife did come out, it was scary. They faced the barrels of seven guns held by lawmen. All other guests had been called and told to stay put.

The motel manager had tipped the authorities that Grandpa was there. Fifteen or twenty FBI agents and other officers responded. Lien got mad at first, but later, he took the whole thing good naturedly.

Since the latter part of February, Grandpa was living at the home of Art Russell, a mile west of Mountain Home in north central Arkansas.

In Arkansas, Grandpa was his own man, as always. An observer could remark, "Anyone who has a mind to take Gordon into custody and throw him in a cage like an animal is apt to go to hell in a hurry. He doesn't bother anyone, and causes no trouble unless he's accosted."

Grandpa's reverie must have wandered back to bygone years, happier times, on occasion. Like the time when Grandma was lecturing him about not letting Yorie and Fred fool around with guns when they were quite young. Grandpa sat at the table, eating and nodding his head affirmatively at his wife. Then Grandma opened the door when someone knocked. There stood the two little tykes, each holding a mallard duck they had shot. Gun safety was drilled into them and became second nature.

A friend of Grandma's was inspired to write:

Ravaged house,
White washed, green trimmed,
Ripped by bullets, windows

Blown away, walls
Splintered.

Heirloom carpets stamped with
Muddied insignia of invading armies.
Rifle butts smashed the mirrors that held

Memories of generations,
Children's monkey faces,
Mothers smiling cheek to cheek with babies,
Babies becoming grandpas in the new land.
The land that promised freedom and justice
For all.

- Maureen Murphy
Heaton, ND

XIX Shenanigans

A day or two after the shootout, a number of telephone maintenance trucks showed up in town. Telephone tapping was anticipated by the entire countryside. They were correct.

Word was passed to residents by the authorities to leave their keys in their vehicles in the countryside. As a tactic, it was better to have Grandpa just to take one than to break into one and short-wire it or to forceably confront them to get a key. Those in the countryside generally complied, with some going a step further and filling the gas tank to the brim. Many neighbors were interrogated extensively.

The neighboring farmer living closest to where the Medina police car had been abandoned was named Glen. He was a close friend of Grandpa's, though not sharing many of his opinions, and was a part-time policeman at Hurdsfield. Like many neighbors, he was visited and questioned many times by the federals during the Kahl hunt. Glen is best described as a tall Swede, perhaps 55 years old.

He once asked the two FBI agents who came to his house for their identification. They did not show it, asking instead, "What are you doing, writing a book?"

"Then you are bums, aren't you?"

"You've got a big mouth," they retorted.

Glen had told the federal agents before they desolated the farmhouse that Grandpa was not there.

"How do you know?" they asked.

"I went over there and their dog told me."

"Oh, you know about that?" the agent responded, knowing that dogs act differently when the place is vacant.

The agents on various visits quizzed him about underground tunnels, mines, army tanks, and the whereabouts of Grandpa. The idea of tunnels came from certain neighbors' children playing in the past at the Kahl homestead. Playing in tall weeds, the small children made pathways through them, with weeds leaning overhead. Thus "tunnels" were a possibility, a reality to the children.

"Where do you and Gordon keep the M4A3 tank the federals were asking about?" a neighbor once asked Glen.

"Right there in the loft," answered Glen with a straight face, pointing to the barn.

When Glen got tired of the agents repeatedly asking him, "Where is Gordon?" he replied, "He's right behind you, probably."

"What do you mean by that?"

"Well, he's on his turf here, and he talks to the animals," Glen replied.

"How's that?" they asked.

"Just to give you an example, we were deer hunting, and suddenly Gordon said that we might as well go home. Someone asked why, and he explained that the magpies had told them where we are so we'd just as well quit. Like I said, he talks to the animals, and if they told him you are here, he might be right behind you."

On one occasion Glen argued with the agents over whether or not Grandpa should be allowed to use his telephone. They threatened him if he did. But Glen contended if Gordon wanted to call and turn himself in, then he could use the telephone, citing the similarity of reporting an accident on the road in front of his home, a legal requirement.

Once when the agents visited, he told one, "I wouldn't sit there!" when an agent had sat on the metal flour bin.

"Why not, what's in it?"

"Dynamite."

Shortly after they left, two different agents came to check out the flour bin.

Glen, tired of the bother from the federals and suspecting his phone was monitored, once said to a friend, Marvin Hammond, "Have you ever been in the army?"

"No."

"Well, we're going to play a little army game. I'll call you later today and tell you to execute Plan A, Schedule 3. Then you call me later."

When Glen called, Marvin's wife answered, as Marvin wasn't home. She assured him that she would give her husband the message "Plan A, Schedule 3 - execute."

Marvin called Glen back the next day and he wasn't home. However, Glen's wife took the message; "Plan A, Schedule 3 has been completed."

Within a few minutes federal agents were at his house, wanting to know what was coming down! "Who is Marvin?"

Once, when federal agents did show Glen their badges, Glen said, "I have one of those, too." He showed them his badge, which he used in his part-time police duties.

The federal agents were never completely convinced that Glen was not harboring Grandpa. For one thing, the federals couldn't understand the people in the countryside calling one another so frequently as they actually did.

Before the SWAT team attacked the Kahl house, Glen wanted to prove to them that Grandpa wasn't there, but their "No Admittance" sign on the road included no admittance for him, too.

Glen had a barn and a round silo next to it. Hay was stacked alongside both of them. The resulting triangular area behind the hay was known as their small daughter's playhouse. When the federal agents queried Glen about the "playhouse" where Grandpa might be hiding, he showed this to them. However, the federal agents would not look behind the hay. Could this reluctance have been from ... oh, well.

For days federal agents foolishly probed for false walls and tunnels. Regarding false walls, "Why didn't they simply measure the outside and inside dimensions?" Glen wondered.

Many of the federals were from cities or from different climates, with the North Dakota prairie being a strange environment. Early one morning, on the theory that the culprit returns to the scene, two agents drove across the frozen field to the clump of trees where the Mercury was abandoned by Scott and Grandpa. They got stuck later when trying to leave. One of their problems was that they were unable to radio their location to others; no reference points. A waitress later told them, "When the frost leaves, the fields become muddy!" as all Dakotans know.

I imagine the other neighbors could provide similar revelations of the task force exploits, but those of Glen are familiar examples, which he stoically shared with the populace of Heaton.

I think maybe the problem with the task force was their philosophical aproach. They are accustomed to dealing with common law criminals - rapists, bank robbers and such - who by and large aren't all that smart, and who do not receive much empathy from friends and acquaintances. Grandpa, though, was highly intelligent and never was rude or unkind to *anyone* in his entire life; he was loved and respected. His behavior while a fugitive was not the norm expected of a criminal.

An ode writer was soon to pen:

"Ring the bells! Sound the war trumpet! A soldier of our race has died. Visions of Vikings standing at the gate to Valhalla - arms outstretched in salute to another brave warrior.

"Listen! Leonidas calls! 'Who is this man that dares to equal the courage of my brave three hundred? Who is this that so boldly treads upon the ground where my men have stood in blood-stained honor for 2500 years?'..."

XX Fracas

Grandpa had visited Timber Lake rancher Byron Dale in South Dakota on January 6 and they had discussed tax laws. Dale was fighting the system from a different angle - unconstitutional debt money. Dale might say that the only good thing about paper bills is the inscription of the national motto, "In God We Trust", which is significantly in quite small print.

The FBI contacted Dale, whose farm was being foreclosed, offering maybe to settle his farm debt if he would tell where Grandpa was hiding. He owed $397,000. He did not know where Grandpa was, and would not have told if he did know. (Bureaucrats are quite liberal with other people's money.)

"That wouldn't take care of the problems this country is facing," Dale explained. "The FBI told me the reward was $25,000, but it could go a lot higher, like whatever my debt was. Gordon Kahl is a quiet and sincere man who has tried to fight this thing through the courts. I can understand his frustration; you can't imagine how corrupt the courts are and how they run over you."

"There could be a lot of people shot yet," Byron continued. "They are trying to steal my place, and when they try to do that, there's going to be a 'hellova' lot of trouble. I am going to stand up and protect my place!"

Byron said that Grandpa had told him that he had been set up by federal authorities when he was convicted of failure to file in 1977, and that if he went back to prison the government might attempt clandestinely to assassinate him with drugs.

During the spring of '83, a court ruled that state police could seize Dale's livestock, machinery and hay for the debt he owed. Governor Bill Janklow told Dale by telephone, "If you point a gun at anyone, they'll flat out kill you!"

"I don't want to die over this thing," Byron said.,

On March 21, thirty officers came to confiscate the property, including Trooper Pat Murphy and Highway Patrol Director Jerry Baum. Dale was wearing a shoulder holster and was near a rifle, while the officers who said they wanted to talk were seated around the kitchen table with him. They were calmly discussing money.

Suddenly, according to Dale, "Murphy grabbed a bottle of ketchup and hit me square on my forehead ... he tried to kill me." Murphy holds a black belt in karate.

After a struggle, Dale was arrested and hospitalized. Ironically, he had earlier tried to pay off his loan with silage and hay, asserting that Federal Reserve Notes were worthless. The Production Credit Association didn't cotton to that! Dale was seriously injured, plus being badly bruised by experts. Two officers got bloody faces in the melee - the blood was all from Dale's injuries.

Attorney General Mark Meierhenry and the Governor had lied to reporters the day before, concerning the planned visit, for "security reasons."

"I wonder if the governor and attorney general make a practice of lying to the people," Dale commented. "I wonder what else they lie to the people about."

Earlier, after the judge had ruled in favor of the confiscation, Dale had said off the wall in umbrage, "I'm not going to apeal anything. I am just going to go about my business and just carry my mini-14 with me, and the first S.O.B. who lays a hand on me will die ... I'm a dead man!"

After the fracas, which was started by lawmen, Dale was tried for obstructing law enforcement officers and resisting the execution of legal process.

Both Byron and Grandpa were interested in the Kansas-centered Farmers' Liberation Army, which actively assists farmers threatened with foreclosures. The FLA believes a systematic drive exists to pick farmers off, one by one, and replace them with super-farms.

After seven weeks of the task force coming up empty-handed in their hunt, DUSM Warren was finally contacted. Can you believe that! The one federal lawman who knew Grandpa well and had his respect - yep, seven weeks! He told them all he knew, including his opinion that the investigation was a bungled farce. Later, he was threaten-

SWAT Team Gear

ed with administrative leave.

Scott remarked, "What scares me about a hunt, be it deer hunt or manhunt, is that the primitive instinct is to fell the prey whenever finally sighted - a John Dillinger, a deer, or a Kahl."

One of the persons interviewed during this period was Grandpa's former employer in the Odessa oil fields. They operated the high pressure transmission pipes from the well-head, which were 2 or 3 miles in length.

"He was the best we ever had," Mrs. Meier explained to the interrogator.

"What was he good at, anything special?"

"Why, Gordon was adept at anything he set his hand to, at anything he tried."

Bud Warren explained to them that there was no way you could put Gordon Kahl in that situation, seeing his son's guts spilled out on the ground, and he not fight back. "Show me any man who won't, and I'll show you a coward. I knew someone would be killed before the marshals ever departed for Medina, but there was nothing I could do about it. If I had tried to discourage it, Muir would have developed an even firmer resolution to go! Mr. Muir had been seriously warned two days earlier."

Well, General Custer was warned about Little Big Horn, too.

It seems that fools rush in where angels fear to tread. Federal officers in Fargo do not live in a communications vacuum. They talk to officials everywhere - Washington, Texas, Bismarck, wherever - by telephone, continually. Who knows what desires concerning Grandpa may have been expressed that week to the marshals, and who knows who did the discussing?

One of the most senseless series of crimes by those sworn to uphold the Constitution and to protect citizens from crime, were those committed against Grandma. Her crime was being the wife of Gordon Kahl. Guilt by association!

Not a scintilla of evidence ever existed to inculpate Grandma in any way. The government agent who swore that she was a murderer and guilty of a number of other charges committed perjury and violated his oath. So did all others who were instrumental in her prosecution, including malfeasance by the grand jury, who should protect citizens.

Two kinds of evidence are used for proof: circumstantial, such as a smoking gun and footprints in the snow, and testimony of witnesses. Not one iota of either type of evidence was ever uncovered against that handsome and noble woman. Does being the wife of a fugitive provide cause for persecution and complete loss of constitutional rights? God forbid, but the legal hounds kept after her all the way, showing no mercy!

They were outraged, not so much because two people were killed, but rather because the wrong two people were fatally shot. Where would be their outrage if, upon arriving at the roadblock, they had killed Grandma as she prayed, first thing, with no one else being shot? I dare say the marshals would claim "death by misadventure", and at most the shooter would be reprimanded for excessive use of force. They wouldn't spend millions to bring the culprit to justice.

Instead, Grandma's character was defamed in the press, she underwent a horrible experience in jail, was kept from

Dining Table/Piano

her critically injured son, her home was heavily damaged and her possessions taken; she was unjustly indicted and tried in federal court, lost her job, and was separated forever from her husband. The jury, which had absolutely no choice in the matter, finally set her free from the federal fanatics.

Grandma later reiterated, "It makes my blood boil that our 'rulers' deem the death of a public servant more important than that of a citizen, whom they supposedly serve."

Jim Wickstrom of Tigerton, Wisconsin, was incensed yet frustrated about the apparent injustice of developments in North Dakota. He tried to help. His well-intentioned but foolish public pronouncements did the Medina Five considerable harm from a public opinion standpoint. He claimed the fictional title of "Director of Counter-Insurgency" for the Posse Comitatuses in America. On TV news, he declared an intention to interview the witnesses. This frightened the Reardons, who said, "They looked pretty tough!" Wickstrom suspected what the court testimony later strongly suggested: that witnesses were heavily coached by the government prosecutors.

The Reardons, who didn't want to leave, were eventually persuaded by the government to take a vacation and visit relatives in Wyoming. They eventually did this, and were paid car mileage for the trip. Rumor has it that they had been promised a much larger sum, covering all their expenses, and were disappointed. Anyway, they turned out to be first-rate witnesses for the government, testifying to "facts" which were absolutely false - all with the identical story, riddled with untruths. Some examples of this were that Yorie shot first, that Yorie "sat" by the pole, that

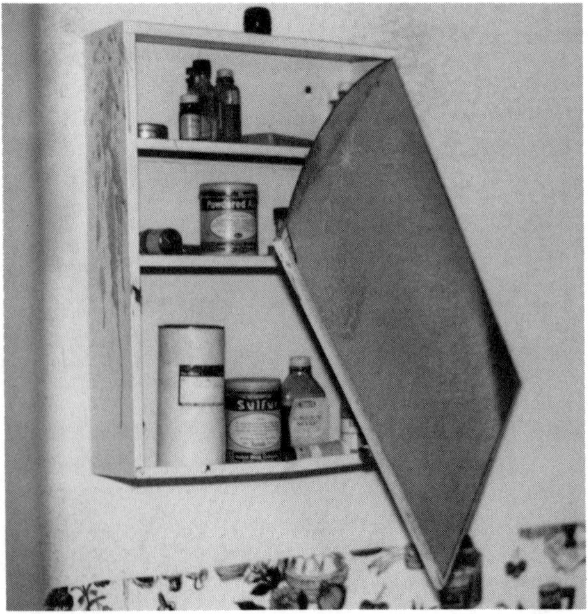

Kahl House Interior

Scott Faul executed Cheshire. (The U.S. attorneys knew that such statements were untrue.)

Anyhow, Wickstrom told reporters, "Kahl was ambushed because he was showing farmers how they were being liquidated illegally."

He would hold press conferences in the name of the Tigerton Posse, and the news media would sensationalize all this brouhaha. It all amounted to very unfavorable publicity for the Medina Five defendants, who were to go on trial in May, even though it was well-intentioned.

Maybe Jim Wickstrom believed that the five didn't stand a Chinaman's chance in the Fargo federal court, anyway. If so, he was right on target!

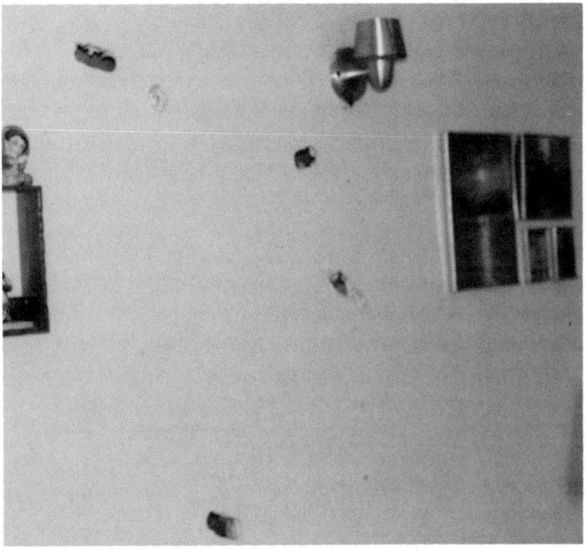

Kahl House Interior

I don't know where Grandpa went the first few days after Medina. I don't want to know, because telling it might cause trouble for some folks, like I said before.

Custom is part of our law, though, as it reflects the will of the people. Anyone who may have helped Grandpa was justified in doing so, however, as the unwritten law gives any person the right to protect another from impromptu mortal assassination. It's a fact that everyone who sheltered Grandpa believed that the federals were out to kill him. They finally did, but not until after the trial of the Medina Four.

I guess you are a little confused about the Medina Six or Five or Four. It was Six before Wegener copped a plea, and Four after Grandma was acquitted.

XXI Caged

Three of the Medina Six were held in the Fargo jail until the trial started - Scott Faul, David Broer, and Yorie. Grandma was out on bond after 16 days in jail. Vernon Wegener plea-bargained his permanent exit after 46 days, with reduced bond. Grandpa remained at large.

All were originally charged by FBI agent Brubaker with first degree murder plus numerous other felonies. After arraignments, grand jury indictments and pretrial hearings, the charges were pretty much firm. Counts 1 and 2 of first degree murder against Yorie and Scott. Counts 3 and 4, forcibly impeding Muir and Cheshire, against all but Grandma. Counts 5 through 8 for impeding the other three in the roadblock were against Scott, Yorie, and David. Count 9, against Grandma plus these same three, charged harboring and concealing Grandpa from the warrant for alleged probation violation. Count 10 was against Vernon Wegener, David and Grandma for hindering the apprehension of murderers. (This count was dropped at mid-trial for Grandma, since no evidence existed whatsoever. Wegener had pled guilty to the false charge, plus another lie, count 11.) Count 11 charged all the Medina Five with conspiracy to interfere with U.S. marshals.

A journalist advised me to do some reading about the myriad of Constitutional violations against Grandpa and his entourage, before, during and after the Medina incident. He referred me to *"Death of a Patriot"* by Andy Mel, Revival Press, Box 3182, Enfield, CT 06082. The author is a paralegal, specializing in the Constitution. He tells of the twelve unsigned search warrants issued to the task force, for example, in their fishing expedition for Grandpa and for evidence. With lucid detail, he lists one constitutional violation after another, even though at times he may be far afield. The seizures in the searches were suppressed by the courts, to the detriment of the Medina Five, which included Grandma.

In reality, the trial of the five was already in progress - in the news media. The vast majority of press, TV and radio coverage, both national and local, was damaging to the defendants. The coverage was chronic and heavy, with many ancillary feature articles. In large measure, the news media survive through exploiting the troubles of individuals.

The fact that Grandpa continued to elude his pursuers, through this period and until the trial was over, did nothing to enhance the chances of the defendants. As Faul's attorney told the jury later, "It's better to hang some feller than no feller!", quoting from Charles Dickens' *"Bleak House".*

Heck, Grandpa's feat wouldn't compare with a farmer named Shamgar, who killed 600 Philistines with an ox-goad (Jude 3).

The government's attorneys and agents went forward with their plans to orchestrate a "fair trial" and then send the defendants to prison. One example of this careful collection of evidence was the Lanengas, who had earlier told the investigators that the first shot was a pistol, no doubt. The agents promised to get back with them and to let them sign their statement, but never did. The long and the short of the judicial masquerade was simply this: Avenge the deaths of two marshals and the injuries to three others. Vengeance, not justice, was the objective.

Irvin B. Nodland was Scott's lawyer; Ralph A. Vingie, David's; Warren Sogard, Yorie's; and Robert A. Ramlo, Grandma's. The government's team was Lynn Crooks, assisted by Dennis Fisher. All of the attorneys were highly competent, articulate and skillful, and they all worked diligently to the end.

To say that the outcome of the upcoming trial was largely a foregone conclusion is not an unwarranted assumption. Such a forecast had little or nothing to do with the facts. The outcome of the trial was to be a function of emotionalism, judicial prejudice, site of the trial, and a dogged determination to obtain a conviction and vengeance by the government. In short, the government was trying its own case.

Perhaps Wegener may have perceived this, and was more pragmatic in falsely confessing, cutting his losses. This conjecture is true, of course, only if he were not an undercover agent in the first place, which some of the other four believe was so, but without proof.

The defense attorneys made motions to sever the cases, rather than to try everyone jointly. This was denied.

Motions were made by those facing the more serious charges for a change of venue, citing media coverage. They contended that a fair and impartial jury could not be empaneled in Fargo. They requested Wyoming. It was denied after being held in abeyance during jury selection.

A motion for Judge Paul Benson to recuse himself was made. It contended his friendship or close working relationship with the unfortunate marshals. Denied!

A motion to suppress all evidence from search was made for David on the basis that the warrant was a general warrant clearly in violation of the Fourth Amendment. The motion failed, as pertinent "evidence" obtained was allowed.

Motions were made to prohibit the "confessions" of Yorie on February 14, 16 and 20, while he was under drugs and isolated. This is when he said, "I might have shot first. I might have shot the man in the white shirt." The one on the 14th was granted, but the later two were to be admitted into evidence.

Lack of success in the motions was so consistent that Nodland was quoted by the press, "Lions 10, Christians 0." The defense attorneys performed nobly, both before and during the trial. However, one must note that certain constraints are on attorneys. They practice their profession in the courts and have no desire to become *persona non grata* by overzealousness in their native courts. In his book, Mel faults them for not pushing constitutional issues more extensively and fervently. However, in a court of equity, such as the Benson court, such efforts would have probably been thwarted. "Just the facts, ma'am!"

The judge decided that the defense lawyers were to have 15 challenges and the government 10 challenges in the jury selection. With two alternate jurors, this meant that 39 jurors needed to be selected by *vior dire*. The judge elected to question prospective jurors, and not the attorneys. They could submit questions for consideration which they desired to be asked.

Although the Medina Four all had remorse that the marshals were killed or disabled, they were optimistic about their chances in court. They were all devout Christians, and their consciences were clear. What had they done that was wrong? None had any trouble sleeping at night because of guilt. They, themselves, were the victims of an assault. The objectives which the marshals sought did not justify the means and methods used. A penchant exists in modern society to blame the victims! They were to be tried on criteria other than that of a Christian conscience or common law wrong.

Later, in answer to a TV reporter, David Broer said, "We shall be acquitted by teling the truth." U.S. attorney Crooks told him the following day that telling the truth would not get him acquitted. Crooks was correct. No other TV interviews were permitted.

Look, these are real names, I'm not making them up - Wigglesworth the elusive, Crooks and Fisher the prosecutors! How ironic!

The government entered a motion in Limine to exclude the philosophies, organizations, religion, taxes and other extraneous subjects from being proper topics of questioning. This was supposedly to keep the trial from being diverted to these side topics. The U.S. attorneys were to later violate their own motion at times, with the effect of biasing the jury against the Medina Four.

What was to be the plan of the government to assure conviction and yet provide, for sake of the appearance, an apparition of a completely, unequivocally fair trial? First, use the kitchen sink approach of charging each defendant with multiple crimes. If accused of enough things, the person must be guilty of something! This could hardly occur without some manipulation of a grand jury, which clearly did not understand its responsibilities. Second, hold the trial in North Dakota, where press coverage and sympathy for the families of the marshals were greatest. Third, use the Benson court, where consistently favorable rulings for the prosecution could be more nearly assured. Fourth, put the widows of the slain marshals and put the disabled marshal on the witness chair, not for evidence, but to prejudice the jury against the Medina Four. Next, hammer on the idea that Yorie shot first, even though the prosecutors were firmly convinced that Muir shot first. This was to be done by mistaken witnesses, such as the Reardons, and by liars, such as Kapp and others. Then, use "expert" evidence, regardless of cost, to implicate the defendants, using photos of gore and blood if possible. Make the jury believe Yorie or Scott actually hit someone, even though the idea is excessively remote, and that Scott "executed" Cheshire. Show a conspiracy, even though none existed in fact. Be insistent that Judge Benson use judicial rulings consistently favorable to the prosecutors. Get two FBI agents rather than the allowable one, to assist with the prosecution; then bring one of them on as a witness. Lastly, be adamant and vitriolic in using emotional language to enflame the jury. Examples of indignation will be terms like "scene of the crime" and "murderers". Again, this was not to be an effort to seek justice, but rather to "win", to get vengeance.

Just as well call a spade a spade! The best laid plans of mice or prosecutors would go awry where evidence is so weak or nonexistent, all other things being equal. The single variable that tips the scales is the judge. The trial is largely subject to his direction by a number of discretionary techniques. The very atmosphere of the trial is under his control in large measure.

One big stick held by the judge is his determination of applicable law. Jurors are improperly intimidated into not questioning his findings in this regard.

It amazes me how a jury that can be so infallible in reaching a conclusion of fact, cannot be trusted to hear and give proper weight to some information. An example of this is Grandpa's letter, which was not to be admitted into evidence. Anyway, the other really big tool of the judge is deciding which information and argument the jury may consider, excluding all others. A verdict often hinges on the judge's discretion in admitting evidence. It can work to favor either adversary.

Jurors, by and large, are common folks who want to do a good job, but are woefully ignorant of the criminal justice system. Since the trial judge is the apparent authority, they typically equate good performance with pleasing the judge. They can sense what he desires them to do. He tells them point blank what they are not to do. Jurors operate in a strange environment which is foreign to them.

Yorie had plenty of time to meditate during his recuperation/incarceration, awaiting trial. At times he thought of his family and his third child, who was soon to be born. He remembered childhood experiences.

Memories are made of such events as when the Kahls made an extra long trip to Crane for the winter. Yorie was eight. They visited relatives in Iowa, then detoured to a short Florida vacation before driving to Texas. They enjoyed the beaches. About halfway to Texas, Freddie said to Grandma, "When are you ever going to bake bread again?" The four car-weary children had tired of snacks and restaurant fare. Grandma had always baked the family's bread. Balking at going into a cafe, all four said they wanted bananas and peanut butter. Grandpa didn't like messes in cars, so Grandma made a deal with them. They wouldn't tell. She bought the items in a grocery and fed the kids monkey style, passing the quickly-snatched peanut butter on banana back between the seats of the station wagon. Grandpa said, "Do I smell peanut butter?" They replied, "We don't smell any, so you couldn't have." Truthful little Lonnie, though, always so good, blurted, "Yes, Daddy, Mama gave us bananas and peanut butter." The stuffed kids then slept for hours. Grandpa never again argued about bananas and peanut butter.

The Medina Four were apprehensive about the Benson court. Their anxieties were justified, as illustrated by the sentencing. First degree murder carries a mandatory life sentence; second degree carries lesser penalties with the life sentence being optional to the judge. Scott and Yorie were to be convicted of second degree murder, even though tried for first degree. Judge Benson sentenced them to life imprisonment on that count. They killed no one. Len Martin reports that one juror later said they were *told* to bring in a second degree conviction.

The strategy for Yorie and Scott at the trial was to be self-defense regarding the shooting and firearms. On the other charges, the Medina Four were to plead that they were innocuously caught in a malevolent circumstance, which was created by others.

XXII Wounded Knee

"Great Spirit," a Sioux proverb goes, "help me never to judge another until I have walked in his moccasins for two weeks."

Two FBI agents were killed at Wounded Knee in 1975. The resultant trial in the Benson court with Lynn Crooks on the prosecution team was a bad omen for the Medina defendants. The following excerpts from the "Crazy Horse Spirit" explains their sobering perplexity, their ominous anxiety:

"In March and April of 1976, the U.S. government presented affidavits purportedly from Myrtle Poor Bear, a mother of a young child from the Pine Ridge Reservation. In the affidavits dated February 23rd and March 31, 1986, Poor Bear claimed she was present at Oglala on June 26, 1975, and saw Leonard Peltier shoot and kill the two FBI agents. This fact was not known to Peltier's lawyers at the time. Myrtle Poor Bear had also signed an affidavit on February 19, 1976, wherein she claimed she had left Oglala the day before the FBI assault and that Leonard Peltier later confessed his feat to her.

"Based upon Myrtle Poor Bear's second two affidavits, and others submitted regarding physical evidence, Leonard Peltier was ordered to be extradited by a Canadian court in Vancouver, B.C.

"It was subsequently learned that the affidavits of Myrtle Poor Bear were a total fabrication by agent David Price and his new partner, William Wood. The two agents had held Myrtle Poor Bear incommunicado for months, separating her from her daughter and friends, and alternately threatened and befriended her. At one point, when Myrtle Poor Bear wanted to back out, they showed her photos of Anna-Mae Aquash's body, telling her the same thing could happen to her. As FBI agents, it seemed they could do 'anything' they wanted to.

"Through the workings of the FBI, the city of Vancouver, B.C. was kept in fear by constant false reports of violent escape plans and terrorism. For Leonard Peltier and his supporters, this meant oppressive security measures for the FBI. It meant control of courtroom proceedings.

"The same basic approach of fear and intimidation was a major government tactic around Peltier's trial in U.S. District Court in Fargo, North Dakota, in early spring, 1977. Local law enforcement and the media were told of large numbers of armed supporters coming to the trial, of threatened escape attempts, and of violence and destruction. Jurors, kept under 24-hour guard by U.S. Marshal SWAT teams during the 6-week trial, were made to believe they were in serious danger from Peltier and his supporters and family.

"The most outrageous government action, however, came during the trial itself. With apparent collusion between Judge Paul Benson and the FBI, the government was permitted to present five weeks of perjured and coerced testimony and often presented manufactured and irrelevant physical evidence. The defense was limited to two days and prohibited from presenting evidence to prove the FBI had created its case against Peltier.

"The defense was prohibited from questioning FBI witnesses about major contradictions in their own reports, about evidence they suddenly discovered, about threatening children caught up in the confrontation, about deals by agents made with a rapist in prison who then signed affidavits that Leonard Peltier or his co-defendants had confessed to them. Judge Benson refused to allow the defense to question RCMP Corporal Parlane about his suddenly remembering incriminating statements at the scene of Peltier's arrest, which were not mentioned until a year and a half later. Another example of the denial of a defense was an attempt to counter FBI agent Frank Coward's testimony that using a 7x rifle scope, he had observed Leonard Peltier, Darelle Butler, Bob Robideau, and James Eagle, running from the scene. The defense was not only prevented from showing Eagle wasn't there that day, but also when a local weapons expert testified that the alleged sighting was impossible due to the distance involved, Judge Benson told the jury the defense was wasting their time. Benson further ruled that Myrtle Poor Bear's testimony about what the FBI did to her would not go before the jury since it would tend to "confuse" them. The judge's actions ensured the verdict the FBI wanted.

"On June 1, 1977, Leonard Peltier was sentenced to two consecutive life sentences for something he claims he did not do. He was immediately sent to Marion, Illinois, the U.S.'s most maximum security prison as well as the location of the government's behavior modification unit.

"Leonard Peltier's attorneys have been actively working on a motion for a new trial since his first appeal was denied by the Supreme Court in 1977. The new appeal must and will be based on newly discovered evidence showing that the government knowingly used false evidence to convict him. From material released recently through the Freedom of Information Act (FOIA) they have succeeded in finding conclusive evidence that the Federal Bureau of Investigation and the United States Prosecutor's Office actively participated in covering up critical evidence that could prove Leonard's innocence. The documents received through the FOIA clearly show that both branches of government manipulated and falsified critical evidence against Leonard.

"Unable to determine who had actually killed the two agents, the government decided to prosecute the three oldest men it could place in the area: Leonard Peltier, Robert Robideau and Darelle Butler.

"In June of 1976, Darelle Butler and Robert Rodideau went on trial in Cedar Rapids, Iowa.

"In July, an all-white jury acquitted Butler and Robideau, who had argued self-defense. When the FBI attacked a camp of women and children, they simply responded. The *evidence against Butler, Robideau and Peltier was the same.*

"During the Butler-Robideau trial, the defense was permitted to show the FBI's conduct during the investigation and the preparation of its case.

"The two co-defendants of Leonard Peltier were able

to present the facts, and they were acquitted.

"Was the Benson 'Railroad' to run again, becoming notorious for disregarding the Constitution? Was this a harbinger of things to come?

"As a retired marshal described Judge Paul Benson, his only qualifications for District Judge were that he had a law degree and an uncle who was a U.S. Senator. Benson had been practicing law for a small law firm in Grand Forks. He had not become one of the more shining members of the firm; his office remained towards the back. After his elderly Republican uncle was nearly beaten in an election, he arranged the appointment of Benson as life-time district judge.

"One might suspect that Paul Benson was ready to discourage the shooting of federal lawmen in the Dakotas, regardless of how justifiable the circumstances."

XXIII The Trial

The trial commenced on May 9, 1983. Defense motions for a continuance of several weeks had been denied. Originally, the trial was scheduled for May 2.

Security in the courtroom was extremely heavy. Perhaps they feared Grandpa would attempt to rescue his family. More plausible, the subtle suggestion to the jurors of the intense precautions was that the prisoners were part of some greater evil scheme. Jurors passing by them, handcuffed to one another, and knowing of the searches, received a definite psychological message. The burden seemed on them to discourage shootouts, they must have thought.

Some of the marshals serving as bailiffs harassed the prisoners. One was told that no gestures or eye contact would be permitted in court. Although the defense attorney got this corrected through the judge, other techniques were used, ranging from rough manhandling to sometimes transporting the prisoners one at a time, thus making them wait after the court day unnecessarily. Absurd rectal inspections for drugs were four-times-a-day affairs.

The trial could not be more eloquently described than was done concisely by Yorie at the time of sentencing. He told the judge, "We are not guilty; this thing was quite a corrupt injustice!" That says it all!

The Chief Justice in the Eighth Circuit Court of Appeals was to agree with the essence of Yorie's conclusion later, although two others did not. Chief Justice Lay wrote, "The record amply demonstrates the defendants did not and could not receive a fair trial in the District of North Dakota. At the time of the trial there existed in that district so great a prejudice against the defendants that they could not obtain a fair and impartial trial at any place fixed by law for holding court in that district."

The Fargo Forum newspaper printed 68 news stories about the matter during the first 44 days relating the Medina incident. These included 22 pictures, many on the front page. TV and radio coverage was extensive.

Concerning these, Chief Justice Lay writes, "Descriptions of Gordon Kahl's fanaticism, the violent and unique nature of the crime, and the feelings of hostility against the defendants were extensive. Marshal Muir (of Fargo) was one of the most respected law enforcement officers in the area. Deputy Marshal Cheshire was also well-liked and respected; according to reports, over 1100 people attended their funeral services. The cold-blooded killing of Cheshire heightened the agitation, not only in the small, peace-loving farm community, but throughout the state. The Governor directed that all state, county and local flags be flown at half-mast in remembrance of the two marshals. Funeral eulogies and editorials condemning the killings and paying tribute to Muir and Cheshire were printed in the district's largest selling newspaper. Anger and shock thus spread across the entire District of North Dakota ... the media created a connection between the defendants and Gordon Kahl.

"Substantial doubts have been raised about the effectiveness of the *voir dire* examinations as a barometer of jury impartiality in this case. *Under any standard of review,* the district wrongly failed to grant venue. In the exercise of this court's supervisory powers, the defendants' convictions should be vacated and a new trial should be granted in a district remote from that of North Dakota."

In another place, Judge Lay noted the failure to change venue failed to meet the American Bar Association's standards for criminal justice. I know that being from Texas as I am, it's hard to be humble, but in all humility and for the life of me, I can't understand any fair-minded person who reads the 16 volumes of trial transcript finding any of the Medina Four guilty of second degree murder and such.

What? Yes, I know there's a town in Texas named Humble. It's misnamed.

Seventy-eight prospective jurors underwent *voir dire* questioning. Half of these (39) were excused as potentially partial due to pretrial publicity or knowledge of persons involved in the prosecution. Were the other half uniquely devoid of media influence or simply less forthright? One of the selected jurors admitted that "his mind was pretty well set" at an earlier date, although he did not claim to have any opinion at the time of *voir dire* questioning. Another selected juror testified that he had formed an opinion, albeit "nothing that I would consider a strong opinion."

Just for fun, assume *ad absurdum* that Gordon Kahl was berserk and insane, and that the four defendants were with him at the roadblock against their will. Given the conduct of the lawmen, would the actions of the four at the roadblock have been significantly different? Hm-m. Food for thought! What about *their* rights?

The government presented its case according to its planned scenario. It was an exercise in drama, cleverly camouflaged to elicit jury sympathy and indignation, punctuated by impressive ballistics and medical experts as figures of authority. As scheduled, it emphasized Yorie firing first and Scott "executing" Cheshire, and, I repeat, both of which were known to be false by the U.S. Attorneys. Efforts were made to defame character, such as Scott's problems with authorities who tried to teach his 6-year-old sex education before instructing him on the ABC's. Impressive displays of weapons were made.

Little or no substantial evidence as to the charges was submitted. In this regard, a preponderance of evidence is not sufficient to convict a person of a felony, nor is "clear and convincing proof" enough. The evidence is supposed to be beyond a reasonable doubt. Could reasonable doubt have been denied the defendants in this case? It would seem so to me.

Perhaps sequestration of the jury for these weeks under the care of the U.S. marshals could have been a factor. No one can prove the marshals influenced the jurors, but few prudent people would doubt it. No doubt exists of their animosity towards the defendants, and who is to say a marshal's gesture or sneer would not have effect, even if no words transpired? Meals to the jurors were catered by a cafe managed by Paul Stalcup, nephew of slain Marshal Muir. To relieve tedium and to pass the time, the marshals participated with the jurors in a softball game on one weekend. Marshal Wigglesworth, one of the alleged victims of assault, was observed with softball gear in a parking lot at the time. My, talk about setting foxes to guard the chickens! Never mind, the appellate court said all this didn't matter.

The prosecutors were overzealous, to say the least, in pushing their obvious advantage with Judge Benson. To illustrate, prior to the trial, the counselors reached an agreement which permitted Scott Faul's statements to the government to be admitted into evidence without objection from the government, provided he took the stand subject to cross examination. When his statement to the FBI was offered into evidence, the prosecutors objected. They welched on the agreement, latently asserting that it only pertained to polygraph results. As usual, the judge sustained and the appellate court agreed. Nevertheless, the instance is a classic demonstration of the nefarious conduct of the trial. Another example: near the trial's end, Fisher showed *colored* photographs of the dead men to the jury, saying, "This is what this case is about!" The defense had stipulated that the men were dead, and had died from gunshot wounds.

The evidence presented by the government did not substantiate the convictions. I'm not saying this just out of the blue. I studied the case. Take David Broer. He only laid on the ground and prayed. Even though he was acquitted of assault, he was convicted of harboring and of conspiracy to assault.

First, the evidence was far below the required level of proof needed for concealing and harboring. (He did neither.)

Second, he was convicted of conspiring to *forcibly* assault, resist, oppose, impede, intimidate or interfere with lawmen. To convict him, it is necessary for the jury unanimously to convict on one of the forcible *means* by which this was done. Of course, the jury didn't do this, because the evidence just wasn't there showing conspiracy to forcibly do anything. The appellate court was no help here, because no objection was made to jury instructions.

Even with two and a half weeks of testimony and scores of exhibits to consider, the jury was not out long in making its decisions. It amounted to about 15 minutes per charge for each defendant.

The defendants each took the witness stand in his own defense. Grandma testified that they were "ambushed". They all had the ring of truth in their answers! Grandma was acquitted on both charges, as *no* evidence existed against her except that she was at the scene. The only other acquittal was the assault charges against Broer.

The judge was pleased at the outcome, but Crooks thought Grandma should have gotten at least ten years.

Sogard, whom defense pathologist Smith said was not too fat, but just too short, conceded during the trial that he felt like David going against Goliath. (He did resemble a little bit a bale of hay with the middle strand busted.) The immense resources and arsenal of weapons available to the Justice Department to prevail in a trial are simply not available to a country lawyer. Government expert witnesses came from Texas and Maryland, for instance, even though one FBI agent surmised the government couldn't afford to procure and store tapes for interviews, with the agents writing their version of what was said being the convenient alternative, sometimes omitting or altering key statements.

The thrust of Judge Benson's position was that there was no such thing as self defense where federal marshals are concerned.

The question to ponder is: just how much guff and oppression must a citizen take off a misbehaving official who is unidentified?

The basic law of any free society is that a person has the right to defend himself and his property from *anyone* unless legal due process has been afforded him to the contrary.

Yorie's pistol with the .38 slug imbedded finally turned up from a trash can plant during closing arguments at the trial. This caused quite a procedural stir, but mainly it confirmed that Muir started the gunfight. "So what?" said Crooks. "He had a right to. I'm just glad he at least got to hit someone before he was killed."

In addition to the life terms for Yorie and Scott, Chief Judge Paul Benson imposed 15 years of *consecutive* sentences. These were four 10-year concurrent sentences for assault charges and five years for harbouring. Another

5-year concurrent sentence for conspiracy to forcibly assault was also imposed.

David Broer, acquitted of assault, was given two consecutive five-year terms for harbouring and conspiracy to forcibly assault.

Lynn Crooks was flown to Washington and was honored for his successful prosecution.

Irvin Nodland waxed eloquent in voicing President Reagan's quotation of C.S. Lewis' *Screwtape Letters*. 'The greatest evil is not done now in the sorted dens of crime that Dickens-like characters paint; it's not even done in concentration camps and labor camps. In those we see but the final result, but it is conceived and ordered and moved and seconded and minuted in clean, carpeted, warm and well-lighted offices by quiet men with white collars and cut fingernails and smooth-shaven cheeks, who do not need to raise their voices.'

"...And the government didn't seem to start out this case talking about those things (philosophies, etc.), implying that these Defendants' beliefs would constitute some sort of creeping insidious threat that had to be destroyed or stamped out, and with calm assurance you were told in the opening statement that what this case is not about is his political beliefs - whether taxes, religion, or philosophy. We could not care less what they said. But, somewhere on the road, they abandoned that stance and they took a pail of slop and they walked over and poured it on top of Scott Faul's head, because things from the evidence of what happened at Medina weren't going the way they thought they would. And 12 hours into the trial we received evidence of things that happened a year ago that we are not prepared to challenge, like we were with Susan Reardon. (They abandoned) what they promised in their opening statement."

He then stated, in effect, that since they haven't been able to get Gordon Kahl, they want to get their pound of flesh from someone.

"This case represents a combination of factors that have come together on the 13th of February to produce madness. There is plenty of fault to spread around, including my client and the other defendants. There is a freak accident, negligence, and there is carelessness. There is machoism and there is insecurity. There is stupidity dripping all over everyone.

"We start this case with a minor misdemeanor violation, the principal penalty of which was inflicted and served by Gordon Kahl. There was a court form reporting violations and a man too stubborn to throw it out because it violated some principle he had. It was over five years gone by from the original conviction, three years of an unserved warrant, meetings and negotiations in lieu of arrest. Finally, there is a directive from the National Marshal Service to file it away, not spend any more time on it, and then it was executed. I think there is something behind this chart that I'd like to get out, that's Government Exhibit 11E, and it represents the response to the national directive of the Marshal Services that it be filed away. That's how it was filed away. It was executed in unmarked cars by ununiformed officers in flak jackets and AR15's on a Sunday afternoon following what we were told was a religious meeting with 11 innocent people and children in the immediate vicinity of the Reardon driveway, and it included among those 11 innocent people my client, who had been driven to virtual paranoia by a false police APB about him or his car, by news articles about circumstances in Utah, by a surveyor with binoculars, by a tip from someone who is unidentified that there is a set up or a trap, and then at the moment when the warrant was executed, there was a tornado of verbal obscenities and threats. 'You're going to die,' 'You're going to have your head blown off,' threats from unmarked, ununiformed people holding fire power with the sufficiency to carry out those threats. And when my client flees from the scene or retreats, as Mr. Crooks called it in his opening statement, he's cut off or contained, as they said, by yet another unidentified and yelling person lying prone some seventy-five to a hundred yards, a football field, away.

"Darrell Graf knew that this was insanity. I think Bud Warren knew that it was insanity. Graf said, 'They are going up there to shoot a tax evader, and this time the police are wrong.' And he called the ambulances and rescue squad and got out a crew. And one of the questions that I have asked myself from the beginning in this case and I can't answer it, as I tried to put myself in Scott's shoes as he was out there, when is a citizen obligated to assume that people who are not acting like police and who do not look like police are nevertheless probably police so as to require immediate submission to authority and to threats of death? Can you throw a hand grenade into a crowd and then demand strict accountability of those who trample others in the panic to escape?

"I think the court will tell you something to the effect that if Scott had *reasonable* grounds to believe and did believe he was in danger of death or serious bodily injury from which he could save himself only by use of deadly force, then he had a right to employ that deadly force. We lived for a number of months thinking that Cheshire's death was the principal issue in this case. You know what I think the principal issue in the case for Scott Faul is now? I think the government has given the testimony of Curtis Pellett as its principal thrust, hoping that somehow or other, because of something that may have happened and may not have happened last year, that you will think, 'Ha, Scott Faul is a bad man and it doesn't matter what happened at Medina.'

"Scott Faul's fate is absolutely in your hands; it's beyond mine, and it's beyond his. He is ready to accept your judgement of his conduct on this day in accordance with the rules of law that the court gives you at the end of these arguments.

"What you have by way of evidence in this case is saturated with mistakes and errors and omissions, but I guess I'm saying to you I don't really think that matters a lot in this case. On this abstract canvas that has been created for you now by the lawyers and the witnesses, I think that you can see the globs of paint that have been heaved in many instances were simply not true. People have come in and said Scott was at a meeting and he said this heinous thing, and ten minutes later said, 'Oh, maybe somebody else said that,' and when Scott explained to you when he was on the stand what that was all about, it turned out to be the opposite of what had been indicated.

"The full force of the federal government has been brought to bear in this case. All of its resources, investigators, its marshals, its FBI, U.S. attorneys. They have put onto pieces of paper what purports to be a preservation of the evidence. Witness after witness then came here, looked at those statements, and said, 'I don't think I said that,' or "They left something out.' Yesterday when Scott was on the stand in surrebuttal of the statement that he gave to the FBI, he made a statement to them that Gordon Kahl told him that he walked around the front of the RAM Charger firing at the door at someone who was crouched down behind the door and finally moved around to finish him off. That statement didn't even find its way into the official 302 report of the FBI. When the printed word fails and there is nothing to establish a preconceived idea that the Government has had here, and there are no video tapes or other tapes, we are given a piece of manufactured evidence. That photograph of the RAM Charger with the streamers coming out of it. The only thing that's accurate about that photograph is the rear end picture of the RAM Charger. It is in fact the RAM Charger. Nothing else on that photograph is actual. But it probably doesn't matter, abstract paintings allow for great poetic license, even when it's done with precision, with careful analysis like autopsies. You heard in this case that experts can vary between a quart of blood and a tea cup in describing the same thing and where you find out how it's measured by sloshing the hand in a cavity.

"The defense we are giving you here is one of self defense that is justified, that was based upon the circumstances, and even though there are parts of the reliance that Scott had, had that latter proved to be inaccurate, that since the APB that was false, that we are entitled to that defense towards any crime that may be charged, whether it is a major offense or whether it is one of those lesser included offenses.

"The government has the right in this case under the rules to go last. That always worried me a great deal because the psychologists tell us that which we hear first and that which we hear last makes the greatest impression upon us. It's called the principle of primacy and regency in the psychology books, and I am concerned about that."

The other defense attorneys made equally impressive arguments, especially against the other kitchen sink charges.

Judge Benson charged the jury not to discuss the jury deliberations or how they had come to the verdicts with anyone after the trial was over. Was there something to hide? (He had no right to do that, as a dismissed juror is no longer under court jurisdiction.)

Robert Ramlo had some interesting comments. Assuming lawmen should use common sense, he said, "Where does it say 'put on badge, park brain'? You can do some wrong things that are legal, and some legal things that are wrong.

"It seems to me that all they wanted to do was arrest Gordon Kahl. I mean, you don't have to know much about law enforcement to know it ain't real smart to arrest some guy that says he ain't going to be arrested and he's got some other guys with him who've got guns. I don't have to read a manual to figure that out, unless you're looking for trouble, unless you want to try to make an example, or unless you think you have got so much authority that nobody dare oppose you, no matter what the circumstances. But, for some reason, they went out there and did that.

"The government's attitude is, 'If you were there you are going to pay for it.' Wonder what a hitchhiker's chances of staying out of jail would have been, had Broer given someone a lift as they left town?

"The only thing dumber (than throwing a kid out of school for truancy) is to put someone in jail for being a tax protester, let him out of jail (even though he says he won't file returns), and make it a condition of his being out of jail that he file taxes, and then he doesn't file taxes, and go looking for him to put him back in jail. Somewhere along the line there ought to be some common sense and reason, (especially) from government. (They should have considered what would happen before they) pulled guns on people and started hollering, 'You're going to die!' and 'We are going to blow your heads off!' "

So the government now has three political prisoners. This cost to taxpayers is roughly $50,000 per year. And so it is that branches developed and some fruit ripened from this poisonous tree planted on the plains of Texas in 1977.

The Supreme Court refused to hear the case. That's not unusual, I'm told, especially for a case related to personal income taxes.

Len Martin estimated the trial costs at $100,000 for taxpayers, with the total Kahl affair being some three million.

XXIV Quo Vadis

You can count the seeds in an apple, but you can't count the apples in a seed. I think this seed of a new era was germinated and precipitated during the fall of 1983. Grandpa had filed for an injunction, with the aid of Ashley's Michael Phillips, to stop the sale of his property by the IRS on November 4. The IRS reported this to the Marshals' Service. Deputy Marshal Carl Wigglesworth, who always seems to be lurking in the background of Grandpa's problems, informed Cheshire in Bismarck, who in turn advised Judge Bruce Van Sickle of Grandpa's "fugitive" status. The clerk did not file the documents, but turned them over to the judge instead.

With all the meetings going on and farm foreclosures occurring, it seems evident that a connection existed. Within four months came the awful tragedy of Medina. Everyone at the roadblock suffered tragedy. Then, three and a half months of the travesties of jailings, federal rampaging, and the mockery semblance of a trial followed.

The central question is: Why all the federal action on a dormant matter?

At the trial, Crooks stated that Wigglesworth was emotionally scarred by events at Medina. The transcript just as accurately mistyped it "scared". He reputedly underwent some psychiatric care, but possibly this was only a continuation of earlier treatment. He had cried while on the witness stand; some observers think the tears were crocodile, because of quick recoveries of composure.

Shauna Faul and her five little children went back to the 1,000 acre farm. She has been plowing the fields and making the crops since the trial.

Friends and neighbors restored the Kahl home, where Yorie and Janice had been living, after the destroyers came. It was no small task. Grandma took both of us girls there to live. Sometimes Grandma would go to Shauna's a few weeks at a time during the busiest farming periods to help. Our store-bought food was purchased with money sent by anonymous givers, marked only "From God, With Love."

A Clinton, Arkansas newspaper, "The Justice Times", was the instigator of this.

Yorie's dog recovered, and hard-earned taxpayer money paid the $150 vet bill.

Darrell Graf became bitter towards the news media, whom he believed portrayed him unfairly as a coward. He had acted very wisely, in fact. He soon lost his position in Medina and law enforcement contracts in three other places.

Dr. Martin retired and moved to western Montana. "It is very clear you don't have the right of association without the Gestapo watching!" he said.

Bradley Kapp continued as Stutsman County deputy, less one index finger, continuing to hate his antagonists. He continues to live in mah-DEE-na, this pronunciation being adopted in 1949, following Judge Harold Medina's trial of 11 Communists in New York. Medina's 520 residents don't like to talk about the shootout, with so many unanswered questions surrounding the incident.

Shauna Faul, who is 29, has been married to Scott for 12 years. She and their five children, like Grandma, take one day at a time. Every day is hard. They try to visit Scott once a month in Wisconsin, 640 miles away. "It's friends and famiily who have kept me together," she is quoted as saying. She has a sparkling personality, and like Scott and Yorie, is deeply religious. She is resentful of news stories which suggest she is indifferent to the families of officers involved in the shootout.

"I believe they are hurting just as much as we are," she said tearfully. "I feel like we are all victims."

Two unsuccessful attempts were made to transfer DUSM Bud Warren, who was a year away from retirement. Some other marshals were ticked off because he testified favorably for the defense. He had no choice, as an honest man, since he was subpoenaed. A local police officer heard the chief marshal talking with Gary Booth, Fargo IRS District Director: "We couldn't transfer him, but we're not through with Warren yet, are we?" Booth said nothing, just smiled from ear to ear. Bud was soon audited. The IRS thought they had him at first, for not reporting some interest income, but the oversight by Bud had been corrected the following year.

The Marshals Service underhandedly broke its tradition of awarding retiring marshals their invalidated badge and credentials when Harold Warren retired at the end of 1983. This was understandably insulting, and Bud felt offended. Several months of correspondence followed. In one letter, he wrote:

> "My 30 years of law enforcement has never wavered from my initial law enforcement interest; being helpful to those who need help; admiring those who don't; despising those that look with scorn at the less fortunate; respecting those that reach out to the less fortunate; never to use my badge and position for any other reason than to serve the needs of the public."

After receiving numerous untruthful letters from the USMS, he finally received a badge embedded in plastic in November, 1984. So far as I know, he was never awarded his plaque and other mementoes ordinarily bestowed, though he continues to try to obtain them.

Honesty and integrity seemed more important to this lawman than popularity and authority.

Lois Muir, 54, is learning to live alone and to adjust to the feelings that threaten to overpower her as a grieving widow. She gets angry, but doesn't blame anyone. "There are so many circumstances that had to come together (for the incident)."

Vernon Wegener, former Streeter policeman, became a self-employed carpenter, after being placed on probation for two years. Saying he wasn't into the Bible much at the trial, he has since become a regular church attender. "Before the incident, I maybe went to church once or twice a year. Now I have only missed two Sundays."

Joni Broer, 39, worked in food service until she had a disagreement with the state concerning sales tax collections. She did not consider herself to be a tax collector for the state. The search by the task force had rendered the Broers' paralegal business inoperative, especially with David in prison. Diabolically and defiantly, Joni and her two children live in a house in Harvey - on welfare - living proof of what unwise tax and subsidy policies can do to work incentives. Joni claims that her husband is a political prisoner and expressed compassion for the families of the slain marshals. Joni told a reporter, "If they (the officers) hadn't been so damn aggressive and more professional, this would never have happened."

Dennis Fisher and Lynn Crooks turned to other matters. "Essentially, the defendants are victims in this crime ..." Crooks said later, blaming Grandpa. "There are more victims than you can count."

Yorie's wife, Janice, and her three small children lived in Richmond, Minnesota for a while, with Grandma. She eventually moved to Carrington, divorcing the imprisoned Yorie two years later.

Lynn Cheshire, widow of Robert, remained in Bismarck with her two small children and attends college.

Wayne Reardon noted that three vehicles parked in his driveway were damaged by the gunfire, and as I mentioned, a federal bullet lodged four feet from his son's crib. He also believes the stress put on his father caused his fatal heart attack during the trial. The courts disagreed when the matter was litigated.

The Fargo *Forum* reported that Len Martin ... who once walked the state with a monkey on his back to protest taxes and later issued citizen's arrest warrants for those who illegally searched his premises, became a lobbyist for the Liberty Lobby, Washington, DC. It must be eerie having such a warrant outstanding against you. He wrote a short booklet about Grandpa that I identified earlier, and a book, "*Medina*", telling of the shootout.

The other two Ashley residents who underwent searches, veterinarian James Coleman and Michael Phillips, moved their families to Canada. "If they (ND Constitutionalists) think they have had trouble up to now, they haven't seen anything yet," President Reagan had said to a slain marshal's wife by telephone.

Yorie went to prison firmly convinced that Freemasons were responsible for his misfortunes in some way to a large extent. Note these excerpts: "...shortly before the trial, when several things were being said and done concerning the

Lodge, the rings began to disappear from the marshals and FBI agents ... My attorney couldn't get a roster of Masons for the state, and the Grand Secretary denied that some persons were Masons, whom I knew were ... We had a 32nd degree Mason who was working with Charlie O'Brien, Sr., of the Constitutional Law Center, who knows Freemasonry well. I wanted to put him on the stand to testify about the subject. He had called me. Judge Benson found out about it and had him jailed until after the trial. We also intended at one point to introduce a copy of *Morals and Dogma* by Albert Pike. My lawyer later decided to avoid the subject at the trial. I wanted Charlie for my counsel, but the judge would not permit it."

By letters and conversations with Yorie, he kept me informed of his plight. He wrote: "After the June 24 sentencing, Scott, Dave and I were soon flown to Leavenworth, Kansas. Security going to the airport was immense. Two marshals accompanied us in flight. The one in charge was a large, impressive Indian. We discussed the Wounded Knee incident and atrocities in general against Indians. Concerning our case, he said, 'You see, we have a brotherhood, and whenever you go against one of us, you have to deal with all of us.' We three glanced at each other knowingly. Typical of today's public servants, his attitude towards other Indians' treatment was, 'Rain on 'em, I got mine!' (Actually, what he said was more vulgar.)

"At Leavenworth, my heirloom Bible and all my addresses and phone numbers were taken from me.

"After several days of being in separate cells, we talked with a Lieutenant. He informed me that 'they' had been monitoring the case since the beginning, and said, 'I don't know what to tell you ... you need to get someone to write a book or something.' He showed his concern and even allowed the three of us to be placed in a large cell together. However, 'higher-ups' found out about it and separated us within two hours.

"Scott was placed in population there, and I have not seen him since. (He was later moved to Oxford, Wisconsin.) I was moved to '63' building, generally used for those who commit offenses in prison. I was placed in a cell with two homosexuals, and for some time I anticipated some serious problems. But I preached to them every day and can only hope I did some good. (God's word does not return void.)

"After a month I was shipped to Lewisburg, Pennsylvania, via Terre Haute and Milan, Michigan. I had the blessing of visiting with David then, who was enroute to Terre Haute. I was held over in the 'hole' in Terre Haute for two weeks; was in Milan for one night, and then to Lewisburg and again the 'hole' for four days. They told me I was 'ultra high priority' when finally placing me in the general population.

"Within ten days, I was again put in the 'hole'. After a week, a hearing was held, strangely, in a utility-like baggage room. The Manager said, 'I don't know why you were locked up. No one in this institution knows why you were locked up. All I know is we got orders to lock you up. The orders were from 'way up'. He looked down at his desk and then back at me, and said, 'Way, way up!' " (Yorie must have recalled the psalmist's scripture: If I make my bed in hell, you'll be there.)

"The ring on his finger told me all I needed to know."

(Coincidental with this lockup was publicity that Joan Kahl and others were to speak at a Gordon Kahl memorial rally in Kansas and then Idaho. However, because of close surveillance and telephoned threats to their safety, their appearance was cancelled. They had learned, also, that the three prisoners had been placed in isolation in different prisons.)

"After a good while, I was taken to El Reno, Oklahoma, and then on to Bastrop, Texas, where the facility looked more like an apartment complex than prison.

"I befriended Ralph Baker, and we discussed government with similar conclusions. One agreed observation was the extraordinary large proportion of prison officials and others in lawmaking and enforcement roles in government who were members of Masonic organizations. A double-headed phoenix, one of their greater symbols, is in Bastrop. Lodges and some federal buildings have cornerstone dates different from our Christian date.

"For reasons we'll never know, Ralph and I were rousted out of bed at 1:00 a.m. on a June night, 1984, and locked in the 'hole'. Next day, they took us to the marshal's office in San Antonio, and that evening to maximum security in the county jail.

"I was returned to Lewisburg and Ralph was sent to Terre Haute. He is a level 2 prisoner and I am level 3, but we are in much tighter security prisons. Contrary to prison policy, also, I am too far from home. Here I am, though, and I try to teach others about Christ. Some knew nothing about Him whatsoever.

"I once talked with a certain prison official in his office. One thing led to another, and he said, 'I know you shouldn't be locked up. You're probably the only prisoner here that I can honestly say should not be here, but you have to look at the government's side of the thing. I'm sure the government assassinated your father. I've worked for this government for many years, and it's no secret that they kill anyone who becomes a thorn in their side. There is nothing I can do ... there is nothing any man can do. Within a few years, we will be a Socialist country, and I'm not going to stick my neck out.'

"I was a pallbearer for Mr. Reinhardt, who was convicted on 'failure to file' charge along with my Dad. A prisoner had called his wife and said 31 inmates were willing to testify that he was murdered in Safford prison. He had a heart attack, which I am satisfied was induced, and for several hours inmates did what they could for him and passing guards refused him any medical help.

"When at Springfield for evaluation, my father met a doctor from Cuba whose government was discussed at length. Previously, Dad had told me that he had met Padre Lance, one time friend to Castro, and learned that Castro was no more than a puppet for the very same 'Internationalists' who financed the Bolshevik Revolution in 1917, from Wall Street. This doctor confirmed all this, including other things, one being Freemasonry's major role in accomplishing these goals. The doctor talked in a very quiet tone, and at the end of the conversation, Dad gave him a 'masonic' handshake. The doctor laughed and said, 'All this time I spoke quietly, and here you are one of us!' The doctor was mistaken.

"Although Dad was supposedly wanted for an alleged probation violation,he was placed under a million-dollar bond before he was arrested. For a misdemeanor? Be sure to note that they wanted to return him to Texas, not for anything he *did*, but because of what he had said. His talk concerned challenges to the 16th Amendment, the Federal Reserve Act, and similar farces, going further and telling of the 'High' Masonic Element that enabled such evils to occur."

Yorie wrote on, indicating how freedom of speech and many other constitutional rights have disappeared, replaced by tyrannical rulers. "How many have been brought to justice for violating their oaths of office?" he wonders, and writes that Cicero said it well:

"A nation can survive its fools and even their ambitions. But it cannot survive treason from within. An enemy at the gates is less formidable, for he is known and carries his banners openly. But the traitor moves among those within the gate freely, his sly whispers rustling through the alleys, heard in the very halls of government itself. For the traitor appears not a traitor, for he speaks in accents familiar to his victims, and he wears their faces that lie deep in the hearts of all men. He rots the soul of a nation, he works secretly and unknown in the night to undermine the pillars of a city, he infects the body politic, so that it can no longer resist. A murderer is less to be feared."

Yorie ends by writing, "The price of freedom and liberty has always been blood, sweat, and so very many tears," and closes with, 'In service to the King of Kings for a return to American ideals."

Yorie is wise beyond his years, and yet has sincere remorse for the tragedies of the marshals. His life will no doubt be shortened from the effects of his own gunshot wounds.

BABYLON, O' BABYLON

Babylon O' Babylon,
You rob the souls of men;
You force them into poverty,
And rob them once again.

You've never given anything
But pain and misery;
Your pleasure is their grievances,
Your red eyes shine with glee;

You rob the widows' houses,
The Orphans you destroy;
You are the works of darkness,
And terror you deploy;

O' how you love your silver,
Your gold's become your pride;
But when the son of God returns,
You'll find no place to hide.

His angels will encircle you,
And stamp you into hell;
Just as your father, Lucifer,
From heaven's war he fell;

Your days are surely numbered,
Your empire shall pass;
Your merchants and your servants
Will cry, "Alas, Alas;

"That great and mighty city,
With burning cinders smell;
She's gone unto her father,
into the pits of hell."

The days of grace have passed you by,
The Judgement now is set;
The gnash of teeth and pestilence,
For reward is what you'll get;

The demons that begat you,
Will dwell eternally;
With Jezebel and Lucifer,
In Judgement's fiery sea;

The whoremongers and Antichrist,
Will share in your reward;
That eternal lake of fire,
Will be your room and board;

You gave up eternal pleasure,
For the artifice of gold;
And when you held it in your hand,
You were powerful and bold;

But now where is your power,
Your golden god is dead;
You've lost your silk and glory,
And the crowns upon your head;

Your rubies now have lost their gleam,
Your diamonds' sparkle fail;
When your memory returns to these,
We'll hear your woeful wail;

Then those of us who gave our lives,
And betrothed the King of Kings;
Who sacrificed thru love and pain,
For splendored eternal things;

We'll gaze upon you briefly,
As we enter thru the gate;
We'll be singing songs of joy,
But for you it's now too late;

You said you were of Abraham,
Of Isaac and Israel;
But Jesus said if you were of us,
That you'd be with us still;

O' Synagogue of Satan,
With your covert societies;
You've spilled the blood of martyrs,
With your murder sprees;

You brought abominations,
And Baalam philosophy;
With you out from Babylon,
From your captivity;

You spread it out through all the lands,
And thought you'd done so well;
And those who bow the knee to you,
Are twice the child of hell;

Praise be to our Father,
And His sacrificial lamb;
And those of you who hate Him,
Will be rewarded as the damned;

O' children of the prince of hell,
Your nature proved your deeds;
Your fruit is of the thistles,
Your gardens grow the weeds;

Life lasts only moments
As a puff of smoke it's gone;
We'll all be pleading mercy,
For all our human wrongs;

But those of us who've cleansed ourselves;
Through the blood of Christ, Jesus;
We'll look back upon our lives,
As if sin never was;

And we'll rejoice exceedingly,
When the scroll of names is read;
And wonderously marvel,
At "Mystery Babylon" - the living dead!

- Yorie Von Kahl

XXV Refuge

Grandpa's heartbreak while fleeing southward must have been that of utter despair, perhaps worse than death, given his love of freedom. He knew that his chances of ever seeing his loved ones again were bleak, nil. He realized his chances of being alive very long were slim. Along with repeated sinking feelings in his stomach and sincere sadness in his heart, he felt strongly a righteous indignation that agents of the "sons of Satan" had accosted him in such a manner. With an overwhelming grief encompassing his entire being, his whole soul, it was difficult to think clearly. He was emotionally exhausted, drained.

Where to go? Who to contact? What routes to take? As Yorie had told Stutsman County lawman Jack Miller, "Grandpa was almost ingenious in survival tactics. You will never catch him or get him alive. He won't contact anyone." Grandpa let his instincts and hunches - perhaps the Holy

Lorna Adkins

Spirit leading - answer the necessary questions for his remaining 111 days of life. If there were refuge and safety, it would be in the hills or vast spaces of the South, not in the less friendly people and hostile climate of the North.

Meanwhile, his daughter, Lorna Adkins (she's 31), of Odessa, was telling the press: "He is a real gentle and quiet person. I know for a fact he would have never shot first. I don't know anyone who could say anything personally bad about him.

"I know for a fact that if they would have wanted to get him, they could have gotten him on several occasions and not involved those other people ...

"I'm sure it was to create an incident, so the people could realize what would happen to them if they didn't pay their taxes. But I'm sure they never realized it would go this far.

"They are looking for a fugitive and a murderer, and he is none of the above. The American people have absolutely nothing to fear that he is dangerous."

Back in North Dakota, Fargo was experiencing more excitement than had existed since June, 1893, when most of the town burned to the ground during the depressed conditions of a financial panic. The mid-winter thaw and unseasonable fog eased Grandpa's flight.

Unlike Carroll's Cheshire Cat of *Alice in Wonderland,* which disappeared leaving only a smile, Grandpa didn't leave a trace or a trail in North Dakota. As Milne's Winnie-the-Pooh would say, that two weeks to the manhunters were "like nothing. A huge, big - well, like a - I don't know - like an enormous big nothing." He seemingly had disappeared into a black hole in space.

As I said earlier, it really wouldn't be proper to tell, even if I knew, which I don't, where Grandpa went or to whom he talked during the next few days of February. It suffices to say that he started roosting in the upstairs, the living area, of Art Russell's home, just outside Mountain Home, Arkansas, a mile to the west, in late February or early March. He had spent one or two days at the Leonard Ginter residence near Smithville sometime prior to his arrival, which was in a mustard and white truck.

Now, let me digress a minute. I don't want to give the

idea that Grandpa was perfect. As the snob says, "There just ain't many of us perfect ones." He had his faults, just like everyone else. For instance, and as Grandma told Dr. Martin, I wish he had adopted Dr. Martin's idea about the Township, which in essence was "love conquers all!" Grandpa was rather stubborn in his beliefs, not prone to yield an inch when it came to his ideologies. He wanted a more exclusive membership. His ideas about Anglo/Nordic/Aryan race exclusiveness were definitely extreme. But, then, who isn't proud of his race? And if the Bill of Rights is the supreme law, can't a person espouse what he believes, whether or not others may think it kooky?

Yep, Grandpa was a lot like William Duncan McDiver, who made a speech back in 1899 in Philadelphia. He said, "I come from a state that raises cotton, corn and cockleburrs. In spite of all your eloquence, gentlemen, you'll have to show me." Maybe Grandpa thought of Missouri's slogan as he traversed the state. He did have firm ideas.

Grandpa did not survive to hear President Reagan in Williamsburg, Virginia, virtually mimic one of his messages, as reported by the Los Angeles Times. On the 220th anniversary of Patrick Henry's speech there, he urged "rebellion" against Washington and expressed sympathy for the "cult of cheating" among American taxpayers:

"It's not considered bad behavior," Reagan said of tax cheating and referring to modern American morals. "After all, goes the thinking, what's immoral about cheating a system that is itself a cheat? That isn't a sin, it's a duty.

"Our federal tax system is, in short, utterly impossible, utterly unjust and completely counter-productive. It has earned a rebellion. And it's time we rebelled."

Patrick Henry's call for "tax reform" prompted immediate cries of "treason", but his speech fueled revolutionary sentiment that culminated 13 months later in the Declaration of Independence.

Speaking on the steps of the colonial capitol where Henry had orated, Reagan said the federal income tax is "so rigged, so unfair, that it corrupts otherwise honest people by encouraging them to cheat ... The current system just doesn't work any more. The underground economy and the cult of cheating prove this is so."

In contrast, IRS Commissioner Roscoe Eggers shortly thereafter announced that enforcement staffing would be increased 20 percent, but that the agency would try to be more courteous, saying "hello" for instance, to audit targets.

As Grandpa made his way southward, praying continually as was his nature and was requisite in his dispairing condition, his meloncholic reverie while in Bunyon's slough of despond must have recalled some of the early rhetoric of sermons in the days of the founding fathers. I'll give you some examples:

"The doctrine of non-resistance and unlimited passive obedience to the worst of tyrants could never have found credit among mankind had the voice of reason been hearkened for a guide, because such a doctrine would immediately have been discerned to be contrary to natural law." - Samuel West, 1776

"The only reason for the institution of civil government, and the only rational ground for submission to it, is the common safety and utility ... Now, as all men are fallible, it cannot be supposed that the public affairs of any state should always be administered in the best manner possible, even by persons of the greatest wisdom and integrity ... Those in authority may abuse their trust and power to such a degree that not any obedience or submission be paid to them; but on the contrary that they should be totally discarded." - Samuel Mayhew, 1750

"All power is originally from God, and civil government his institution, and is designed to advance the happiness of his creatures. Civil power ought therefore ever to be employed agreeable to the nature and will of the supreme Sovereign and Guardian of all our rights." - Ben Stevens, 1761

"God never gives men up to be slaves till they lose their national virtue, and abandon themselves to slavery." - Richard Salter, 1768

"Life, liberty, and property are the gifts of the Creator." - Daniel Shute, 1768

"Unlimited submission and obedience is due to none but

God alone." - Samuel West, 1776

"The scriptures cannot be rightfully expounded without explaining them in a manner friendly to the cause of freedom." - Charles Turner, 1773

"If God be for us, who can be against us? The enemy has reproached us for calling on his name, and professing our trust in him. They have made a mockery of our solemn fasts, and every appearance of serious Christianity in the land. On this account, by way of contempt, they call us saints; and that they themselves may keep at the greatest distance from this character, their mouths are full of horrid blasphemies, cursing, and bitterness, and vent all the rage of malice and barbarity. And may we not be confident that the Most High, who regards those things, will vindicate his own honor, and plead our righteous cause against such enemies to his government, as well as our liberties. O, may our camp be free from every accursed thing! May our land be purged from all its sins! May we be truly a holy people, and all our towns cities of righteousness." - Samuel Langdon, 1775

"Men did not purchase their freedom, nor was it the grant of kings, nor from charter ... nor in any proper sense from man: but from God. They were born free!" - Samuel Webster, 1777

"It is not easy to determine who is the more criminal - they who would make their way to places of power and trust by indirect means, or they who have so little concern for the welfare of their country as to hearken to them. No civil rulers are to be obeyed when they enjoin things that are inconsistent with the commands of God. All such disobedience is lawful and glorious." J. Mayhew, 1754

Some modern-day preachers are again taking up the cry, such as James Kennedy of Coral Ridge Presbyterian in Fort Lauderdale.

Little doubt exists that Grandpa pondered such thoughts as he followed the mallards southward. Ned Rorem said, "Nothing is a waste that makes a memory." His freedom at the time was akin to that of the truck driver suitor of Bobbie McGee in the popular song. The driver moaned, "Freedom's just another name for nothing left to lose!" Were it not for his walk with God, Grandpa's flight would have been an exercise engulfed in utter hopelessness. He undoubtedly thought of II Cor. 4:8-9: "We are hard pressed on every side, but not crushed; perplexed, but not abandoned; struck down, but not destroyed."

And Habakkuk 1: "How long, O Lord, must I call for help, but you do not listen? Or cry out to you, 'Violence!' but you do not save? Why do you make me look at injustice? Why do you tolerate wrong? Destruction and violence are before me; there is strife, and conflict abounds. Therefore, the law is paralyzed, and justice never prevails. The wicked hem in the righteous, so that justice is perverted."

Art and Grandpa had numerous conversations, varying from subjects profound to paltry trivia. To illustrate the latter, one can imagine Art saying to Grandpa, "You know how a squirrel will get on the opposite side of a tree trunk when a hunter approaches? Well, suppose the hunter walks a big circle around the tree, as is often the case. The squirrel will keep moving around the tree to keep the trunk between him and the hunter. The riddle I can't figger out is this: When the hunter has completed his walk around the tree, has he circled the squirrel the same as he has the tree?

The two were good entertainment for one another. They discussed the book of Revelation.

Karen Russell Robertson, who was 28, was the youngest of Art's ten children, and had always been a special problem to the family. "During childbirth," Art explained, "her mother was given this drug which permanently affected the baby (as I had mentioned). While growing up, her behavior was sometimes erratic. Once she took the family car and ran off. Typically, when a sudden loud noise occurred, she would run from it, screaming."

Karen's marriage to Mike had been somewhat stormy. Mike was easy-going, but not Karen. For one thing, Karen was notoriously averse to housekeeping. Relating an incident during one marital spat, Karen asserted, "Dad tried to assault Mike through the car window, come in after him!" Whether or not such an event occurred is open to conjecture. It kinda reminds me of Mark Twain who said, "When I was younger, I had a good memory of events, whether they happened or not." The jovial Arthur is in his mid-70's and would be no match for Mike. Karen called the sheriff to her father in this instance.

Since Mrs. Russell had died two years earlier, Art had lived alone, the children long scattered all over the country. Through the years, if any of them were down on their luck, they would come home for a while and recoup. All had good relationships with their parents; that is, all except Karen, who resented her father. He loved her, though.

Art's property was worth perhaps $200,000, including $75,000 of silver bars (later confiscated by the FBI) that he kept upstairs. Everything was placed in a trust for the children, with Art managing the trust. On one occasion, Karen tried to get other siblings - it required three in all - to have her father committed to a mental institution. O'course, none of the others would go along with that. Karen harbored childhood resentments from spankings and such, but mainly feared that Art would let his friends trick him out of his wealth. She especially disliked Rev. Ed Udey from nearby Cotter, who was retired but sold health foods from his home, conducted Bible studies, and whose wife was a naprapath, helping others with health problems. Karen had an intense but false fear that Ed was after Art's money.

Karen and Mike divorced in mid-November; that was in '82. She and her two daughters, Michelle, 7, and Beth, 4, came to live with Art. "By cracky, Karen," Arthur would counsel her, "you've got to pull yourself together and start keeping the girls clean and get your life together. Make a fresh start!" Such petitions had little effect on Karen. It fell on Art to support the three for the next seven months, which he did not begrudge. It was rather nice to have a woman in the house, even if it fell his lot to do the housecleaning and most of the cooking. However, Art was not entirely retired. He continued to repair pumps for old customers, and on occasion, put down a well for someone in the Ozark countryside.

On a gorgeous, warm Sunday morning ending February in the hills, Grandpa arrived at Art's home as a passenger in a Dodge Omni driven by one Leonard Ginter, according to one report, probably inaccurate. More about Leonard later. Art agreed to let him stay a spell, when it was explained that the Feds were trying to kill him. When Karen and the girls returned from church, Grandpa was introduced to her as Herman "Sam" Louden. Art called him "Curly", perhaps because his bald dome resembled one of the Three Stooges. Anyway, they did not attempt to keep his identity from Karen, who called him "Gordon" in conversations. Grandpa stayed there for about ninety days.

This hill country of Arkansas was the epitome of God's handiwork as springtime blossomed. The natives had their endemic customs and humor in those parts. Were a stranger to ask, "How far is it to Little Rock?" he might well get a trite reply at first: "Little Rock? Well, now, it's about two lengths of a fool. If you don't believe me, lie down and measure it sometime." After having their fun, the gracious Arkansasyers would help anyone in any way possible. That's just the nature of these hospitable people, and goes a long way in explaining why Grandpa resided with Art Russell during his final spring. Thanks in part to Karen, he would not live to see summer. He would see June come, though, which is a decent attempt by nature to try to top springtime in the Ozarks.

Art warned Karen, right from the first, "Don't mention to anyone that a man is here, *or else*..." (She didn't, until after he left. Some believe she became emotionally attached to Grandpa, and resented his leaving.) Michelle and Beth quickly became attached to "Uncle Sam", and he often helped dress the children and tend to their needs. Grandpa kept his mini-14 and pistol in his bedroom, away from the children. Karen often went out "job hunting", but never seemed to have much luck in this endeavor. Grandpa once bought the children some clothes.

He passed the time by helping put in a garden, watching TV and helping with the housework. Karen lent him a book relating to natural gardening, building up the soil, entitled *"The One-Straw Revolution"*. As I said earlier, Grandpa and Karen spent long hours discussing the Bible. Art rather enjoyed his guest and the good company of a Christian man and an excellent conversationalist, who seemed really to know about the things they discussed. They both thought the same way about the IRS and the threatening directions being taken by the federal government. The friendly, jocular Art especially appreciated Grandpa's not smoking. As a young man, Grandpa had once smoked for a brief period. After returning from hunting one day, he remarked to his wife that it affected his aim - and never smoked again.

Grandpa would give Karen money when she went to the grocery store, more than enough for his food, but not extravagant amounts. He did not know low long his $5,000 would have to last him. It's ironic, I guess, yet typical for Grandpa to have been eligible to draw Social Security for the past year or two, but yet refused to take such payments. As Ylva said when she wrote a newspaper in North Dakota about this time, "Gordon is always ready to lend a helping hand, but never to take a handout. Gordon Kahl is my brother, and doesn't deserve this bad press."

Everyone in the house watched a TV report dealing with Grandpa in one instance. The children did not register a connection with "Uncle Sam".

It is curious that although he was the most "wanted" man in America, Grandpa was not on the FBI's "Ten Most Wanted" list, simply because no vacancies on the list had opened.

Unusual for a man of his age, Art kept a diary in which he recorded both trivia and significant daily events. One such entry, "Curly arrived today." would be used later as evidence against Art when charged with harboring a fugitive.

Ed Udey met Grandpa during that spring. They shook hands and Ed expressed his admiration for a "great man". Karen testified in error that on one occasion Ed called and invited Grandpa to come to his house for dinner. Karen said she took the call, and that Ed then drove over and took Grandpa to his home in Cotter, leaving Art a note to come over for dinner, also. Actually, Ed did come by and leave a note, but the reference was to another friend of Art's. Grandpa was not mentioned in the note, nor in any telephone call. That evening, Art got cleaned up and drove over, returning with Grandpa. At one time or another, Ed made an entry in the margin of his Bible, among other entries, writing, "Gordon Kahl delivered." The entry was made in the book of Acts, by the passage where Peter was delivered from Roman soldiers under cover of a divine fog. The authorities interpreted this differently, alluding to his delivery to Art Russell's residence. The notation was unfairly used against Ed Udey in his trial later.

Karen later testified that a confab occurred in mid-May among several persons in the mobile home trailer located in Art's front yard. Ed Udey, Gordon Kahl, and Leonard Ginter discussed Grandpa's situation. The gist of it was the possibility that the FBI may be getting close. According to Karen, Bill Wade was introduced to Grandpa about that time. However, at this time Bill Wade was nowhere near. He was in the Bahamas at a health clinic for a diabetic treatment, and then in Reno, Nevada. Art didn't participate in the discussion. For one thing, he was hard of hearing, like Grandpa was, but even more so, being older. More important, though, was that Art was just a lovable, congenial good neighbor, available to help others in any way he could. It was not his forte to tell friends what they should do. Unknown to Art, the FBI had placed him under intermittent surveillance during the preceding eight years, following his attendance at a "patriot" meeting of some type years ago.

Federal agencies considered the north-Arkansas Ozarks as an area reeking with "extremists" and "survivalist" groups and as a refuge for tax protesters and others who might be at loggerheads with the government. Art had had his problems with the IRS since he retired. "By jiminy, they think I make just as much money since I retired as I did when I worked full time," he once exclaimed. Assessments and liens had recently been made against him by the IRS.

One of the pastimes in the small towns of Arkansas is to assemble at the local cafes for talk and coffee. A typical impromptu revelation during hunting season would be something like: "They wuz two does come over the rise with a spike buck behind 'em. I'uz in a tree stand we'd built last week. I let 'em pass and then an eight-pointer come from the same direction. I kilt it, an' when I went to gut it, doggone ifen it wudn't a doe, a female; I'd heard about that happenin' before, but it 'uz the fust time I evah seen it."

"Hey, sugah-lump, how about a refill? Whatcha' doin' tonight?"

"Here's the coffee, but excuse me if I don't look at you. I've already seen one train wreck."

"Here's your beans and cornbread," said the waitress to a patron. "That'll stick to your ribs."

Yarns are common at such gatherings. For example, one fellow might say, "Did I ever tell you the story my granddad told me about what happened to him in Oklahoma, when Geronimo was there? He told me a war party chased him into a dead end gulch, no way out. What happened? He said, 'They killed me, of course!' "

I'm glad that school has started again, even if it does mean the North Dakota winter will soon be here.

They say a 17-year-old often vacillates from smiles to tears, but I reckon everyone has his ups and downs. But sometimes it seems that life just isn't fair. Take the boys at school, for instance. Why is it that the ones always wanting to talk with me are creeps, while the one or two guys I really like don't pay me the time of day? Just doesn't seem right.

Pardon me for being personal. Mine is not the story you're after. Let me get back to Arkansas.

XXVI Betrayal

Grandpa had been able to keep his spirits high under the circumstances until mid-May, when the pressures began to demoralize him. He thought of Joan and Yorie currently being tried in Fargo, along with his friends, David Broer and Scott Faul. He pondered the travesty, thinking, "With all that silly courtroom security, any jury would convict the judge - and now that I mention it, they ought to - in that court. They don't stand a chance." By late May, the verdicts were rendered and Grandpa became both despondent and morose.

On Memorial Day, Leonard and Norma Ginter came by the Russell residence during the morning. Grandpa said, "I want to go home with you."

"You can't," replied Leonard.

"I've got to. The federals are closing in," retorted Grandpa, whose intuition was always fairly reliable and a mystery to those who knew him.

Leonard Ginter was a retired carpenter who departed Wisconsin six or eight years earlier for the Ozarks, partly to escape that state's higher taxes. His only income was a V.A. insurance benefit of $166 per month, owing from the death of his son in the Viet Nam conflict. He lived in a trailer for a while, and then made a gentleman's lease agreement with Bill Wade to construct a home on Bill's farm, halfway between Smithville and Imboden. He then built an earthen home of concrete, covered on three sides and on top by dirt, to conserve energy. The only wood in the building was for cross partitions, cabinets, and doors. The long, center partition was concrete. The back rooms were vented through a single roof vent. A two-story garage was attached to the west end of the building. Leonard's son had lived in another house nearby and across the creek in the same vale for a while. The place was located about two miles from the state road connecting the two towns. He sank all his life savings into that house, containing everything he owned.

Leonard backed his cream-colored Omni to the house

and loaded Grandpa and his meager possessions, including a shotgun and a mini-14. Ed Udey was also at the Russells' on that morning. Karen had noticed the two vehicles before she left the house that day; when she returned both cars and Grandpa were gone.

The enticing reward money loomed large on her mind. She was tired of being broke. The next day she provided the government with the long sought-after lead. Karen drove to the E-Z Mart on Highway 5 South and called the FBI in Little Rock, telling them she knew where Gordon Kahl had been. For this and her subsequent cooperation, she received $1196 for interim expenses plus $25,000 reward money, and was granted immunity from prosecution. Grandpa had told her earlier that the reward for him was the highest ever offered. It was not tax-free.

Karen was told to stand by, and FBI Agent Jack Knox of Fayetteville called her back a few minutes later. They arranged a meeting in Mountain Home for the next evening, June 1, and in discussing possible code names for the agent, Karen suggested "Fort Knox". Whether this was prompted by his last name or a way to get the gold needed for her school ambitions is open to conjecture.

They met in a park at the appointed time. The interview was taped. She told him all she knew about events of the past three months. He told her about the reward, which might be "as much as ten or fifteen thousand dollars." She volunteered to be an undercover agent of sorts, "play along with these people," and keep the Bureau informed. He gave her some expense money. She pushed for immunity from prosecution for her father, but was told they didn't know whether they could do that or not. The two discarded the "Fort Knox" code name, maybe because it sounded a bit mercenary. Agent Knox pressured her to help determine the location of Grandpa, who was to be killed in cold blood within 48 hours.

For the next eighteen days, Karen continued to live with her father. As requested by the FBI, she gave them evidence of Grandpa's having been there. This included a handkerchief purported to be his, the book she had lent him, and two other documents for fingerprint analysis. One of these was a drawing of the Beast from Revelation. His fingerprints were also later found on a prune juice jar obtained in a search of the house.

As a result of Karen's betrayal and testimony, five people were to be charged in federal court with harboring a fugitive and for conspiring to do so. As Clarence Darrow had stated years ago, "Stealing a dime is no big deal, but conspiring to do so can get you 20 years." Irene Udey was finally acquitted by the judge for lack of evidence. With the most paltry of evidence, Rev. Edwin Udey, at age 72, was found guilty and later sent to prison for five years. Evidently, Karen's intercession on behalf of her father had results. The judge, remarking that Art was the kind of person one would want for a grandfather, meted out a 6-month sentence at a low security institution in Texarkana. Art, who was 74, later remarked, "By cracky, I'll tell you, it was not a correctional prison, it was an educational institution. They meant to teach you that they were the boss." Leonard Ginter got eight years and was sent to a prison in Oklahoma. The incarceration of Norma Ginter was commuted to time served in jail.

About three weeks after Grandpa had left, Art came home to find Karen extremely upset.

"I'm scared to death," Karen said. "They brought a subpoena to me to appear at the grand jury."

Art tried to console her and said, "I'll bet they have one for me, too."

Karen admitted that this was so, and Art made arrangements to get the subpoena from the federal authorities, who sought to avoid coming onto his premises.

Art's was a false summons, as no one desired for him to appear before the grand jury. As Lord Acton said, "The struggle for liberty is the struggle to contain government power." This despicable use of a false subpoena goes to show the pits to which the noble grand jury institution has sunk in present day America. Pure fraud by government agents! Shades of Magna Charta!

"I'm sorry to do it this way," said Agent Knox, "but you're under arrest and this is the only way I could take you into custody without a risk."

On the same day and after Art had left home, FBI agent Richard Brazzile and others searched Art's place. Besides taking his diary, patriot literature, prune juice jars and other items, they stole his cache of silver in the name of the federal government. "We couldn't just leave it there unguarded." Nothing in the search warrant allowed such confiscation. Art was not permitted to use this for bail bond. In fact, he never got the silver back, but is taking legal action to obtain payment, like I said before. If he should ever get compensated, most of it will go for lawyer's fees and other legal expenses.

When Art was arrested, the FBI placed Karen in the witness protection program. She and her daughters were moved, first to Fayetteville and then elsewhere, under an assumed name. She lacked two months of an English course when she quit high school and said that she wanted to get a G.E.D. and go to college. Her relatives do not know where she is, except possibly her ex-husband, Mike, who has visitation rights with the children.

Art has expressed his contempt for the government action, avering that Karen is not and never was in any danger. "They (the federals) mistakenly attach their morals and values to people like me and my friends. The whole thing is silly and ridiculous. Christians don't operate like the Mafia." Art is concerned about her after her reward money is spent.

Everyone knows that state governments steal people's kids all the time, under the guise of child welfare, but it seems to me that the federals have stolen Art's grandchildren. As the psalmist said, "The wicked freely strut about when what is vile is honored among men." (Psalms 12:8)

I think when governments interfere with people's lives, regardless of how noble their intentions, they are apt to do more harm than good. Beware of any government employee who is going to do you good.

XXVII Pursuit

Leonard Ginter and his wife, Norma, lived in their "earth home", about four miles out of town. Their home was in the rolling foothills, a long mile off State Highway 115. Following up on Karen's lead, the FBI verified that Leonard's Omni had been in Smithville on Memorial Day afternoon.

The chief FBI agent, James T. Blasingame of the Little Rock office, took charge of the search. A light observation airplane was utilized for agents Downing and Blasingame intermittently to fly over or lazily circle the Ginter residence, joining the field hawks in search of prey. They spotted Leonard's car, and on one occasion saw two people outside the house. This was on June 2nd. The car was registered to the Life Science Church.

Leonard warned Grandpa about the flyovers, that it was probably the federals. However, he seemed apathetic, tired of running, and unconcerned. News of the Fargo trial outcome had made him despondent. After settling down in one of the bedrooms, he passed the time by going for walks in the surrounding woods and sometimes watching television. Maybe he really wanted the Lord to call him home, what the psychologists would call a "death wish". He seemed uninterested in relocating elsewhere, even though the Ginter residence had only one entrance.

It is interesting to note that he had done nothing to alter his appearance since leaving North Dakota - no toupee, no mustache - nothing. He simply was not prone to deception.

To be forewarned, as the airplane surveillance provided, was to be forearmed, if Grandpa were inclined to do so. He was not. To get to the Ginter house, a vehicle must travel for a mile or so down a one-lane gravel road, heavily fenced on both sides, then turn right for half a mile similarly fenced, up and down hills. It would be extremely dangerous for any armed aggressor to invade such territory, if apt defenders were inclined to keep a vigil and use armed resistance. But this is exactly what the FBI was to plan to do.

Blasingame began making plans for an armed task force search of the Ginter property. It was to be a coordinated and joint effort of the FBI, the Marshals service, the State Police, and the Lawrence County Sheriff's Department, including civilian posse members. SWAT teams of both the FBI and the Marshals' Service were to be included. Sheriff Gene Matthews was to be notified and involved in both the planning and execution of the search, because failure to do so would risk years of ill-feeling and non-cooperation with federal authorities in the area, according to Blasingame. Another reason was that Matthews knew the area and the people.

(The fiasco to come was the worst and most inexcusable task force snafu in Arkansas since FBI Agent Milton Purvis and Team assaulted the "Machine Gun" Kelly gang. That happened on Grandpa's birthday one frosty January dawn, over a half century ago at a rural residence in Pulaski County near Little Rock. Copious blood was spilled foolishly on both sides during the ensuing shootout, which might have been avoided. George Kelly, his moll, and another escaped with a suitcase of stolen money during the firefight. Local lawmen had been relegated to a distant back-up role in the raid. One of Kelly's captured friends then told Purvis where George was headed. In this instance, when Purvis encountered him a few days later in a Memphis hotel, the notorious gangster was arrested, not killed. Kelly later originated the term "G-Man".)

A decision early on must have been made not to attempt to obtain a federal search warrant. This was evidently because of the uncertainty of getting one, a lack of probable cause. A federal magistrate might not accept an FBi affidavit that "...informant X told agent Y that Gordon Kahl was seen traveling with Leonard Ginter in a cream-colored 1980 Dodge Omni. Leonard Ginter was at the Russell residence at Mountain Home," to be probable cause for a search of Ginter's house (Karen had only said "...a cream-colored compact car was at the house"). Maybe Grandpa's position that government agents tell lies has some merit. That's nothing to compare with prevarications to follow later.

An agent later testified in court that in all his years of service he had never known of a federal warrant being obtained through a state or local official. But a state warrant was obtained from Larry Hayes in Walnut Ridge on June 3, which was not shown to the Ginters until a week after their house was torched. The warrant had dubious validity, since Mr. Hayes wore several hats, part-time jobs. One of these was being City Attorney for Walnut Ridge, a prosecutorial function. Warrants are legally issued by non-partisan judiciary members only. Ostensibly because higher judicial officers were "not available," this municipal judge for Hoxie, who was also the Juvenile Judge for Lawrence County, was to be used.

"I was called by Mr. Stallcup. I went down to his office ... there were some people at his office. They had a warrant. I looked at it and I signed it ... something was said about someone's life being in danger," testified Larry Hayes in court. That happened after lunch on June 3rd.

James Stallcup is the Prosecutor for Lawrence County, thought by some to be politically ambitious. Some citizens aver that bad blood existed between Stallcup and Gene Matthews. They allege that a few days earlier Stallcup had gone to the sheriff's office and was trying to tell Matthews how to run his department. The ensuing argument ended, it is said, by the robust Matthews decking Stallcup and threatening to kill him if he returned.

Sheriff Matthews, serving his second term as sheriff, had had his share of tragedy and personal problems. He was divorced. During the preceding summer, he was visiting a physician's home where his small son could swim in the pool. His son drowned, but survived, but has since been totally incapacitated. On the job, Sheriff Matthews was known as a take-charge sort of guy. His funeral was to be heavily attended within a few days at Walnut Ridge.

The plan was to have Blasingame in charge. If his Arkansas assignment was not the FBI's relegation of him to Dogpatch and Bureau exile to lower Slobbovia, the snafu of the search operation to come certainly justified it. His subsequent retirement from the FBI at a relatively young age in 1985 may have been related to those events of June 3, 1983, and civil lawsuits arising therefrom.

His plan was for a motorcade of armed law enforcement officers to drive to the Ginter residence. The bull horn on the vehicle was to be used to call everyone out of the home. One separate team was to approach the house by a trek through the woods from the highway. Lawmen armed with automatic weapons and shotguns traveling in the convoy would surround the house. A roadblock would be established at the highway. No portable bull horn would be carried, believing it was unnecessary. This time, the federals would have the machine guns.

The motorcade arrived at the Ginter residence about 5:50 on the afternoon. Events did not go according to plan, starting with the separate SWAT team getting lost in the woods.

Marshall Kupferer, the head of Fugitive Apprehension, who was active in the North Dakota search, was enroute from Washington. Perplexingly, this high ranking Justice Department official, who arrived at the botched scene a couple of hours later, did not take command of the operations, leaving Blasingame in charge.

XXVIII Menslaughter

Leonard Ginter had eaten supper and told the others he was going fishing. He put his .22 rifle, fishing pole and bait in the back seat of his car and started to drive away. His real purpose was to reconnoiter for surveillance activity. Grandpa was sitting at the kitchen table, watching the evening news on TV and eating his supper of weiners and green beans. The kitchen-living room was all one long room, with the bedrooms going off from it across the back. Because of the distance to the TV and his difficulty in hearing, the volume on the set was loud.

The SWAT team which was securing the inner perimeter at this time radioed to the roadblock and convoy at the top of the hill that Ginter was leaving. Shortly after exiting his driveway, Leonard observed the vehicles coming towards him. He backed his vehicle some distance into his driveway and stopped. Upon seeing the visitors brandishing rifles, he reached down and tossed his .22 pistol from its holster onto the passenger seat.

The four people who played primary roles in this affair - Matthews, Blasingame, Hall and Fitzpatrick - all arrived in the same car. You know who the first two are. To identify the other two, Jim Hall was a Deputy U.S. Marshal, and Ed Fitzpatrick was Criminal Investigator for the Arkansas State Police. All the shooting that was done initially in the confrontation was done by the three accompanying Blasingame. Grandpa never fired a single shot, nor did Sheriff Matthews, in all probability. Hall was armed with a .38 calibre pistol and maybe a shotgun, Fitzpatrick had a shotgun, and Matthews his .41 calibre magnum pistol. The sheriff's magnum was fired one time, but it is highly doubtful that he fired it. A round was expended from Grandpa's mini-14, due to heat from the house fire, not from a firing pin. Fitzpatrick fired his shotgun five times - buckshot. How many shots Hall fired is uncertain. He has since sold or disposed of his .38 calibre pistol.

FBI agent Jerry A. King was the first person to have contact with Leonard Ginter. He was about a hundred yards from the Ginter driveway in his pickup truck. "Just stop this man, don't let him come out," he was radioed. King drove towards the driveway and waved him to go back up.

King then yelled, "FBI. Get out of the car with your hands up," waving his badge out the window. Then, pointing his shotgun, he hollered, "Get out of there, now!"

Ginter got out, but did not raise his hands, presuming that if they intended to shoot, it wouldn't matter whether his hands were up or down.

The four lawmen then drove around the pickup in their car and surrounded Leonard, taking his snake guns from the car and covering him with their weapons. Others followed.

Blasingame identified himself, explaining that he was looking for Gordon Kahl, "This is not a tax case; this is a murder case. Who's in the house?"

"My wife is."

"Come on," and the group walked down to the northwest corner of the house, the outer corner of the garage.

"Would you call your wife out of the house?" agent Blasingame asked.

"Norma, come on out here; THE FBI WANTS to talk to you."

Norma could not hear what he said, but went outside to see what he was yelling about. The Ginters' guest remained at the table, eating and watching the blaring TV, with his back to the house entrance, located just past the refrigerator to his right. The house is somewhat soundproof.

"I'm mighty proud you come out, Mrs. Ginter," Sheriff Matthews exclaimed.

"Who's in the house?"

"Nobody that I know of," she answered, glancing at Leonard and agent Blasingame.

"Who?"

"Nobody."

The time was now 6:00 p.m.

"Do you have a warrant?" Leonard asked.

"We've got one. Is Gordon Kahl in there?"

"Do you have a warrant?"

Agent in charge Blasingame began looking in his folder

for the warrant, after several such verbal exchanges. No warrant was produced.

Now, it should be made clear that on one occasion before the sheriff went inside, when they were repeatedly asking him if anybody was in there, he admitted it.

Leonard replied, "Yes, there is somebody else in there, but do you have a search warrant?"

An FBI agent as well as the Ginters attest to this.

"Is Gordon Kahl in there?"

"Do you have a search warrant?"

While this was transpiring, Sheriff Matthews gave instructions for Leonard to be handcuffed, which was done. He then said, "Come on!" to whoever would, and entered the house, followed by USDM Hall and State Policeman Fitzpatrick. They also handcuffed Norma shortly thereafter. Did Hall have a vendetta for the marshals in Dakota?

One first must enter the utility room to go into the house. This can be done either from inside the first level of the 2-story garage by going onto the stoop or directly from the covered stoop porch. At the rear of the garage is a root cellar with a dirt floor, mud at the time. At the left rear of the utility room as one enters, is an entrance door into the kitchen, next to the refrigerator, and into the living quarters. The kitchen range was within inches of the refrigerator, with overhead cabinets above it and around the kitchen. A full-length cabinet filled the space between the range and refrigerator. Hunting ammo was kept in it. As I said, the living room and kitchen were one big room.

Within seconds of their entry, shooting erupted in the kitchen/dining area. Grandpa was killed instantly in cold blood by a downward pistol shot, the bullet entering above and behind his right ear. He fell from the chair at the table, where he had been eating, onto the floor.

After Grandpa was killed, Sheriff Matthews was shot and injured inside the house. It's hard to say just which shots hit Matthews inside the house, or who fired them, as a fusillade was fired at him a few minutes later when he exited through the garage door and rounded the garage corner. Someone had yelled, "He's coming out!" His arm was raised when he was shot then. The fatal bullet entered and exited the sheriff's arm, then entered his chest over the flak jacket, below the armpit.

One may doubt Fitzpatrick's testimony of having gone into the kitchen, based, if nothing else, on his description of shots fired from behind the ice box area, a nonexistent area, at the sheriff "20 feet" into the living room. Grandpa fired no weapon. Fitzpatrick said that he fired his shotgun one time blindly around the refrigerator at someone shooting from the dining table area. He then ran outside and fired four times through the picture window, which would be approximately across Grandpa's body and towards the refrigerator area. He said the injured sheriff was lying on the living room floor when he left to go outside, with agent Hall being in the utility room. He also alleged the pellets in his shells to be smaller than those imbedded in the sheriff's flak jacket and bodies of the slain pair. His testimony seemed to be mostly nonsense. Based on his incorrect description of the house interior, he most likely never entered the living or dining area.

The time between shots of the two or three pistol shots from inside the house is in dispute, as is the number of shots.

Ginter House

Hall's version of what happened in the house was that two shots were fired, two or three seconds apart. He observed smoke from the refrigerator/range area. Then the injured sheriff allegedly started walking toward him, to the doorway. Other shots were then fired in the kitchen area, evidently by Fitzpatrick from outside at the time. He helped the sheriff into the garage and couldn't carry him any further. He went outside, then the barrage of fire from the lawmen commenced. No blood was on the floor where Hall said he laid the sheriff and tried to stop the bleeding.

No one seemed to be in control of the operation. When the shooting of the dining area of the house ended, lawmen surrounding the house began to fire in earnest. These groups were in three main locations: one to the north, directly in front of the house, one behind a nearby woodpile to the front and west of the garage, and one to the west rear of the garage, up the hill a ways in a clump of trees. It was probably this latter group who fatally shot the sheriff, as the bullet which killed him entered his arm in a downward direction while his arm was raised, then exited his arm, entering the side of his chest at a downward slant. The bullet damaged organs and vertebrae. I think he died when the missile hit his backbone, even though the official version was that death came from excessive bleeding. Blood spatters and pock marks were on the wall of the garage at the corner. No life signs existed at the time he was moved from the scene, which was immediately, to get medical attention. His trousers were muddy, the only mud being in the root cellar.

A rainstorm was approaching the area, maybe heaven's way of protesting such carnage.

Earlier, while the motorcade was enroute, several citizens and area law enforcement officers with police scanners reported hearing comments transmitted about burning "him" out and killing him.

The task force started out being about 28 people, but eventually swelled to over 40. The roar of their periphery firing continued for a while. Included in this were about ten tear gas cartridges. Tear gas is a fine powder which irritates the eyes; it is not a flammable vapor. Eleven gas masks had been found at Grandpa's North Dakota farmhouse earlier. In the absence of highly flammable substances, tear gas cartridges seldom start conflagrations. The firing left scores of pock marks on the outside of the building, with all windows shattered.

A blurb was broadcast over the police scanner that Bill Wade had been shot. Bill owned the land on which the house sat, and closely resembled Grandpa, being bald with a round face, and near the same age and of like build.

The federal fanatics were not through; they had a ways to go yet. Within the hour, diesel fuel had been obtained to set the house on fire, to force Gordon Kahl to come out before dark. Agent Hall later testified that Gene Matthews had told him, "I'm hit, he's dead," while they were in the building. These may have been his last words, if indeed he spoke them.

Ginter House

The way the burning happened was that FBI agent James Handley, Jr. was involved in a discussion with others about obtaining gasoline. He then told State Policeman Robert Speer, "Get the gas!" Deputy Sheriff Tom D. Lee was enroute to the scene, having been summoned from

Ravenden by the sheriff's office. Upon arriving at the roadblock where the gravel road turns off Highway 115, a call came over the radio that they needed some gas. Jimmy Jones at the roadblock told Lee where he could probably get some. Lee went a mile towards Imboden, where a farmer gave him a can of diesel fuel, after Lee said that he needed some. When Lee arrived with the fuel, there was no shooting, other than FBI agent King and another agent trying to shoot the fan off the vent top, sticking up through the soil on top of the house. Later, another shot was expended by accident.

Agent King asked Lee and State Policeman Steve Huddleston if they could place the can over the vent. Lee set the can over the vent, and Huddleston shot the can twice - once towards the bottom to let the fuel drain and at the top for air venting. Some witnesses say Huddleston also spread fuel on the walls in the house. The state and local officers and Posse Comitatus members considered themselves to be under the direction of the federal officers. This is consistent with the government's position that Schnable and Kapp were functioning as federal marshals at Medina. Smoke and tear gas grenades were dropped down the vent. "We gutted it the best we could," said a deputy later.

Forensic fire experts from Texas were later hired by some citizens to investigate the fire. They determined that an accelerant was also used in the kitchen on a mattress. Wonder how the mattress got into the kitchen by Grandpa's body? A gallon kerosene can was in the kitchen. Prosecutor Stallcup later implied that he might arrest and prosecute the Texas experts if they returned to testify, should someone file a complaint, since they were not licensed in Arkansas.

Everything flammable in the house burned. Everything else was destroyed by the 1800° F heat. A can of firecrackers, Leonard's box of .22 calibre ammunition and other miscellaneous rounds created a noisy fire at times.

Lee and Deputy Sheriff John Hitchcock of Jonesboro (in Craighead County) went inside the house after the fire subsided much later, using special equipment. A copper jacket from bullet - .41 calibre - was seen perched on top of Gordon's head on oozing brain tissue by people outside the picture window. Lee was told to retrieve it, which he did. Hitchcock pitchforked and shoveled the charred body out the picture window, along with another body part which he said may have been a foot, where it was placed into a body bag.

The storm that started around eight o'clock had no effect on the earthen home. It was a total loss, except for the garage. A fire truck eventually arrived, not used for a time, overtly because of "exploding ammo."

Prosecutor Stallcup, learning of the sheriff's demise, armed himself and drove to the scene, apparently to fill the sheriff's role. He remarked that the Ginters might be prosecuted for murder by the state. Blasingame retorted that they might have a federal case on harboring. Kupferer had arrived like Captain Ahab pursuing Moby Dick but did not participate in these exchanges, evidently. He didn't bring a bull horn, either. Each seemed to think the other would be responsible for protecting the evidence and securing the premises. "What say ye, Starbuck?"

Ginter House

One reported incident is noteworthy. State Police Director Tommy Goodwin was called in Fairfield Bay by a trooper dispatched to Matthews' office to obtain a helicopter gunship during the operation and a bazooka. Radio calls for a flame-thrower were made by someone, also.

Goodwin, in turn, contacted Governor Clinton. If the request were approved, the logistics of assembling the crew and ammo must have precluded its use. It never arrived. Maybe, as some hill people claim, the climate is so good that a man must be killed twice to stay dead. Some think the objective may have been to destroy the house - and evidence. Had they killed the wrong man?

Grandpa had come to the Land of Opportunity, the state's motto. Singer Joe Roper had said that when he got the opportunity, he left. Unfortunately for Grandpa, he didn't.

FBI agent Dero Downing of Jonesboro was at the scene. It's peculiar that he soon resigned from the Bureau. He had traced the Omni car ownership and had participated in the aerial surveillance. He was the first to use the word "arson", a serious crime, at a legal hearing, saying, "I'm not an experienced arson investigator."

"Why did you use the word 'arson'?" the attorney inquired. "Isn't arson a criminal offense as opposed to just setting a fire? There are legal ways to do it, and illegal."

"Objection!"

"Sustained."

As Seneca wrote may centuries ago, "One crime is committed to conceal another crime."

What would the other crime be, if any?

The most striking story of all is not what happened that night so much as the contradictions in the various stories of the participants. And, not only that, but the changing stories, official and unofficial, which evolved over the following months. At first, they tried to blame the tear gas for the fire. Stories changed as to when the Ginters were "under arrest" or handcuffed. The number of people who went into the house has varied as well as the number of shots fired inside. The Ginters were charged with capital murder for not telling the authorities that Gordon was in the house. After many months and several hearings, these charges were dropped, perhaps in reality because he did tell them someone was inside and no warrant was produced. James Blasingame eventually told the *Arkansas Democrat* reporter that the Bureau wasn't subject to an "administrative inquiry" by a newspaper, declining to disclose the internal FBI report on the incident. Prosecutor Stallcup soon stonewalled and instructed lawmen not to talk to media about the affair, overtly in order not to lose venue. Gordon's extremities and several of his teeth disappeared, not only without a trace, but also without any official explanation. Could a flame-thrower have been used to destroy them? Dr. Malak testified that no accelerant was found on the body, and teeth are virtually impossible to destroy in the fire as described. Sifting ashes did not find bones or teeth; where did they go?

When I was a little tyke, we had a short play quip that we would say to one another from time to time:

"Back to back we faced each other,
drew our swords and shot one another."

XXIX MYSTERY

We learned a useful verse in school once:

I have some six and noble friends
Who've served me long and true,
Their names are what and where and when
And how and why and who?

This jibes with a later statement by Circuit Judge Andrew J. Ponder of Newport, who said, "The truth is a beautiful thing." Trouble is, neither he nor other officials, federal or state, have seriously tried to determine what happened on the stormy June 3rd, in the face of continual clamor by media and citizens to do do.

Dirty Harry in the movie, "Magnum Force," said, "This is a magnum .44, the most powerful handgun in the world. It'll blow your head clean off." Clint Eastwood was correct; a Magnum .41 will do the same. It will penetrate through half a set of encyclopedias. The lead, striking a bone will tend to disintegrate. Yet, the .41 cal. missile incredibly remaining in and then removed from Grandpa's head is said to be virtually reloadable by one observer. In the same movie, Harry said, "When cops become the executioners, where and will it all end? Next thing will be executions for jaywalking."

Could it be, as some postulate, that the head was severed from the body at the scene? Under this hypothesis, a local deputy would then dig a .38-cal. bullet from the brain with a pocket knife, replacing it with a .41 cal. from the Sheriff's gun, fired say, into the mattress. Local Deputy Tom Lee said that this is exactly what he did, dig the .38 out. Even though neither victim was shot from the front, the official report is that they did, indeed, kill one another. Most of the news media parroted this story. Some eventually questioned it.

When Jess Beard, a reporter, was asked why he was taking pictures of the garage floor, he replied, "I want to see where a man bled to death and there is no blood." (It is conceded that a person may bleed internally, but how did Hall get blood on the front of his clothes? Was it from helping the sheriff? From multilation?)

Blood spots were furnished by citizens to a lab from splatters on the outside of the garage corner where the Sheriff last fell. No analysis was ever made, some say. Others say the lab flip-flopped in its determination.

No forensic fire investigation was ordered by the authorities.

The legs below the knees were missing on the Kahl body, as was a hand, and some teeth. The jaw and teeth, originally retained by state forensic examiner Fahmy Malak were forced by the family's attorney to be released later. The ones sent to North Dakota were not those belonging to my grandpa; those jaws had a perfect full set of teeth, not yellow, or not showing spaces where Kahl's teeth were shot out in wartime battles and probably more that evening.

Malak's autopsy was somewhat strange. Little mention was made of the missing body parts. An FBI agent (McElhaney) was present during the autopsy, a fact possibly suggesting intimidation. Dr. Malak states that the head was severed to facilitate x-rays, which seems unnecessary to a layman and is not standard procedure elsewhere. Malek's conduct is despised by the patriot community.

One story circulating in the grapevine is that possibly the Federals killed Grandpa, and then the Sheriff said, in effect, "My God, you've shot Bill Wade!" The Sheriff may have then been shot, because he may have protested such conduct. As this scenario goes, the injured Sheriff would have gotten up while others were busy severing the parts of the body commonly used for identification, slipping into the muddy root cellar to hide.

Now, be sure to realize that I'm not accusing anyone or implying guilt of wrong doing to a particular person at the scene. If something happened that was improper, though, the responsibility rests with the person in charge. He can delegate authority but cannot dodge responsibility.

A number of perplexing facts cry for explanations. Powder traces were not found on Matthews' hand, evidence that he never fired his Magnum pistol. The autopsy never discussed a bullet which entered the Sheriff's upper right chest or lower shoulder with a large hole in the back, where it exited. The picture of the body had a band-aid over the small hole in front. The question also arises as to why buckshot was found imbedded in the Sheriff and in his flak jacket, even if the shots did little damage.

While the Sheriff was in the garage, or the root cellar to the rear of the garage, the firing from groups outside started. The Sheriff was driven out by tear gas shot through the garage windows. He exited through one of the garage doors which fold together, rather than through the covered stoop from whence he entered. He turned left, west, to the garage corner, then turned left again and fell. Pock marks on the wall at the point indicate firing from the group up the hill. Most weapons at the scene were .223 calibre rifles or shotguns.

About a month later, Jim Barden, a New York Times reporter, found a charred foot in the ashes. A Jonesboro TV station reported that observers believed the foot was severed by a sharp instrument, striking the foot from two different directions. Charred blood on the end of bone suggested this may have been done prior to the fire. The authorities (Malak) sent the foot to a mortuary in North Dakota. By the time the family arrived at the funeral home for it, the foot had been destroyed. Why? At whose instruction? Wonder what happened to the lower leg bones, the missing hand, and the other foot? Unanswered questions.

Uncertainty existed in the minds of many as to whether or not the charred body was Gordon Kahl. A comb was reported found in his pocket; he only used a wash rag on his head, not a comb. He was wearing a print shirt. Joan once said, "He wouldn't be caught dead in a print shirt." Fingerprint identification was impossible, but despite some seventeen discrepancies in dental analysis, the dental analysis determined the body to be Grandpa's as did war shrapnel found in his hip, plus some other evidence.

A meat cleaver which ordinarily hung in the Ginters' kitchen is missing. Should it happen to turn up there might be blood stains on it if any multilation occurred. Identification of such stains would go a long way towards settling the controversy.

Grandpa had the practice of squirreling away his money in safe crevices. The remainder of his $5,000 was later found and purportedly returned to the family, except for any he may have been carrying in his pocket, according to those in the vicinity. Joan did not receive any money.

XXX HARBORERS

As soon as she was outside, Norma Ginter was told, "Come around and you be quiet." She was then handcuffed. The FBI contends, however, that the Ginters were not under arrest.

"Cease fire," is a phrase never yelled at the scene. Why Swat Teams began firing at the house, with the Sheriff known to be alive and inside, is strange indeed. Agent Hall had been told by the Sheriff that Grandpa was dead, but later testified to the effect that maybe the Sheriff was confused.

When the firing started, Blasingame had Norma lie on the ground by the end of the garage, at first. Leonard was led a few steps away with very tight handcuffs and he was told to get on the ground. At first he did not, but was forced to do so.

No one bothered to move Leonard's car nor drive the vehicle with the P.A. system around it, so that anyone in the building could be warned. Nor, could it be used to control and direct the task force. The bedrooms were never checked to see if maybe the Ginter grandchildren were hiding in them before all the destruction began, according to the lawmen.

As at Heaton, the task force encountered a dog on the farm. Buddy was a solid white young dog with some German Shepherd blood. In contrast with the black Labrador up north, he was frightened and ended up in the back car seat between the Ginters, at the dog's insistence. A special agent later explained that the official policy is to observe a dog's behavior before taking measures to harm a dog. When the dog cowered towards his master, Leonard told them, "He's more scared of you than you are of him." Leonard was permitted to lead Buddy inside a neighbor's fenced back yard.

Anyone is apt to "stretch the blanket a bit" in ones' own defense, as the hill folks say. However, the Ginter's observed that the eyes of some of those appointed to guard them at the scene were glazed, as if on drugs. Such a comment is not likely to be a fabrication, especially when the behavior of such guards was bizarre, even for ones who are frightened. Ginter reported that the deputy sheriff, first standing over him after he was pushed down, had such symptoms and was weaving back and forth, repeatedly saying, "I'm going to kill you, sonofabitch." Leonard thinks this was Bob Johnson. (Remember now, I don't use words like that.)

The Ginters were then jerked to their feet and taken further from the house, toward the drive that leads to the upper garage, then pushed to the ground again.

Norma later testified about her feelings while on her stomach by the garage, hands cuffed behind her back. "There was all kinds of gunfire and it sounded like a big army there. There was lots of stuff whizzing around...I was so scared I got a spasm in my back. I thought I was going to pass out. The ground was shaking under me; it was really vibrating. I thought I had had it. I had a nervous condition prior to all that, and I'm still on medication...I just went limp and they says, "Oh, hell, she's fainted, we don't have to watch her anymore!"

During the early stages of the firing, the sheriff yelled from inside the garage, "I'm hit, somone help me!" Or did he? It's not for sure; no one came to his aid. They just kept pouring bullets into a house *where no one was shooting back!*

After being moved up the hill, the Ginters were soon moved to the backseat of a sedan on the road. The handcuff brutality ended when Blasingame instructed that the cuffs be moved to the front. Leonard was handcuffed to the door post. A woman officer there, possibly FBI Agent Deveta Tyer King, is reported by Leonard as, "...weaving back and forth like the male cop, pointing her gun at us and her eyes looked like she was on drugs. She did not say much; just went from one hand to two hands on the gun and acted like she was looking for something to shoot at." The frightened dog came up and insisted on entering the car. Soon one of the male cops came up and urinated right ahead of me and my wife. Trooper Huddleston's car, evacuating the blood-splattered Sheriff, passed by."

A poster of Grandpa was shown to Leonard, who agreed that it was the man in the house.

FBI Agent Warner Calhoun moved the pair to another automobile further up the road about 6:30. The dog was penned at this time. Deputy Sheriff Morris Bowles drove the three to the Walnut Ridge jail. After being read their Miranda rights while enroute, Norma declined to talk, but not Leonard. Leonard vouched that Gordon was there because the government was wrong; if he had the choice, he'd do it all over again. Leonard stated that he was protecting Kahl from the government, which had tried to poison Kahl's family. Two days later he would tell jailer John Hitchcock in Jonesboro, "I told a friend if we'd moved him a week sooner, all this wouldn't have happened...I can't trade anybody in for 30 pieces of silver."

Before they left the premises, their home was being burned. "I saw someone walking with a can of gas," said Leonard. Mrs. Ginter later said, "I heard 'em hollering for gas—they needed more gas, they said. Then, when we was going to the second car, why, I was looking back to see if I could tell what was going on with my home. And, I seen smoke coming from it, and I thought: Oh my God, there goes the only thing I own." Later investigation revealed that an additional two-gallon can of fuel may have been splashed on the living room walls.

When Leonard was put into his isolated cell, the mattress, blankets, and toilet paper were removed. He relates, "I did not sleep all night. There was laughter and merriment all night long, like people on drugs. Next day, we were moved to Jonesboro. Before going into the cell, I was told by Jailer Hitchcock that if I asked for anything there, he would beat the hell out of me, and a state trooper with him said he sure would. The cell was stripped clean, except for a filthy mattress. On Monday, we were taken by convoy to court in Walnut Ridge, where we were denied bail. We were taken back to Jonesboro via Conway. The sheriff had men all over with M-14s and shotguns."

While at the Jonesboro jail, Ginter was told that two men were stopped at Bono who were enroute to kill him. Bono is a village just to the west of Jonesboro.

At 12:30 the night of their arrest, the Ginters were interrogated, despite Mrs. Ginter's earlier assertion that she chose to remain silent. Incarcerated, knowing their house and possessions were all destroyed and that two had been killed, and finally having Leonard's life threatened, they were hardly in a state of mind to protest or resist. Mrs. Ginter told Deputy Sheriff Perry Webb all she knew, sobbing at times, in order to end the questioning as quickly as possible. When Leonard was asked about waiving his right to an attorney, he replied, "I don't plan on it." Nevertheless, to his detriment later, he answered their questions.

Most states require a grand jury to indict for a capital offense, as required by the Constitution. Arkansas paid scant regard to this provision, charging the Ginters on an "Information" by the Prosecutor. Compounding this problem, prosecutors are not required to be attorneys, although all of them are. In this way, they do not fall under the jurisdiction of the ethics committee of the bar association nor under a similar committee for judges. In Arkansas, prosecutors are entrusted with great and unbridled authority, offering opportunity for oppressive government at its worst. Of course, I don't know that all this is so, but it's what some of a citizens' committee said.

"What are you so happy about?" Murray Grider reportedly asked Judge Andrew Ponder in the library. The judge responded, "At last I've got the sonofabitch!" They then discussed Leonard Ginter. Jame Dauer said that he overheard this talk. The judge and Mr. Grider later denied the damaging details, so Dauer volunteered to take a lie detector test. It cost interested citizens $100. He passed the polygraph exam cleanly. Judge Ponder refused to recuse himself from the case, nevertheless, and the local bar refused to force him to do so at a hearing. Leonard had caused ill feelings with the Judge earlier by once picketing a church he attended and by certain *pro se* type amateur legal counseling. Leonard has a big mouth and has a way of rubbing people the wrong way. He hardly ever misses an opportunity to criticize the authorities.

The Ginters next questioning, on June 4, was by Sgt. Mike Coy, Arkansas State Police. This revealed that Leonard had met Grandpa at an Israel Identity Church meeting. When Mrs. Ginter suggested that Grandpa should not stay at their house, Leonard asserted his authority as head of the house and said, "Let me worry about that." Grandpa was sitting at the table eating when Norma was called outside that fateful night. His weapons were in the bedroom. Grandpa could hear nothing going on outside. Leonard said "I have known Gordon for about 2 years... Gordon is my friend and he told me that he shot the marshals because they shot first and he thought that the government was trying to kill him. I was trying to work out an agreement through a lawyer for him to turn himself in...I told the officer at the house that because they did not show me a warrant, I was not going to say anything." Leonard incorrectly asserted that both were members of the Indentity Church. Grandpa was not, but shared many of their beliefs.

After a day or two in Jonesboro, Leonard was moved to the Ash Flat jail. Jail atrocities continued. According to Ginter, first the Deputy and then both the Deputy and Sheriff Powell of Sharp County threatened to kill him if he asked for anything, again stripping the cell. Leonard's arthritic back caused this to be extra harsh treatment. As in the other jails, no phone calls or visitors were allowed. FBI agents corrected the cell conditions when they visited him.

More jails and interrogations were to follow. At a hearing later, Norma was questioned by her attorney:

Q. Did you have any resources to hire an attorney?

A. No

Q. Did it ever occur to you to ask them to use a phone?

A. No sir. I was so shook up, I just wanted to do whatever they told me so they wouldn't kill me.

Q. Did anyone ever threaten you at the jail?

A. No, but after what I seen out at our house, I thought they'd do anything to a person. I didn't figure you had any rights anymore.

The Ginters faced an unusual dual prosecution in Federal and State courts from charges arising out of the same set of facts. To avoid this technicality, the harboring charges were limited to activities at Mountain Home, in another Federal District from Smithville, which was in the Eastern District.

I wonder if there is any merit in the rumor that FBI Director William Webster came to Arkansas and reviewed the case with Judge Waters before any hearings were held?

XXXI JUSTICE?

As things worked out, the State capital murder charges against the Ginters were put on hold while U.S. Attorney Asa Hutchinson of Fort Smith prosecuted the quintet of elderly "villains." The judge was H. Franklin Waters, headquartered in Fort Smith. The actual trial situs was Harrison in October, 1983.

Ominous signs these. Fort Smith was once the site of "Hanging Judge" Isaac C. Parker for about 20 years, 1875-96, when Oklahoma was a territory. Defendants Art Russell, Leonard Ginter, and Edwin Udey had picketed the Waters court in times past, which had been shown on TV news. Perhaps because of motions for recusal, in part, Judge Waters gave a great effort to appear fair in the actual trial, although some bias seems clearly evident in the sentencing. Where doubt and controversy exist, why wouldn't a judge recuse himself?

Joe A. Izen, Jr. of Houston, Texas, an intellectual in legal matters, was attorney for the group in the early going. Fees were paid in part by donations from sympathizers. When motions for severance were unsuccessful, other lawyers were brought into the defense, because of possible conflict of interests. Michael Minns, who had never lost a criminal case in his seven years of practice, defended the Udeys. Reared in Hot Springs, he practiced law on the outskirts of Houston. Both Izen and Minns are Jewish. Charles Karr of Ft. Smith was the Ginters' court-appointed attorney. Izen represented Art Russell.

To illustrate Minns' sagaciousness, he once questioned an Arkansas trooper thusly:

"Do you know why they poured fuel into the house?

"Yes, I know why," he answered as Minns was coming closer and getting right in the trooper's face.

"Then, *tell me why?*"

Knowing Minns, he would probably smile the biggest were a wag to tease the legal profession by saying: Know how to tell when a lawyer's lying? Answer: when his lips are moving!

The atmosphere of the trial was strikingly different from that in North Dakota. Hostile vindictiveness was not openly apparent on the part of the Federal attorney and judge. The advocates for the defendants were more sophisticated and seemingly highly knowledgeable about criminal law. They pulled no punches and took no guff. Minns especially was a trial scrapper. One of U.S. Attorney Hutchinson's most questionable acts was rudely to take courtroom seats requested by the defense. The defense had requested specific seats, so the jury could see that the defendants were not "animals" as depicted by the press. Another difference in the Arkansas case was that the defendants did not take the stand. The jury was not sequestered by the judge. The judge was careful that deliberations did not conflict with the opening of deer season or the Arkansas-Texas football game.

Can you imagine that a bureaucrat U.S. attorney would have the audacity to think the people of Arkansas would permit him to guard their freedoms as a U.S. Senator? He did.

Some aspects of the trial were similar to the one in Fargo. Adverse publicity had been heavy. Real doubt exists of Asa Hutchinson's properly furnishing the defense timely information following the Discovery Motion. Security was especially heavy, with the jury parking lot isolated. Two of the Marshals Service court staff were allowed to sit behind the defendants and scowl for a time. The judge had been upset by murmurings in the courtroom audience during earlier hearings. The sympathizers were saying "We'll go underground." The trial was in a small city, with a heavy concentration of Masons. Motions for venue change, suppression of statements and other evidence, psychologist evaluation, etc. were denied. Judge Waters was the first to violate his own instructions not to mention tax protesting. The jury must swear to adhere to the judge's interpretation of the law. The format was geared towards a conviction, as is invariably the case. Attorney Izen remarked, "(It was) 30 percent chance of hopeless prejudice and 70 percent chance of ignorant bliss, without anyone knowing what is going on."

At the end of the government's presentation, Minns was not surprised by the dismissal of charges against Irene Udey. The only evidence against her was by Karen, who saw her at the Russell house once, carrying a purse. Minns *was* surprised when Pastor Ed Udey did not receive the same treatment. Karen's testimony of his participating in a confab regarding FBI closing in, of inviting Grandpa to dinner, calling Grandpa, "a hero" and writing "Gordon Kahl delivered" in his Bible was sufficient to get a conviction. Karen had incorrectly sworn that Ed was a member of the posse. It is not a law violation to know the location of a fugitive and not to report it.

Udey was sentenced to five years on the conspiracy count. The case was appealed to the Eighth Circuit, where both the Fargo and Harrison cases were considered all together by the Appeals Court. The Chief Justice said there was no case at all against Udey, but two other justices affirmed. This was reconsidered by the full court. Four of the justices found lack of evidence, but the other five said that he was guilty by inference. One of these had his office in Harrison. Some people may question the substitution of inference for evidence.

Udey, 72, was in jail about 39 days before getting out on bail initially. He finally went to prison in August, 1985. Being more than a health food faddist, as the minister's religion was interwoven with nutrition in some way, he immediately protested the prison food by fasting. He was hospitalized and force-fed intravenously. This impasse remained for many weeks. Other faiths reportedly have prison food consistent with their beliefs. Minns had finally lost a case!

If one reads the many hundreds of pages of trial transcript, he must conclude that Ed was really found guilty by association. Had the trial been severed, Rev. Udey most likely would have been acquitted. In many instances, the judge instructed the jurors that certain testimony applied only to certain defendants. The jury was left with the impossible task of sorting it all out. Joe Izen remarked about the cartoon where the jury was instructed to disregard the hole in the attorney's head.

"The proof of the pie is in the eating." Seems to me that if a defense based on necessity and justification had been allowed and pursued, the defendants may have fared better. It's cut and dried: they feared my Grandpa would be killed if found. And wasn't he? Did they not prevent the greater crime as long as possible?

Leonard Ginter has been in jail or prison continuosly since June 3, 1983. When he became eligible for parole, it was denied without explanation. He has filed a couple of lawsuits pro se, one protesting prison overcrowding. Maybe this was a reason for keeping him, or maybe it's his propensity to speak out or sound off.

Since all three families lived long lives as good citizens, one must wonder why they were jailed and all the men imprisoned. None are a threat to society. No penitence for their actions will be developed. To the contrary, their disrespect for the legal system is intensified. Why prison, then, rather than parole and a great savings of tax dollars? The action must be simply to set an example for others. The lesson learned by those of like mind is to be more cautious next time. They acted in good conscience.

XXXII ARKANSTYLE

Additional hearings were held in Walnut Ridge on the capital murder charges against the Ginters. In these hearings or motions, many details of events at the Ginter residence came to light. As is often the case, the answering of one question generates another which remains unanswered. Adversarial procedure is a clumsy method to get at the truth; an inquiry, such as by a grand jury, is much superior, I would think.

Unlike the federal case two months earlier, the atmosphere of the Prosecutor and Circuit Judge was undeniably hostile to the defendants and their attorneys, Izen and Minns. Little success was achieved in obtaining favorable rulings on motions, but the hearings were useful for obtaining information excluded from the Federal trial.

The State had little chance of convicting the two persons of a capital offense, when they were handcuffed and in custody when the killings occurred. A lesser included offense conviction was probably the Prosecutor's objective.

For whatever reasons, including the fact that Leonard was imprisoned, Prosecutor Stallcup decided later to drop the charges against Leonard and to prosecute Norma only. This delighted Norma's attorney, Minns, because of two things: It lessened her chances of conviction, and the trial would be used to collect much needed information on the events of June 3. He and Izen planned on suing some folks. As it turned out, the court eventually dismissed the charges against Norma Ginter.

This infuriated Prosecutor Stallcup, probably because he then anticipated that civil actions against him would be forthcoming. They were.

Citizens concerned about the deaths of two men and the conflicting and illogical reports relating to the affair began calling for a grand jury investigation of the matter. For example, officials said thousands of rounds exploded inside the house, but very few shell casings were found.

One of these concerned citizens was Bill Wade, who owned the farm and the house which was burned. Now, Bill is accused of being a tax protestor but actually is not, believing the Government has exceeded its authority in oppressing the people in many ways, misapplying the law. I've already told you how he resembled Grandpa physically. Bill is a veteran of World War II and had held leadership positions over the years in many civic, veterans, and farmer organizations, including acting as President of the State Cattlemen's Association. He was suspected of helping harbor Grandpa, but scant evidence was available in this regard. He organized regional and county Development Councils. He is respected as a lay speaker in the Methodist Church. Recently, he formed a group of about 20 persons, who meet to study the Constitution from time to time. He has been placed in position No. 32 on the insulting list of notorious or nefarious persons publicized by the Arkansas State Police.

Bill's son, Ray Wade, is 33 and is highly educated in agricultural matters. He is a 150 percent Arkansan, being half fox and all razorback. His farming interests center on self-sufficient farms, emphasizing such things as small-scale energy technology and crop diversity. His picture was widely circulated holding Grandpa's severed foot. His role in the Kahl affair got him into a "whole heap of trouble." He wanted a grand jury investigation.

Ed Gran of Little Rock was another who was calling for a grand jury. He is a physics professor for the State University and leader of the Central Arkansas Patriots, a group advocating a return to government in accordance with the Constitution.

No grand jury was to be called. Formal requests for grand jury were sent to the U.S. Attorney and Federal judges in both East and West Districts, Prosecutor Stallcup, Circuit Judge Andrew Ponder, the State Supreme Court, and Governor Clinton—to no avail.

Bob Sherman of Mena asked Gov. Bill Clinton at a Clinton coffee shop why he had not used the power of his office to see that a grand jury was empaneled? Since Sherman thought Ed Gran to be especially informed about the Smithville incident, he requested that Governor Clinton give Ed an audience. The Governor agreed and said that Ed Gran should contact his aide for an appointment. Ed made several attempts to get an appointment through the aide, but was never granted one.

After all, no grand jury had been called in Lawrence County since 1970. At that time, a judge was allegedly accused of improprieties with County assets, a finger-in-the-pie deal.

One should note that a grand jury also has an annual monitoring role, such as auditing county property. But, not if it's never convened.

Now, if I've said anything that's inaccurate in this story, it is certainly not intended. Whose fault are inaccuracies, anyway, with no grand jury to seek the truth? However, Judge Ponder, who has the principal responsibility for convening a jury in this case saw no need of one.

A small group of people formed a Citizens Committee to investigate the shootings and house burning, since no grand jury was called. Ed Gran and Ray Wade were elected co-chairmen. Having no subpoena power, witnesses were invited to come forward, with assurance of privacy and confidentiality. The Committee has made good progress, even though with limited results.

By the way have you heard the silly rumor about the University Medical Center in Little Rock? They're going to start using lawyers instead of little mice for their experiments. It seems that there are plenty of attorneys, and you don't get so attached to them.

XXXIII BACKLASH

"A newspaper," said Mark Twain, "is not just for reporting the news; it is to get people mad enough to do something about it."

Gene Nail, *Arkansas Democrat* reporter at the time, did a masterful job of investigative reporting on the two shootings and house burning. He raised a lot more questions than he answered. His notoriety perhaps cost him his job. Gene's country home is secluded and somewhat distant from the main road at the front. However, to the rear, his house is quite observable from across a road. A portable cabin suddenly appeared on the property to the rear of his property. After being occupied for a few days, it was vacated. I understand there was a windfall gain for the property owner who gave some men permission to put it there.

As Euripedes wrote long ago, "A coward turns away, while a brave man seeks danger." Ray Wade's activities irritated the Lawrence County authorities. He was the principal spokesman for the Committee. He was jailed for six days on June 8, 1984, and then for 93 days starting October 8, 1984, for "terroristic threatening of his ex-wife," charged by Proescutor Stallcup. The State Supreme Court refused to grant his Writ of Habeas Corpus. Associate Justice John L. Purtle, in dissenting, reflects the pits to which Lawrence County justice has sunk in only 150 years and the general disregard of constitutional rights by the Supreme Court and lower courts.

I think it is a perfect example of what Grandpa had been warning about. Purtle wrote:

> I disagree with the majority because I think the petitioner is entitled to relief whether by way of Habeas Corpus or release on his own recognizance.

On June 5, 1984, the prosecuting attorney filed an information in which Ray Wade was charged with terroristic threatening. An attached affidavit executed by Jim Stallcup reads as follows: "I have investigated this matter and the facts justify the filing of this charge." No other affidavit or statement is in the record. A bench warrant was served on June 8, 1984, at which time petitioner was taken into custody and detained in the Lawrence County jail.

On June 11, 1984, the appellant was advised of his constitutional rights. The first advice given to the petitioner was, "YOU HAVE THE RIGHT TO REMAIN SILENT." On June 12, 1984, the petitioner filed for a Writ of Habeas Corpus in the Lawrence County Circuit Court. The following day he filed a petition to be released on his own recognizance. The same day about 36 friends and relatives of the petitioner presented a statement in support of the petitioner's request for release on his recognizance.

He was taken before Municipal Judge Harry Ponder on June 14, 1984, and was released on his own recognizance on condition that he not disturb his wife.

So far as the record revealed, nothing offically transpired in this case until October 8th, 1984, at which time the petitioner voluntarily appeared before the Lawrence County Circuit Court, Judge Andrew Ponder presiding, for arraignment on the charge of terroristic threatening. The court informed petitioner that he would have to give spoken answers, which he refused to do. The court stated, "Can you not hear me? But you don't want to answer me? Is that what it is? Alright." He was placed in the sheriff's custody. On the same date the state filed a petition and the court entered an order the next day, committing the petitioner to the State Hospital for observation for a period of not less than 30 days. He was transported to the state hospital on December 13, 1984. An answer to petitioner's request for Habeas Corpus was filed, on behalf of the respondents, by attorney Harry L. Ponder, (Andrew's brother) on October 19, 1984.

On or about October 29, 1984, petitioner and his friends commenced filing pleadings in this court. The original pleadings were subsequently filed in the Lawrence County Circuit Court and in this court. A trial of some sort was commenced in the Lawrence County Circuit Court on the first day of November, 1984. On some previous date an attorney had been appointed by the court to represent the petitioner. The first question presented to the court by the attorney was "Your Honor, for my benefit, could the court state the grounds for Mr. Wade being in jail at present?" Response by the court was as follows: "Mr. Westerfield, you won't have to inquire. The reason I had him brought around was not at your request, but—I will make myself clear." The court then explained that it had attempted to inquire of Mr. Wade about setting bond and explaining the charges on October 8, 1984. The court stated that since Mr. Wade would not respond, he was asked whether he could hear the questions by the court and he nodded in the affirmative. "...He was placed in jail because it appeared to the court that he was not competent at the time to appear without an attorney. And the court could get no responses from him." The court went on to explain why petitioner was being held in jail by stating, "He is not being held for punishment of any sort. He's being held because they can't take him at the State Hospital and his behavior has been bizarre enough that the state felt that a defense of insanity might well be sought." The court then went on to explain that he would be inclined to let petitioner out on some sort of bond if there was assurance that he would report to the sheriff's office when it came time to take him to the State Hospital. Mr. Westerfield then informed the court that the petitioner did not desire Westerfield's assistance. Mr. Westerfield then told the court that petitioner had informed him "(that Ray) would report back to the court at whatever time the court appointed. He was, I believe, on some type of bond, perhaps an O.R. Bond,...from June until October. And Mr. Wade, from talking with him, has advised me that if the court tells him to be back here on December 3, or whenever, he will be here...whether it's for court or whether it's for transportation to the State Hospital for observation." The court then inquired whether Mr. Wade wanted to tell the court that he would be back when the court told him to. The appointed attorney then asked petitioner if he would be back. The court replied, "No, Mr. Westerfield, I am not talking about from Wade to Westerfield to Stallcup to Ponder. And you want to assure this court that you will be back here whenever we want you back? (No answer) All right. That concludes this hearing." Petitioner was then returned to jail.

This court entered Certiorari on November 27, 1984, but ordered the expense of the record to be paid by the petitioner. A statement of indigency was filed in this court but it was not acted upon; the petitioner's friend paid a filing fee of $100.00. The clerk charged $295.55 and the court reporter $30.00 for the 150 page record, including the 11 pages of testimony and court proceedings. The record was lodged in this court on December 6, 1984. Petitioner was committed to the State Hospital for observation on December 13, 1984. He was found without mental disease or defect and released to the Lawrence County Sheriff on December 24, 1984. In addition to the numerous allegations previously filed the latest amended petition alleges that petitioner is suffering from diabetes for which treatment is required but refused by the Lawrence County Sheriff's Department. This amended petition also points out that petitioner was denied access to the law library and books as well as writing materials.

The facts of this case are indeed unusual. Petitioner was picked up on a charge of terroristic threatening. There is no supporting factual affidavit by any one which even attempts to describe any act of terroristic threatening. In fact, the wife, who may have been the complaining party, has filed an affidavit wherein she declares she is not afraid of petitioner and joins in a request for his release. It has been more than seven months since peitioner was arrested and placed in jail. He was sent to the State Hospital on the motion of the state even though there had been absolutely no hint that he would plead mental disease as a defense. To this date the record does not show that he has entered a plea or even been read the charge against him. Apparently he is in limbo at this time.

The criminal charge of terroristic threatening was filed against the petitioner many weeks after the information alleges the threat occurred. If the wife was the source of the information upon which the charge was founded, it seems the likelihood of conviction would be slim because she has recanted if, in fact, she ever told anyone she was afraid of her husband. Judge Harry Ponder released the man on his own recognizance at the probable cause hearing. Judge Andrew Ponder apparently revoked this bond even though the accused appeared at the time and place scheduled for a plea and arraignment. The *reason appears that petitioner stood upon his right to remain silent* as he had been informed he had the right to do. He was held in jail because he elected to stand upon his constitutional right to remain silent. He had been a resident of the same county for over 35 years and a host of friends and neighbors attempted to point out to the court that petitioner was entitled to be released upon his own recognizance. His parents agreed to cooperate in seeing that he would report as directed by the court. He suffers from a life threatening disease for which he was allegedly denied treatment while being held in a county jail.

It seems to me the courts are being used to coerce the petitioner into talking to the judge. No reason is shown which would have prevented this prisoner from already having been tried. From the appearance of the record, the trial limit within the meaning of the Constitution is a period of time less than those enumerated in our Rules of Criminal Procedure. Our Rules set the outside limits within which a person must be tried or released.

The defendant should be granted his freedom pending a fair and impartial trial at the earliest possible convenience of the court. He is entitled to be convicted or found not guilty promptly, or he is entitled to be released pending trial.

The order sending petitioner for observation requires that he be kept for *not less than 30 days.* Arkansas law requires that the period of observation *not be more than 30 days.* Obviously it took the hospital far less than 30 days to determine the accused was not suffering from mental disease or disability. Petitioner did not request nor did he desire to be committed for observation. He gave no indication that he would make a defense based upon his mental condition. The effect of the commitment was to prolong his incarceration rather than protect him. Such commitments are expensive and wasteful of the human resources of the state and should be used only when there is some clear indication that the defense of mental disease will be employed."

One day in January, 1985, the jailer ordered Ray to leave the jail. Strange! No writ had been granted. Perhaps a discreet telephone call was made by a Supreme Court justice.

They finally got around to arraigning Ray in December, 1985, but, instead, dropped the charge at that time.

One deterrent to malicious prosecution and criminal or negligent misbehavior by government officials is by suing them for damages under various laws, including the Civil Rights Act.

In this way and as defendants to various suits based on laws they believe unconstitutional, a myriad of "Patriot" groups use the courts to fight their battles, even though they hold a general disdain for the legal system as it exists. Patriot groups by and large vocally abhor violence, holding that it is something to use for self defense only, according to media reports. A tiny percentage in this movement will sometimes take up arms to make a point. This gives the Constitutionalists a bad name. Even more serious, it has caused the Justice Department to brand the movement incorrectly as militant extremists who seek to gain their ends by force. In contrast, patriot housewife Penny Wilson said, "I don't want Asa Hutchinson representing my dog, much less Senator."

Patriots are characterized as the Christian counterpart of the Muslim Kurds of the Near East, a people with no country though residing in five countries in constant armed defiance. Battles are frequent. These Kurdish "Wolves of Freedom" seek only independence from oppression, but they have no Constitution to back them up, as do the Christian Patriots in America. Iraq recently destroyed the Kurds' university by aerial bombing. In America, destruction of personal property is a criminal act, as are other violations of inalienable rights guaranteed by the highest law of the land. Officials all have sworn to uphold the Constitution; many fail to keep their oath. As columnist Sidney Harris wrote in 1985, "Almost everyone professes to believe in 'freedom' in the abstract, but most people are really afraid of freedom, in any concrete or psychological sense, and want to suppress the freedoms they do not specifically favor." Like a river steadily eroding a riverbank, we have lost our freedoms, bit by bit. The "small incursions" on freedom are always rationalized as for some greater good. But, the end result is that we have no freedoms left, according to columnist James Kilpatrick. Freedom is a scary thing these days.

The laws being passed currently differ from their proper function of protecting persons and property from being harmed by others, to those of positive social control. Instead of prohibiting certain things, like spitting on the sidewalk, laws are now compelling action—fasten seat belts or buy this social insurance.

To celebrate their Sesquicentennial, the good people of Arkansas possibly may start sweeping with a new broom by voting themselves new faces at the top in the judicial and executive branches. At lower levels, memories of distinguished circuit judges, such as the late Bill Lee of Clarendon, might remind them that changes may be in order at that level. A resurgence of the love for freedom may occur, causing displacement of those who oppress citizens or who prefer taxes and subsidies to the fruits of liberty or would make a drainage ditch of Cache River.

Multi-million-dollar lawsuits have been filed, for some as much to gain information as to obtain damages. Norma Ginter is suing some eight people for fifty-two millions in actual and punitive damages, using attorney Mike Minns. Bill Wade is suing some twenty officals who were at the scene of the house burning, *pro se.* He also has an attorney suing the State Police for defamation of character. Art Russell is seeking damages and recovery of his stolen silver, with attorney Joe Izen. Joan Kahl, in Heaton, is suing for Task Force damages to her home and personal property. Ray Wade is suing *pro se* Judge Andrew Ponder, Prosecutor James Stallcup, Sheriff Bob Tomlinson, Deputies Stanley Witt, Warren Williams, and Hubert Adams for three million collectively.

A TV reporter asked Bill Wade why he bothered with the patriot movement, which took so much of his time?

He tilted his cap back, scratched his head, and looking squarely into the camera said, "Isn't freedom worth it?

XXXIV GOODBYE

Most of Gordon's badly charred body was returned to the family in North Dakota.

A request for military burial was made for the war hero to the Minot Air Force Base, which in turn coordinated with Maxwell Field in Nebraska. The request was denied, "considering the circumstances." Air Force Headquarters later said they knew nothing about this and were apologetic.

When Dagmer Taborsky, a teenager in Florida who had immigrated from Czechoslovakia at age 4, heard about this treatment, she was incensed. She returned the honors the Air Force had given her for winning their science fair competition. She had developed a water flea which ate raw sewage. Dagmer said, "I dont' know if they're holding something out, or if they (U.S. officials) are covering something up."

Thanks to some members of a nearby veterans organization, my grandpa was accorded a military funeral. A 12-year-old bravely played taps the best he could.

Rev. Peter Dyck conducted the service. The Seventh Day Adventist Church lent us its facilities for the purpose. Many people came—a lot more than the newspapers reported. I think you will appreciate what Rev. Dyck has to say. The proceedings:

We are gathered on this occasion to pay tribute to a friend, a neighbor, a loved one, and to be of some consolation and solace to the immediate family.

There are many things in this life here on this earth that we do not understand. Many mysteries we cannot understand. Many wonderful things we do not understand, and certainly there are, unfortunately, many sad things in this world that we do not understand. God's people one day will understand all things perfectly, by and by...

1 Cor. 15. ...So, when this corruptible shall put on incorruption and this mortal shall have put on immortality, then shall be brought to pass the saying that which is written: Death is swallowed up in victory. Oh death, where

is thy sting; oh grave, where is thy victory? The sting of death is sin, and the strength of sin is the law. But, thanks be to God which giveth us the victory through our Lord Jesus Christ. Therefore, my beloved brethen, be ye steadfast, unmoveable, always abounding in the work of the Lord, for as much as you know your labor is not in vain.

(The music of the old hymn, "It Is Well With My Soul" penetrated the stillness.)

Gordon W. Kahl was 63 years of age. His address was Heaton, North Dakota. He died on June the third, 1983. He was born on January the eighth, 1920, on his parents' farm south of Heaton. He was a son of Frederick and Edna Kahl. He was reared on the farm, and graduated from Heaton High School in the late 1930s. As a boy he began farming with his father, remaining on the farm until 1942, when he enlisted in the Army Air Corps, serving in World War II. Following his discharge in 1945 from the Army Air Corps, he returned to North Dakota, and it was at that time he married Joan Seil on January 6, 1945, at Mandan. They together lived on the Kahl family farm near Heaton. He later took over the farming operation from his father, continuing to farm until retiring in the early 1970s. They since have lived in the Heaton area, spending winters in Odessa, Texas, however. Mr. Kahl was a member of the Disabled American Veterans. And, surviving him are these family members: His wife, Joan; sons Yorie Von Kahl of Heaton and Frederick Von Kahl of Crosby; daughters Linda Holder and Lorna Adkins of Odessa, Lonnie Jo Kahl of Carrington, Loreen Kahl of Heaton, and six grandchildren. He also has a brother, Clarence Kahl, of East Grand Forks, Minnesota; sisters Delores Everest from Telespa, Montana, Ylva Zanious of Long Beach, California.

As we all realize, the events surrounding this funeral are most unusual in nature. And, I think it behooves us to have an unusual funeral, since the circumstances, the man, and the events are of unusual nature. I would like to say that we honor this country. We teach the great American history to our youngsters. We tell them the tremendous stories of early American history, such as the story behind the Star Spangled Banner, the flag under which so many of our men on foreign soils have fought. It is a tremendous story, heart moving. So, we love this country, and we can say that this man really loved his country and was willing so ably to serve his country.

I would like you to know that I did everything I could to prevent these events from occuring. Two years ago, I succeeded in getting the current marshal at that time together with Mr. Kahl. Neighbors and friends came, and we had a very cordial meeting, which resulted in complete tranquility of the situation for two years. While the events were beginning to unfold on the news just last week, I was on the telephone, talking to the head FBI man in the Little Rock office, pleading with him to do something, even to the degree of allowing me to come down if Gordon would talk to me—just to pull back and—but that effort was in vain. Some have tried, and perhaps some of us have failed. But, in an occasion such as this, to say nothing, I feel in my own heart, would be cowardly.

So, bear with me a minute, and we will talk a little bit about this man. Gordon Kahl was a very unusual man. He was different in many respects from the average American. He served his country well in the military as a gunner. He was seriously wounded at one time, and returned to active duty in a flash of heroism, earning many medals and several purple hearts. However, on his return home, he came back to his farm and continued farming. It is then that he encountered problems with some government agencies. His problems increased and compounded over the years, leading up to events of recent months.

Perhaps the life of Gordon Kahl may be summarized under three headings: The first, that he was a controversial man. There were many who loved him and liked him, and there were also many who disagreed with him. He had, however, strong beliefs when it came to liberty and freedom. He saw his beloved nation being eroded by the enemy, and he felt he must speak up. This brought him controversy from fellow citizens, and this brought him into controversy with government agencies. To say that he was a controversial figure is really the understatement of the day. On this quiet, humble community today, we have the

eyes and ears of the entire nation upon us.

Second, he was a dedicated man. He served his nation under the Stars and Stripes with dedication, and he worked hard with dedication to seek to preserve this nation from falling into serious pitfalls of tyranny. Any other man would have been discouraged long ago in pursuing his efforts, but his dedication kept him going while many of his countrymen turned against him.

Third, this man was a sacrificial man. He sacrificed everything he had for his cause. The family, along with him, sacrificed a lot of things. They paid a great price emotionally and materially in their attempt to awaken up us pacifistic public to the dangers facing these great United States of America.

I want everyone to know today that I am not here because I sought to do this. I am here because Gordon, on several occasions, indicated that in the event something happened to him, he wanted me to take his funeral. The family also requested that I fulfill his wish. You may well realize that this is not an easy duty, today, but I feel in my heart that this is really what the Lord would have me do. Gordon did not ask me to do this because I believe everything he believes. He and I disagreed on a lot of things. He did not ask that I serve his family in this manner because I would necessarily champion his cause. However, the reason may be because he thought I understood him better than most in what he tried to do. So, please do not feel ill of me today if I tell you in just a few words what I believe he was concerned about. I shall reach back in American history and refer to an illustration or two.

Patrick Henry, the eloquent attorney of the colony of Virginia saw a preacher of the gospel flogged publicly one day, because he preached without a license. The gruesome scene made an indelible impression on Henry, and shortly afterward, he rose to his feet in the Virginia convention, on March 23, 1775, and addressed the Convention with his famous powerful speech, and he concluded that great address with these words: "Is life so dear or peace so sweet as to be purchased with the price of chains and slavery? Forbid it, Almighty God. I know not what course others may take, but as for me, give me liberty, or give me death!" I think I can say here today that Gordon Kahl emphatically believed that. In the preamble to the Declaration of Independence we read these words, "...accordingly, all experience hath shown that mankind are more disposed to suffer while evils are sufferable than to right themselves by abolishing the forms to which they are accustomed. But, when a long train of abuses and usurpations pursuing invariably the same object evinces a design to reduce them under absolute despotism, it is their right, it is their duty, to throw off such government and to provide new guards for their future security."

I believe I can say here today that Gordon Kahl really believed that, and he felt that by speaking up, he must resist the rising despotism that he saw in our nation. Paul Revere rode through the night and cried in a loud voice to arouse the people, saying, "The British are coming. The British are coming!" But, this man has traveled all across this country, and in his way, and bound by his conscience, has cried, "The tyrants are coming! The tyrants are coming!" Hardly anyone paid any attention to the warning. People didn't believe in a lot of his political and religious beliefs, so they discounted everything he said

Patrick Henry did not believe in all that the Baptist preacher preached, but he believed, with all his soul, that he should be free to preach what he believed. On one occasion, he rode fifty miles on horseback to be at the trial of three Baptist preachers. And, he immediately set those three men free, he stood in their behalf. So, that's how devoted this man was. He believed that men ought to be free!

We may sharply disagree on many things that this man believed, and I am sure that many people do, and many people disagree with what he did. But, should he not have the privilege of free speech? Just like the press? It is a matter of indisputable record that he lived peaceably, and graciously, and very generously with his friends and with his neighbors. And, he used only words—no violence ever, of any kind in all the years of his verbal battles with the

authorities. Is this here today, a mute and eloquent evidence that the tyrants did come?

If he has done things which you do not agree with, or if he believed things which you do not agree with, would you not forgive him now? Would you not forgive his family? If this man must be buried in infamy, perhaps I am, and sir, perhaps you are, partially to blame for being too uninvolved in seeking to rectify some of our evils. Maybe this is a good day for all of us to search our hearts and to pray for our country and really work for its betterment. Maybe, the whole tragedy of four dead and five in custody need not be in vain. May God help us that it be not in vain. Amen.

A few days later Gordon's grandson was born. Yorie and Janice named him Gordon Wendell Kahl II. Reckon he'll be a good shot? His forebears did hail from Defiance, you know.

We'll use words for ammunition and keep shooting at those who would destroy the Constitution. We can't afford to miss.

Goodbye, Grandpa. I loved you and I miss you so much. When you last left North Dakota, you did not know what the future *held,* but you did know Him well who *held* the future. Some Christians are so distant in their walk with God that He must yell at them and even chastise them. Others, like you, walked so closely that you could hear His heartbeat and be sensitive to the soft and gentle whisper of his will. That's what I want to do Grandpa. I want to walk so close to Him each day that whoever looks at me will see Christ. I can do all things through Christ who strengthens me.

I wondered why you had to die? I think I have figured that out: You, like Jesus, died so that others can be free. Bitterness only destroys us. We must forgive those who did it, because they knew not what they did.

I'll see you in heaven.

—THE END—

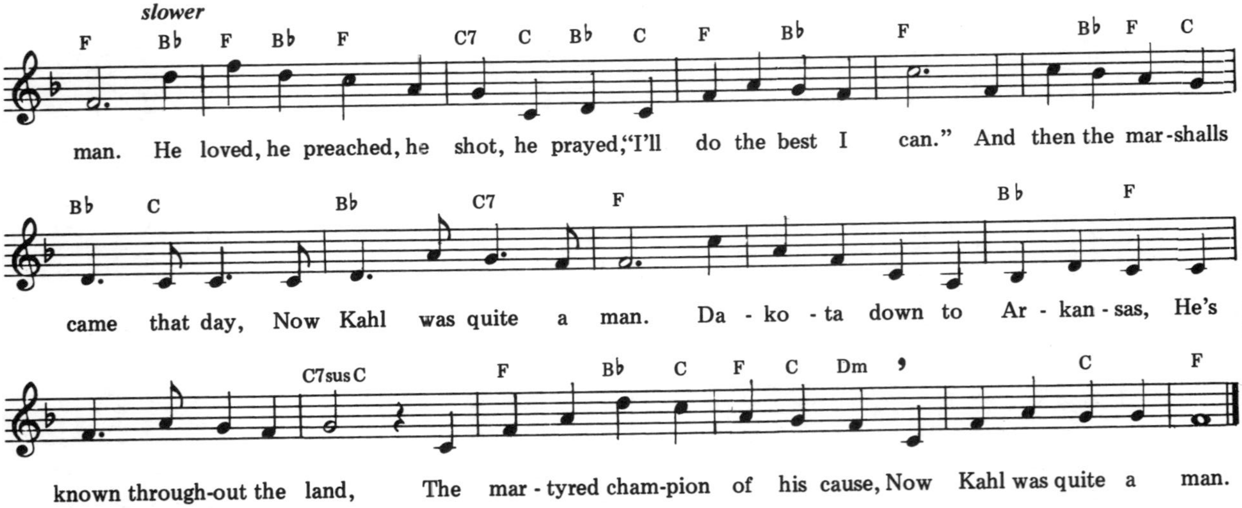
slower
F Bb F Bb F C7 C Bb C F Bb F Bb F C
man. He loved, he preached, he shot, he prayed, "I'll do the best I can." And then the mar-shalls
Bb C Bb C7 F Bb F
came that day, Now Kahl was quite a man. Da - ko - ta down to Ar - kan - sas, He's
C7sus C F Bb C F C Dm C F
known through-out the land, The mar - tyred cham-pion of his cause, Now Kahl was quite a man.

Ballad of Gordon Kahl

Words & Music by
Capstan Turner

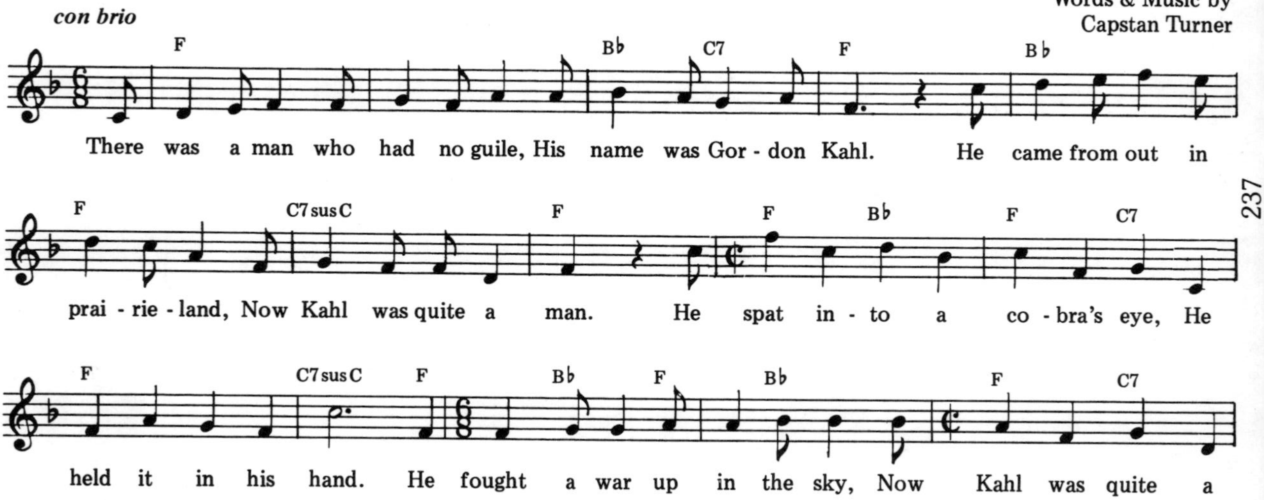

Ballad of Gordon Kahl

Words & Music by
Capstan Turner

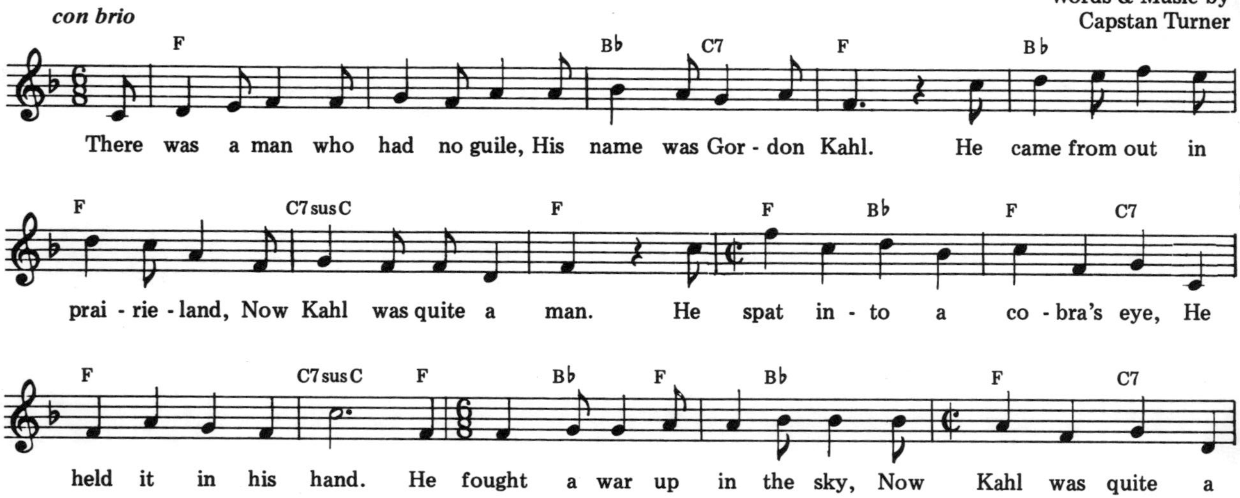